Nobody's Angels

Reading
WOMEN
Writing

a series edited by
Shari Benstock and Celeste Schenck

Reading Women Writing is dedicated to furthering international feminist debate. The series publishes books on all aspects of feminist theory and textual practice. *Reading Women Writing* especially welcomes books that address cultures, histories, and experience beyond first-world academic boundaries. A complete list of titles in the series appears at the end of the book.

Nobody's Angels

MIDDLE-CLASS WOMEN AND DOMESTIC IDEOLOGY IN VICTORIAN CULTURE

Elizabeth Langland

Cornell University Press

ITHACA AND LONDON

First published 1995 by Cornell University Press.

—

Printed in the United States of America

An earlier version of Chapter 7 was published under the same title in *Narrative* 2, no. 2 (May 1994) and is reprinted by permission. Copyright 1994 by the Ohio State University Press. All rights reserved.

⊗ The paper in this book meets the minimum requirements of the American National Standard for Information Sciences–Permanence of Paper for Printed Library Materials, ANSI Z39.48-1984.

Library of Congress Cataloging-in-Publication Data

Langland, Elizabeth.
    Nobody's angels : middle-class women and domestic ideology in
  Victorian culture / Elizabeth Langland.
        p.   cm. — (Reading women writing)
    Includes bibliographical references and index.
    ISBN 0-8014-3045-3 (alk. paper). — ISBN 0-8014-8220-8 (pbk. :
  alk. paper)
        1. Middle class women—Great Britain—History—19th century.
  2. Middle class in literature. 3. English fiction—19th century—
  History and criticism.   I. Title.   II. Series.
  HT690.G7L35   1995
  305.5'5'082—dc20   94-24393

For Jerry

Contents

Acknowledgments

At the completion of a book, it is always a pleasure to thank those who have contributed so significantly to it. I wish particularly to acknowledge Donald Ault and Daniel Cottom, whose stimulating writing and conversation inspired the best parts of my own and who read and provided invaluable commentary on the entire manuscript. Alistair Duckworth and David Leverenz also read and responded to substantial portions of the manuscript in ways that have made this a better book than it would otherwise have been. It is with a keen sense of gratitude that I also acknowledge the friendship of Laura Claridge, who not only encouraged the project all along the way but also invested time reading and responding to drafts.

The constant presence of many people who provided intellectual stimulation has continually benefited my thinking on these issues. In addition to those mentioned above, I am indebted to Elizabeth Abel, Lori Amy, Maryellen Burke, Patricia Craddock, Caryl Flinn, Jeff Franklin, Aeron Haynie, Anne Jones, MaryAnn Leiby, John Murchek, James Phelan, Peter Rabinowitz, Ofelia Schutte, Stephanie Smith, Marlene Tromp, Maureen Turim, and Christa Zorn-Belde. I also thank the Women's Studies Colloquium and the Feminist Reading Group at the University of Florida for providing a context in which some of these conversations could take place.

I am indebted to Margaret Homans and Coral Lansbury, readers for *PMLA*, who provided valuable input on an article that was the germ of this book. I acknowledge as well the anonymous readers for Cornell University Press, whose comments at the end of this process helped sharpen the dimensions of my argument. I extend my thanks to Bernhard Kendler of Cornell University Press, who has been a model editor in all aspects connected to the production of this book.

I am grateful to the University of Florida for a sabbatical and for twice providing summer grants to support the research and writing on this project. For other research help, I thank John Van Hook and Angelika Ilg, who unearthed the titles of hundreds of obscure nineteenth-century etiquette guides and management manuals, and the staff of the British Library for their prompt and efficient help in securing the volumes I needed. I also am indebted to Linda Bourassa, a photographer fortuituously met in London, who provided companionship after the libraries had closed and who enlisted me as photographer's assistant on a fascinating night shoot at the Victoria and Albert Museum.

Finally, I wish to acknowledge and thank Jerald Jahn, to whom this book is dedicated, for generously providing unstinting intellectual and practical support and for sharing with me a philosophy and practice of household management in the twentieth century.

E. L.

Nobody's Angels

1

Introduction

I began this project with a plot: a young servant girl marries her master, a man significantly her social superior. Ian Watt's classic work, *The Rise of the Novel*, cited this pattern in Richardson's *Pamela* as a prototype for the courtship plot that dominates the domestic novel in the succeeding century.[1] But the story of the working-class heroine who secures her master's hand in marriage, in fact, disappears from the novel. Although men and women still marry, the classes do not intermarry in nineteenth-century fiction.

Lizzie Hexam and Eugene Wrayburn from Dickens's *Our Mutual Friend* may seem a notable exception, but that relationship is skewed by Eugene's dissolute behavior, the savage attempt on his life, and his rebirth at Lizzie's hands. Moreover, the marriage culminates in social seclusion instead of social accommodation. A few governesses, like Jane Eyre and Becky Sharp, snare their masters' hands in marriage, or at least secure proposals, but these are not "working girls"; they are educated and impoverished gentlewomen forced to the expedient of working. The absolute class barrier makes its dramatic presence felt in the doomed romances of such couples as Little Emily and Steerforth, Hetty Sorrel and Arthur Donnithorne, Ruth Hilton and Henry Bellingham, Tess Durbeyfield and Angel Clare, where the pretty little innocent who aspires to be a lady ends up transported, dead, or dying. Marriage between a working-class woman and a higher-class man has become non-narratable. Why?

It is worth at least acknowledging that marriages between ser-

[1] On the question of a heroine's social elevation, Watt also claims that "Pamela initiated a fairly constant feature in the novel . . . a rise in the social and economic status of the bride. . . . Hypergamy, though not a convention of modern society, is a fairly constant convention of the novel" (154).

vants and masters actually did occur. There are celebrated instances of interclass marriage in the nineteenth century: Sir Henry Fetherstonhaugh of Uppark wed his dairymaid; Lord Robert Montague, his nurserymaid; the Marquess of Westmeath, a scullery maid; and Arthur Munby, a maid-of-all-work (Lummis and Marsh 130). But such examples from the nineteenth century did not engender new versions of *Pamela*.[2] So we return again to the question of why Richardson's eighteenth-century "probable" plot becomes a nineteenth-century narrative impossibility.

Henry Fielding, who recognized that the historicity of an event did not necessarily make it believable in a narrative, early established a famous distinction between fictional probability and factual possibility, which takes us back to antiquity. The commentator of *Tom Jones* elaborates: "Nor is possibility alone sufficient to justify us; we must keep likewise within the rules of probability" (334). For Fielding, historical possibility must always be informed by considerations of narrative plausibility, and he expands upon this insight: "In the last place, the actions should be such as may not only be within the compass of human agency, and which human agents may probably be supposed to do, but they should be likely for the very actors and characters themselves to have performed; for what may be only wonderful and surprising in one man, may become improbable, or indeed impossible, when related of another" (337).

But Fielding's formal criterion, here consistency of character and motivation, takes us no further than a simple historical explanation. The question why something becomes impossible to narrate, or nonnarratable, remains unanswered by a focus on the formal dimensions of novels. Close textual analysis of the characters' consistency and motivation, the pertinent themes, the relationships of plot to story, and the commensurability of parts to wholes cannot explain why an established formal paradigm should cease to be viable during a particular period.

When critics have focused on the limitation of traditional formalist approaches, their emphasis has fallen on how those approaches instantiate a vision of the subject as coherent and install in literature possibilities of wholeness, unity, and transcendence while concealing its ideological bearings and incoherence. But even a poststructuralist approach to form, which responds to these objections and

---

[2] Indeed, in the continuation to the novel, Pamela herself cautions that her example is not to be taken as a precedent that others should expect to follow. Her virtue and beauty may win Mr. B's love, but only her adept mastery of the domestic discourses that were emerging can secure it.

emphasizes the self-referential textuality of novels, the instability of signifier and signified, stops short of resolving the dilemma of why a particular plot becomes non-narratable. However useful it is in exposing the gaps, the elisions, the aporia within a text—and it will be invaluable in my analyses of novels and tracts here—a textual approach to form cannot explain why certain paradigms have play in certain cultures and not in others.

The question raised, then, finds a satisfactory answer neither in an examination of the historical record nor in a scrutiny of novels conceived as formal wholes or self-referential structures. It suggests, instead, the limitations of any history of the novel that so circumscribes itself, and, further, argues for a theory acknowledging that cultural events cannot be understood apart from politics, history, and economics. Such a theory forces us to engage other ways of thinking about novels, to see narratives as discursive practices bound up in and implicated in other discursive practices through which a culture's meanings are articulated.[3]

The objects of this analysis, then, are not simply fictional representations but the interacting texts through which a culture represents itself and the shared and conflicting ideological economies that inform these discursive formations. "Discourse" in this view refers to signifying practices of all kinds, including those broadly formulated within institutions, such as law or medicine, those articulated within our systematically organized fields of knowledge, such as history, politics, economics, or sociology, those focused in the home, such as etiquette and charitable work, and those governing our quotidian, prosaic relationships and interactions. In regulating what is sayable, how it can be articulated, who can speak, where, under what conditions, and within which social relationships, discursive practices constitute knowledge and structure the network of power relations in a society (Foucault, *History of Sexuality* 18).

The insights of Michel Foucault, Walter Benjamin, neo-Marxist theorists, and new historicist and cultural materialist critics provide

[3] Leonore Davidoff cautions critics against using popular publications and fiction as a "source for sociological analysis," but we may equally warn against excluding such materials and automatically privileging certain historical archives over other versions of the past (*Best Circles* 18). Fredric Jameson reminds us that history is "inaccessible to us except in textual form," insisting that "our approach to [history] and to the Real itself necessarily passes through its prior textualization" (35). In a related argument, developing the concept of emplotment, Hayden White points to the analogous relations between historical narratives and verbal fictions: "By emplotment I mean simply the encodation of the facts contained in the chronicle as components of specific *kinds* of plot structures, in precisely the way that [Northrop] Frye has suggested is the case with 'fictions' in general" (83).

some paradigms for considering discursive intertextuality, identifying how the literary discourse of the domestic novel cooperates with, extends, and is extended by other signifying practices of the Victorian age. I investigate a text's formal ruptures not simply as evidence of self-reflexive textuality but as signs of disruptive tensions within the interacting sign systems. In this way, a formalist study of the novel becomes historically and materially informed.[4]

In light of the intertextuality of discursive formations—here, of domesticity—we find out why certain plots become non-narratable in a particular historical moment. Plots are informed by a culture's ideologies, its assessment of value and meaning and possibility.

Foucault has drawn attention to how different discursive formations operate and cooperate as a technique or "form of power which makes individuals subjects," both "subject to someone else by control and dependence, and tied to [their] own identit[ies] by a conscience or self-knowledge" ("Subject and Power" 212). Such signifying practices, then, formulate, transmit, and reproduce the ideologies of a culture through the production of subjects. This is the process through which particular and local beliefs of a group become naturalized as truth.

Foucault's theories have been powerfully applied to illuminate the Victorian novel in its cooperation with other discourses, particularly carceral discipline (David A. Miller, *The Novel and the Police*) and sexual desire (Nancy Armstrong, *Desire and Domestic Fiction*).[5] Whereas Miller's study concentrates on the way transgression is used as a mechanism for stabilizing the status quo, Armstrong's demonstrates how the desiring subject is used as a mechanism in fiction to consolidate middle-class identity by transforming political issues into psychological ones requiring regulation and surveillance.

Foucault's insights on the particular mechanisms of power rela-

[4] Jonathan Culler's summary in "Literary Theory" is apt here: "literature is a space that offers special opportunities for observing the construction of the natural and its exposure as a construction and thus for reflecting on the significance of both the processes of construction and the act of critical analysis" (208–9).

[5] Miller, drawing from Foucault's *Discipline and Punish*, points to the way characters are all policed within a disciplinary grid of bourgeois values just as the novel itself acts to discipline the reader to the routines of middle-class life. The novel becomes a relentless machine inculcating cultural mythology, all attempts at resistance already anticipated and coopted. Armstrong both borrows from and revises Foucault's *History of Sexuality*, addressing questions of gender differentiation and defining in terms of gender and class the forces that Foucault describes merely as power. Although Armstrong locates an active agent in the figure of the woman writer, she binds her to an ultimately passive position in the machinery of patriarchal middle-class ideology and so sets up a similar grid by which the novel constitutes an inescapable cultural hegemony.

tions in Western culture are profitably explored in both these studies, which culminate in compelling narratives of the emergence of the bourgeois subject, but neither Miller nor Armstrong adequately explores the possibility of discursive instability as a site for social change, especially in the role of middle-class women. Foucault writes:

> Discourses are not once and for all subservient to power or raised up against it, any more than silences are. We must make allowance for the complex and unstable process whereby discourse can be both an instrument and an effect of power, but also a hindrance, a stumbling-block, a point of resistance and a starting point for an opposing strategy. Discourse transmits and produces power; it reinforces it, but also undermines and exposes it, renders it fragile and makes it possible to thwart it. (*History of Sexuality* 100–101)

Nor do Miller's and Armstrong's totalizing narratives of the bourgeois subject address the way Foucault's analysis feeds his larger goal of reenvisioning history by introducing "discontinuity into our very being" (*Reader* 88). The seamless narrative of an idealized history accounting for the origins of a middle-class subject that emerges from *The Novel and the Police* and *Desire and Domestic Fiction* inadequately accounts for Foucault's notion of genealogy and his warning that "the traditional devices for constructing a comprehensive view of history and for retracing the past as a patient and continuous development must be systematically dismantled" (*Reader* 88). Genealogy, according to Foucault, "seeks to make visible all of those discontinuities that cross us" (*Reader* 95). Gaps that for Foucault point out the shortcomings in a monological history are for Miller and Armstrong recuperated into a narrative that reifies historical continuity.[6]

The perspective I engage favors a less idealized, more discontinuous historical method, and it draws not only on Foucauldian concepts of discursive instability and genealogy but also on Walter Benjamin's critique of phantasmagoria, which he defines as the dream of progress through a capitalist system at the expense of the suppression of traces of labor. Benjamin developed these ideas in

---

[6] For example, Armstrong's focus on conduct books guarantees that she will discover a fairly seamless portrait of emerging subjectivity from the early eighteenth to the twentieth century. A more subtle genealogy focuses on shifts in subject formation that these other studies elide—the gradual disappearance of conduct books in the 1820s and the dramatic and sudden emergence in the 1830s and 1840s of a distinctively new set of discursive practices.

notes for his *Passagen-Werk* or Arcades project. Although he did not live to complete even a draft of this manuscript, his notes, as gathered and interpreted by Susan Buck-Morss, develop several important ideas. Like Foucault, Benjamin wishes to forge a different way of doing history, one that frees the historian from the captivity of the phantasmagoria or the hegemony of bourgeois liberalism. Benjamin's, too, is a history of discontinuity, built out of cracks and fissures. He posits the continuity of traditional historical narrative as "that of oppressors"; but he notes that this narrative is composed of those "'rough and jagged places' at which the continuity of tradition breaks down, and the objects reveal 'cracks' providing 'a hold for anyone wishing to get beyond those points'" (quoted in Buck-Morss 290). The materials of this new history are the ephemera and trivia of a culture. This history emerges in part from representations of, by, and for women. In an appropriately feminized image, Benjamin speaks of this materialist history—a history of things such as gloves, bustles, hoops—as a Sleeping Beauty, "asleep within the 'once upon a time' of classical historical narration" (quoted in Buck-Morss 49).

Benjamin shifts from Karl Marx's definition of phantasmagoria, which emphasized use and exchange value, to a focus on the representational value of objects (Buck-Morss 81). This shift begins to move us from class defined in economic terms to class defined through cultural representations, and it enables a fuller understanding of women's participation within nineteenth-century political economy, because, as we will see, women controlled representations of the middle class. Benjamin interprets the great urban exhibitions of the nineteenth century, such as the London Exhibition of 1851, as "folk festivals of Capitalism," which worked to deny the very existence of class antagonisms: "The message of the world exhibitions as fairylands was the promise of social progress for the masses without revolution" (Buck-Morss 86). In this insight, Benjamin suggests the force of representations in Victorian life. The conjunctions that Benjamin spells out—among the ephemera of daily life, representational versus use value, and stagings of the bourgeois myth of progress—point to a history that not only includes women but also focuses on women. To women, as we will see, belong the ephemera of fashion, the privileging of representational value over use value, and the deployment of representations in managing class unrest.

I maintain that women were active in *producing* representations and so became prominent players in the historical scene. In so arguing, of course, I am insisting that class determinants be understood in more complex and complicating ways than a traditional Marxist analysis allows. My perspective emphasizes the close imbrication of economic conditions with cultural constructions, where financial resources cannot position individuals more irrevocably than do the networks of representations through which they negotiate their daily lives. In this dimension of cultural currency as opposed to economic capital, women dominated Victorian society. Although Benjamin is useful in stimulating this understanding of women's role in capitalism, he himself sees women largely in clichéd ways. He lodges the feminine within a dialectic of fecundity versus mechanical productivity and interprets women as consumers of representations—a classic positioning. I part ways, too, with Benjamin when he posits "blasting out" of the old classical narrative into a new narrative telos. I wish to concentrate on the "garbage" of history to assess women's role as producers of representations and thus to disrupt certain historical narratives we have constructed.[7] This exploration of complex competition in the formation of identity, competing versions of reality within the same moment of time, frees history from the linear pattern of developmental narrative and refuses the simple binary opposition represented by male versus female. When we add class and the traces of labor to questions of gender representations, we can begin to upset some fairly stable cultural encodings.

I examine how domestic practices almost exclusively in the hands of women, what Catherine Gallagher calls the "micro-politics of daily life" ("Marxism" 43), coalesced into their own institutional articulation. To make this move from discursive formations largely in the hands of men to those practices shaping women's lives opens up a new way of thinking about middle-class homemakers in nineteenth-century Britain. It takes what has seemed to many a trivial

[7] Nancy Armstrong has argued eloquently for a gendered history that includes material formerly relegated to the "status of junk": "It is this kind of residual cultural information that can supplement the structures determining reality at a given moment of time. And . . . [it will] call for a more adequate model of history that includes the history of sexuality and that accounts for ourselves as gendered selves" (258–59). At this point late in her argument and then earlier when she seeks a way of talking about a form of resistance that could "allow for such heterogeneity—the overlapping of competing versions of reality within the same moment of time—[so that] the past would elude the linear pattern of a developmental narrative" (23), Armstrong is herself resisting producing what she criticizes in Foucault: "a story of power [that] often describes what seems to be the inexorable unfolding of order" (282n.22). Yet her study ironically produces just that narrative, as she concludes: "In fact, a central purpose of my argument has been to show how the novel exercised tremendous power by producing oppositions that translated the complex and competing ways of representing human identity into a simple binary opposition represented by male versus female" (253).

world of etiquette, household management, and charitable visiting and reveals how effectively power may operate when its manifestations appear insignificant and inconsequential. In one way, it is to carry out a suggestion of Foucault, who parenthetically noted that it would be interesting to show "how intra-familial relations . . . have become 'disciplined'" (*Discipline and Punish* 215). It is also to bring to light, following Benjamin, the representations out of which historical narratives are built and the hidden traces of labor.

My book focuses on the intersection of class and gender ideologies in a Victorian icon: the Angel in the House. It shows that a Victorian wife, the presiding hearth angel of Victorian social myth, actually performed a more significant and extensive economic and political function than is usually perceived. Prevailing ideology held the house as haven, a private sphere opposed to the public, commercial sphere. In fact, the house and its mistress served as a significant adjunct to a man's commercial endeavors. Whereas men earned the money, women had the important task of managing those funds toward the acquisition of social and political status.

Running the middle-class household, which by definition became "middle class" in its possession of at least one servant, was an exercise in class management, a process both inscribed and exposed in the Victorian novel.[8] Although the nineteenth-century novel presented the household as a moral haven secure from economic and political storms, alongside this figuration one may discern another process at work: the active management of class power.[9] The novel, in sum, stages the conflict between the ideology of the domestic Angel in the House and its ideological Other (the Worker or Servant), exposing through women represented in fiction the mechanisms of middle-class control, including those mechanisms that were themselves fictions, stratagems of desire.

Thus, the story of the working-class wife for the middle-class man

[8] Pamela Horn notes that "when Seebohm Rowntree conducted his survey of York in 1899, he took 'the keeping or not keeping of domestic servants' as the dividing line between 'the working classes and those of a higher social scale,'" a practice that had long been in effect (17). E. J. Hobsbawm comments that "the safest way of distinguishing oneself from the laborers was to employ labor oneself" (85). This thesis has been challenged by Edward Higgs, who notes that some members of the working class could afford to employ a charity girl to labor in their homes. But Higgs's observation simply implicates representational practices (as I have argued they are implicated) as well as economic factors in the determination of class status.

[9] Theresa M. McBride lays out a supporting argument in *The Domestic Revolution*, claiming that domestic servitude initiated middle-class women in the role of manager and employer. McBride, however, focuses less on *class* management than on the middle-class prerogative of labor management in general.

became non-narratable because a mid-Victorian man depended on his wife to perform the ideological work of managing the class question and displaying the signs of middle-class status, toward which he contributed a disposable income. In 1839 Sarah Ellis put the matter succinctly: "Society is to the daughters of a family, what business is to the son" (*Daughters of England* 255). The bourgeois wife must fulfill a range of representational functions. A lower-class wife, a working girl, would not be sufficiently conversant with the semiotics of middle-class life and could not, therefore, guarantee her husband's place in society.[10] The home, often figured as a haven with its attending angel, can be decoded so that we recognize it as a theater for the staging of a family's social position, a staging that depends on a group of prescribed domestic practices.

These signifying practices range widely from increasingly complex rules of etiquette and dress, to the growing formalization of Society and the Season, to the proliferation of household-help manuals, to the institution of household prayer and the custom of house-to-house visiting, to cookery and eating behavior; they even encompass major changes in household architecture. To say that beginning in the 1830s and 1840s middle-class women controlled significant discursive practices is to argue that they controlled the dissemination of certain knowledges and thus helped to ensure a middle-class hegemony in mid-Victorian England.

In order to understand the process by which women, isolated from the realms of politics and economic production, became key players in consolidating power, we may refer to the work of Pierre Bourdieu, whose analysis of symbolic power is relevant to the Victorian semiotics of status deployed by women although Bourdieu's own applications seem largely oblivious to the roles women might play in generating what he calls cultural capital.[11] He dissects the

[10] John Kasson, writing about social manners in nineteenth-century America, comments, "Semiotics, the science of signs, acquired its theoreticians (the Swiss linguist Ferdinand de Saussure and the American philosopher Charles Sanders Peirce) only at the end of [the nineteenth century]; yet, considered as the broad enterprise of understanding the life of signs and their meanings within society, it was a popular endeavor throughout the nineteenth century. . . . by far the richest single source is the profusion of etiquette manuals" (5).

[11] For example, Bourdieu speaks of public institutions, such as education and the arts (not domestic discursive practices in women's hands), as examples of cultural capital. Yet he makes clear that an "institution is not necessarily a particular organization . . . but is any relatively durable set of social relations which *endows* individuals with power, status and resources of various kinds" (John B. Thompson 8). Bourdieu defines the different fields in which agents in the social space are positioned: "These are, principally, economic capital (in its different kinds), cultural capital, and social capital, as well as symbolic capital, commonly called prestige, reputation, fame etc.

mechanisms through which power is deployed in social interactions, not as physical coercion, but as a symbolic force that he elucidates as "violence." Bourdieu points to the interaction and interpenetration of material and cultural capital, in which the former is transmuted into the latter, securing "a real transubstantiation of the relations of power by rendering recognizable and misrecognizable the violence they objectively contain and thus by transforming them into symbolic power, capable of producing real effects without any apparent expenditure of energy" (*Language and Symbolic Power* 170). Expanding Bourdieu's idea of cultural capital to include the practices of everyday life, we may see that the very rhetoric that insisted on the separation of private from public spheres in Victorian England and depicted Victorian women as disinterested cultural guardians facilitated the operation of this symbolic violence in which the "structured and structuring instruments of communication and knowledge . . . help to ensure that one class dominates another" (167). Bourdieu elucidates: "Even when [interests] give every appearance of disinterestedness because they escape the logic of 'economic' interest (in the narrow sense) and are oriented towards non-material stakes that are not easily quantified, as in . . . the cultural sphere of capitalist societies, practices never cease to comply with an economic logic" (*Logic of Practice* 122).

Thus, the mystifications of the Angel in the House, the polar representations of bourgeois women as either redemptive or idle, all fed their ability to wield symbolic violence through "misrecognized" and "invisible power which can be exercised only with the complicity of those who do not want to know that they are subject to it or even that they themselves exercise it" (*Language* 164). Whereas genteel women oriented themselves toward specific goals of class hegemony, their actions were rarely the product of conscious deliberation and calculation, rather the result of an unconscious disposition (inscribed even in the body through speech and bearing) to act in certain ways.[12]

-----

which is the form assumed by these different kinds of capital when they are perceived and recognized as legitimate" (*Language and Symbolic Power* 230). Although Bourdieu speaks here of "social capital" apart from "cultural capital," he often seems to comprehend the former in the latter. Because Bourdieu's analyses tend to employ the term "cultural capital" in a wide variety of instances, I have appropriated that term for my analysis; furthermore, Bourdieu's postulation of "social capital" as a category indicates that he has in mind the phenomena I identify.

[12] Bourdieu terms this disposition to act and to orient oneself in specific ways a *habitus*. He remarks that "it must be clearly remembered that [social] *status*, like the habitus generated within it, are [sic] products of history, subject to being transformed, with more or less difficulty, by history" (*Language and Symbolic Power* 248).

In a reciprocal process, then, middle-class women were produced by domestic discourses even as they reproduced them to consolidate middle-class control. Such a reinterpretation of the subject and agency complicates more traditional analyses of women's roles in Victorian society and forestalls a view of women as victims passively suffering under patriarchal social structures; it equally prevents a picture of them as heroines supporting unproblematic values in the way they deal with society on issues of gender and class. This perspective stresses the constructed nature of experience and the politics of its construction and thus allows us better to account for the complexities of social change and human agency. While drawing on previous approaches to the ideology of Victorian novels, this approach also challenges them, providing a more comprehensive view of the angel icon and lingering on a drama generally overlooked even in well-known texts such as *David Copperfield*.

In this book I focus on Victorian discursive formations of domesticity and the construction of the middle-class wife, with several goals in view. I want, first, to complicate and enrich our ideas of the female subject, the Victorian wife, and her Other, the Victorian domestic servant. Second, to point to women's critical role in consolidating the genteel middle class, as opposed to both the working class and the petite bourgeoisie, or lower-middle class. Third, to examine literature's relation to other discursive formations. Fourth, to reread novels for stories often overlooked. And, fifth, to explore how conflictual inscriptions of the female subject in nineteenth-century culture became a mechanism for change. My objects of examination are the texts of domestic novels in conjunction with other, nonliterary representations of domesticity: domestic tracts, etiquette guides, household management manuals, ladies' magazines, cookery books, charitable treatises, and architectural directories. My central concerns are the revision of historical narratives of the female subject, the elucidation of literature, and the illumination of a changing conception of bourgeois woman.

The pioneering work of social historians such as Leonore Davidoff, Carol Dyhouse, Catherine Hall, and Anne Summers has already begun to challenge the historical portrait of Victorian women as the passive, dependent, and idle creatures of prevailing ideology. In *The Best Circles*, Davidoff examines the effect of the social conventions governing polite society as a "linking factor between the family and political and economic institutions" (14–15). Society itself she defines as "a system of quasi-kinship relationships which was used to 'place' mobile individuals during the period of structural differentiation fostered by industrialisation and urbanisation" (15). Society so conceived allows Davidoff to tie women's explicit exclusion from the marketplace with their social role in drawing the lines of rank. In a later work, *Family Fortunes,* Davidoff and her coauthor, Catherine Hall, argue for the "centrality of the sexual division of labour within families for the development of the capitalist enterprise" (13). They do not explore what they term "an important but different story," "the relation between the middle class and other strata" (13). This is the narrative that engages me, especially for what it has to say about middle-class women as employers and managers and their role in the emplacement of class through domestic signifying practices. This story is told only obliquely and partially, however, constantly contested and occluded by countervailing ideologies. It receives a compelling articulation in the Victorian domestic novel. I examine the role that the novel played in sustaining mythologies of the middle-class homemaker even as it exposed through rupture and tensions the very mythology it sedulously portrayed. Thus, this analysis reads narrative form both for its reproduction of ideology and for its revelations of the paradoxes and contradictions in representations of the Victorian Angel.

Although the inquiry I propose focuses on the mid-Victorian novel, it also extends back to the late eighteenth- and early nineteenth-century novel and looks forward to late-Victorian novels in order to consider changes in the discursive construction of the female subject. Because literature is deeply imbricated in the multiple discourses or technologies by which individuals become subjects, it has a great deal to tell us about changing technologies of the subject. In this case, it offers special insight into a group or type: the everyday housewife and her evolution.

Recent revisionary interpretations from other literary critics explore the ideological work of gender and the political dimensions of domestic life. Mary Poovey's *Uneven Developments* presents women's lives through public and professional debate on women, illuminating, for example, the ideology of gender at work in institutions such as medicine and law. Nancy Armstrong, as I noted, shows how texts "informed by discourse on gender acted upon representations of class, modern institutions, and class relations" (Newton 157). And Catherine Gallagher, in *The Industrial Reformation of English Fiction*, structures her analysis of class issues on linkages between domestic and social discourse. But the prosaic household arrangements of domestic life are not engaged; the materiality of women's lives is not examined. A focus on the material practices that shaped women's lives offers a bridge between the perspectives of critics such as Poovey and Armstrong, the former of whom stress women's oppression, the latter, women's primary role in the construction of the modern individual. It provides a way to move beyond both celebrations of middle-class Victorian women as possessed of personal and redemptive power and opposing critiques of those women as invidious apologists for and perpetuators of bourgeois hegemony. It points to assessments as multiple and contradictory as the complex subject positions these individuals inhabited.

I have written thus far of the middle and working classes as if those were not contended concepts. But to engage these constructs is to enter a debate. For Marxist critics, class is usually defined in economic terms as the relations between labor and management. For example, Fredric Jameson identifies the "constitutive form of class relationships" as "always that between a dominant and a laboring class," and he differentiates this use from "conventional sociological analysis of society into strata, subgroups, professional elites and the like" (83–84). Patrick Joyce expands this grounding definition: "It was in the sphere of work and operations of the trade union that class became more decidedly by evident . . . : conceptions of social relations as turning centrally upon the relationship of labour and capital, of the relationship as tending to conflict, and of society as more exclusive than inclusive in character" (329). Yet Joyce elaborates this classic definition to make the claim that class consciousness so understood "developed most markedly in the early twentieth century, especially post-1914" (329) and not in the early nineteenth century. What was termed "management of class" in Victorian England actually focused on moral vocabulary; "betokening instead distinctions of morality or social status, and not carrying all the distinctions of sub- and super-ordination, of solidarity and struggle, and of the exaltation of manual labour alone which were later to accrue around class" (335). Joyce's conclusion, which pushes ahead the development of a Marxian class consciousness to the early twentieth century, may startle readers. And though one may contest his conclusions, he forces a rethinking of class issues in Victorian England.

Joyce ultimately applies this point to purposes different from my own, but his researches encourage us to ask questions about domestic service and the construction of class in Victorian England, especially because, with the exception of farm work, domestic service employed more workers than did any other occupation in the nineteenth century (Davidoff, Hawthorn 11). Lawrence Stone notes, too, that "the only employment for women that continued to increase through the nineteenth century was as domestic servants to the increasing number of affluent middle class" (*Family* 418).[13] A management of class focused on moral vocabulary found its logical expression in the Victorian home rather than in the factory. It was in the home, with its select, few workers, each under the surveillance of another in a rigid hierarchic chain, that the moral dimensions of class could be most fully and effectively articulated and enforced. Domestic workers were entirely under the supervision of their masters and mistresses; lower servants under the supervision of the upper. Servants were "bound to give up their *whole* time to their masters or mistresses and to obey all their lawful orders in relation to their employment" (Baylis 2).[14] Their limited round of acquaintance made organizing virtually impossible.[15] Further, the mystique of the happy, harmonious Victorian home as a refuge from the competitive sphere diffused serious complaints by domestic servants and also made it difficult for a public to articulate conflicting interests between management and labor.

The persistent myth of idle women in the home, isolated from industrial strife and class conflict and unriven by class contradiction, testifies to the power of domestic ideology and familial values that persist stubbornly today. Of course, by employing domestic servants, Victorians were introducing class issues directly into the home and setting up the home as a site for all the conflicts between labor and management that afflicted the nineteenth century generally. That they and others have refused to recognize this phenomenon testifies to effective management of conflicts within a regulatory

[13] Other analysts confirm this same statistic. Horn notes that "by 1901 [domestic service] was not only the major employer of women in the country, but, with a total labour force of nearly one and a half million persons, it formed the largest occupational grouping of any kind—bigger than mining, engineering or agriculture" (13).

[14] Horn discusses at length the vulnerability of domestic servants to their masters, particularly in chapters 3 and 7. Very few laws existed to protect domestic servants from arbitrary or abusive employers. Physical violence against servants became such a problem that it led to the passage of the Apprentices and Servants Act in 1851, although physical brutality continued throughout the century. Also, a vengeful mistress could refuse to give a good reference to a servant who tried to leave her employment and, in effect, deprive her of her livelihood. Not until the early years of the twentieth century did members of Parliament attempt to bring in a bill "'to make it compulsory upon employers to supply a Reference Note to a person leaving their employment and deserving one', but . . . it never progressed beyond the first reading" (Horn 46).

[15] Horn charts the many abortive attempts to unionize domestic servants, beginning in 1872. She concludes that "these organisations have had a negligible influence, and the most significant expression of workers' views on domestic service has been the way they have voted with their feet—abandoning the sweeping-brush and the kitchen sink for the typewriter and the factory machine" (180).

system that masked domestic labor. Ironically, although other gender, racial, class, and ethnic representations are currently contested, this image of the middle-class homemaker remains firmly in place, serving, in part, to ground other categories being questioned.[16]

Through precise signifying practices, servants were installed within a rigid class hierarchy where a moral vocabulary performed the function of naturalizing an elaborate system of beliefs about men and women, middle and lower classes. "Contact with servants," argue Davidoff and Hawthorn, "was one of the ways in which middle- and upper-class children were introduced to their social and economic world. They had to learn very early in life that servants were different from themselves. They walked, talked, ate, even smelled differently" (84–85).

Domestic ideology not only positioned the bourgeois home at a distance from class conflict, it also represented domestic service as an ideal occupation for a young girl because it kept her under surveillance and out of trouble even as it trained her for running her own household upon marriage. Ironically, however, "almost all wives of working men had to work to earn money at some time in their lives. . . . A girlhood spent in domestic service was of little practical use in facing this basic fact of economic life" (Davidoff, Hawthorn 89). Phillis Browne's *Common-Sense Housekeeping* made a related point in 1877: "It is a notorious fact that the women who make the worst wives for working men are those who have been domestic servants in English homes. They become accustomed to a lavish style of living" (58). Once again we see domestic servitude and the home interpreted more through myth than investigated through analysis.[17]

[16] See, for example, the work of Jenny Sharpe, who asks that we rethink racial stereotypes that inform representations of Indian men and women but then relies on the stereotypical understanding of Victorian bourgeois women. Sharpe writes, "One of the intersecting lines of narration I trace in colonial writings is the Victorian doctrine of female self-immolation, which demanded from the domestic woman an absolute devotion to her family, and the Indian practice of *sati*, which was the religious obligation of a Hindu widow to burn herself on her husband's funeral pyre. The resemblance between the two forms of female self-immolation suggests to both nineteenth-century and contemporary Western feminists the shared oppression of Victorian and Indian women" (14).

[17] Edward Higgs has also argued that historical accounts tend to uphold "a certain stereotyped image of domestic service" in nineteenth-century England. He claims that historians' reliance on domestic manuals such as Mrs. Beeton's *Book of Household Management*, which reflect middle-class aspirations, not actual circumstances, have given them a distorted picture of domestic service as a "bridging occupation" for the working classes (125–50). My analysis here reads those manuals for what they say about historical representations but also recognizes that the manuals are, in fact, documents of the middle class.

Whereas writers depicted factory conditions, factory workers, and class conflict in the industrial novels, no novels specifically address domestic service and the millions of female servants.[18] That story is told only obliquely; but that is the story I want to linger on for what its very obliqueness tells us about the operations of cultural ideology and power, about the development of gender and gender consciousness, class and class consciousness in the nineteenth century.[19]

It has been easy and tempting for critics to take at face value the domestic ideology of the Victorians and unwittingly reproduce crucial aspects of the very ideology they have set out to critique. Catherine Gallagher, for example, distinguishes between two views of the social order: social paternalism and the ideology of domesticity, each meant to manage the gap between society, "based on the disintegrative principle of competition," and the family, "based on the cohesive principle of cooperation" (*Industrial Reformation* 116). In positing the latter as cohesive, Gallagher reproduces the very myth that rationalized the continuing exploitation of servants in the home. These ideological models unquestionably existed, but we must examine how this ideology of domesticity was itself contested by the managerial function of the bourgeois housewife and the tendentious construction of class that underwrote household arrangements.

These observations prompt the more eclectic approach to class that I have suggested above. Gareth Stedman Jones's work in analyzing the linguistic content of class and its conceptual references has proved helpful for socialist feminist critics: "Because there are different languages of class, one should not proceed upon the assumption that 'class' as an elementary counter of official social description, 'class' as an effect of theoretical discourse about distribu-

[18] In *The Servant's Hand*, Bruce Robbins analyzes in detail the limited representations of servants in the novel, often reduced to a metonym, the "helping hand." Servants existed as "signs of their master's status," not as individuals with autonomous and compelling lives (15). Robbins cites Thorstein Veblen's account of domestic service in *The Theory of the Working Class*. "For Veblen, 'the chief use of servants is the evidence they afford of the master's ability to pay'" (16). Robbins focuses on the decentering effect of the servant's presence, "producing effects incongruous with [this figure's] social position and moments of vision incongruous with literary functionality" (xi). Whether such tangential characters can so destabilize a narrative is an interesting question. In any case, Robbins tells a different story from the one I narrate here on the managing mistress, yet my analyses of the dynamic between mistress and maid do not share his idealism. One might compare, for example, Robbins's analysis of *Cranford* with my comments in Chapter 5.

[19] Servants, who worked grueling days (often from 5 or 6 A.M. until 10 or 11 P.M.), had little leisure time for reading or writing and so rarely told their own stories. Elizabeth Mary Parker, author of *Rose of Avondale* (1872), is "supposedly the only servant maid in the Victorian period to have written and published a novel for the circulating libraries" (Sutherland 489).

tion or productive relations, 'class' as the summary of a cluster of culturally signifying practices or 'class' as a species of political or ideological self-definition, share a single reference point in anterior social reality" (7–8). Cora Kaplan seizes upon the feminist implications of Stedman Jones's observations: "These distinctions put a useful space between the economic overview of class—the Marxist or socialist analysis—and the actual rhetoric of class as it appears in a novel. . . . Fiction refuses the notion of a genderless class subjectivity, and resists any simple reduction of class meaning and class identity to productive forces" (163–64). In a related vein, Bourdieu moves away from a definition of class focused on "a group mobilized for struggle" to develop the concept of class as a "set of agents who occupy similar positions and who, being placed in similar conditions and submitted to similar types of conditioning, have every chance of having similar dispositions and interests, and thus of producing similar practices and adopting similar stances" (*Language and Symbolic Power* 231).

In general, Bourdieu's sociological approach to class as representation, enriched by his post-Saussurian understanding of the differential and arbitrary character of signifiers, provides a framework within which to theorize Victorian class constructions through more than economic terms. Further, Bourdieu's approach, which addresses the discursive construction of "classed" bodies, points in two other directions with implications for feminist theories of subjectivity. First, it works to break down simple notions of agency and intention in the production of effects and thereby complicates the simple binaries of credit or blame, celebration or critique, frequently deployed in studies of Victorian women. Second, an understanding of class as bodily inscription, such as Bourdieu unfolds in his concept of "bodily hexis," provides a way to theorize the multiple dimensions through which subjectivity is simultaneously constituted. Bourdieu defines corporeal or bodily "hexis" as "the political mythology realized, *em-bodied*, turned into a permanent disposition, a durable way of standing, speaking, walking, and thereby of feeling and thinking" (*Logic* 69–70).

A focus on the moral and bodily dimensions of class makes a distinction between the upper- and lower-middle classes of an importance equal to the difference drawn between middle and working classes. The signifying practices on which I will concentrate belong to the genteel bourgeoisie, and they functioned not only to manage working-class dissent but to police the borders of polite society from the incursions of the vulgar middle class or the petite bourgeoisie.

Both historical and fictional representations of class have been inadequately addressed as they subtend domestic ideology. They have been occluded by Marxists and socialists committed to investigating class as manifested in struggle and solidarity and by feminist critics oriented toward questions of gender when examining the home. Attention to the multiple representations of gender and class in domestic novels, domestic tracts, and management manuals provides for a richer and more complex picture of subject formation in mid-Victorian England. The rifts and discontinuities within these works yield privileged insight into the complex roles of Victorian homemakers. They expose as an "ideological mirage" (to use Jameson's phrase) the appearance of formal unification in the novels and of explanatory cohesion in the image of the wife.

We must recognize, in other words, that domestic ideology is an unstable amalgam of at least two other major ideologies: a patriarchal ideology regulating interactions between men and women and a bourgeois ideology justifying the class system and supporting the social status quo.[20] Frequently interpreted only as victims of patriarchal oppression, bourgeois women were both oppressed as women and oppressors as middle-class managers. And they helped facilitate change not as agents fighting against oppression to generate new opportunities, but as subjects positioned unevenly within those power operations.

Bourdieu's grasp of the body as "the site of incorporated history" suggests a fruitful way to intervene in the current debates on subjectivity, which have articulated the way in which the sex/gender system has been privileged as a primary term in subject construction, leaving inscriptions of race, class, ethnicity and so on to take a secondary determining status. The pressure to theorize these complex and multiple determinants of subjectivity has given rise to attempts to think through terms of identity together to forestall a collapse into the simple categories of identity decried in much recent criticism. Although it has become popular now to invoke what Brook Thomas dubbed the "new trinity of class, race, and gender" (200)—an "all-too-familiar mantra" as Kobena Mercer put it (58)—and critics rightly note that this strategy's ritualistic character threatens to reproduce the stable identity categories it sets out to dismantle, nonetheless, it remains critically productive to think through these terms as interacting "vectors of power," to consider, in Judith Butler's

[20] I use these broad terms—"patriarchal" and "bourgeois"—heuristically to encourage a continual examination of the different power relations in which individuals, depending on gender and class positions, may participate.

words, "what it might mean to have one's sexuality formed through race—to understand one's sexuality as racialized."[21] Similarly, a focus on class consistently foregrounds bodies as cultural products multiply constituted. And to worry here about what it means to have one's sexuality formed through class or one's class inflected through sexuality offers a way to disrupt the totalizing tendencies of a Foucauldian praxis. Moreover, it works to dislodge gender as a single determinative term.[22]

Manifestations of power and power itself are always shifting, and one must respond to those changes. So I am troubled when Judith Lowder Newton, in a piece I otherwise admire, defines the politics of feminism as manifest in "the degree to which [a critic] expresses a political predisposition to see social change and human agency as possible." She talks about this end being realized when a critic deals "with the power relations of gender and with women's oppression" (162). "Oppression" coupled with "opposition" become key organizing words. Newton wants to hear the voice of "organized feminist protest" (163). Her insistence that we "produce 'history' in a way which allows us better to account for social change and human agency" (165) comes uncomfortably close to calling for a feminist theory that is restricted by a feminist praxis and to simplifying our assessments of individuals positioned wittingly or unwittingly within the struggle. It confuses theory and praxis to claim that "to any persons engaged in progressive politics which they still feel to be vital, such models of history . . . are at once more useful and have greater explanatory power than those which tend to deny or to mute radically the possibility of change and agency both" (165). Change, of course, occurs; the problem is its relationship to "agency," which here implies intentional, organized opposition. To

[21] In an interview with Liz Kotz, Butler argues that those who are trying to "think race and sexuality together . . . [are] asking some pretty interesting questions. . . . That questioning is very different. . . . I don't believe that gender, race, or sexuality have to be identities. I think that they're vectors of power" (Kotz 85). Other feminist critics, notably Cora Kaplan and Teresa de Lauretis, earlier called attention to multiply constituted subjects. De Lauretis, for example, points to a subject "en-gendered in the experiencing of race and class, as well as sexual relations; a subject, therefore, not unified but rather multiple, and not so much divided as contradicted" (*Technologies of Gender* 2). Kaplan, writing on Victorian literature, argues that "to understand how gender and class—to take two categories only—are articulated together transforms our analysis of each of them" and asks that we "come to grips with the relationship between female subjectivity and class identity" ("Pandora's Box" 148, 151).

[22] In *Bodies That Matter*, Butler delineates such a process in Nella Larsen's *Passing*. She notes that "the social regulation of race emerges not simply as another, fully separable, domain of power from sexual difference or sexuality"; rather, "its 'addition' subverts the monolithic workings of the heterosexual imperative" (18).

equate change with an agency so defined is to stifle the articulation of other possibilities and to install a radically simplified scheme of moral judgment.

Butler develops a related point at length in *Gender Trouble*, arguing that "the identity categories often presumed to be foundational to feminist politics . . . simultaneously work to limit and constrain in advance the very cultural possibilities that feminism is supposed to open up" (147). She adds that "paradoxically, the reconceptualization of identity as an *effect*, that is, as *produced* or *generated*, opens up possibilities of 'agency' that are insidiously foreclosed by positions that take identity categories as foundational and fixed" (147). Butler thus concludes that "construction is not opposed to agency; it is the necessary scene of agency, the very terms in which agency is articulated and becomes culturally intelligible" (147).

We need to distinguish between contemporary political feminism, which expresses our commitment to protest and change, and academic feminism, which often forces upon us the realization that those philosophically committed to the status quo may have done as much to bring about change as those opposed to the status quo. This is not a cynical reflection, merely a pragmatic recognition that our efforts may not bear the fruit we intend within a complex dynamics of power. Jameson eloquently develops this point in *The Political Unconscious*: "History is what hurts, it is what refuses desire and sets inexorable limits to individual as well as collective praxis, which its 'ruses' turn into grisly and ironic reversals of their overt intention" (102).[23] This recognition does not absolve us from participating in the politics of change, although it might make us humble about what we have accomplished.

Of course, I must submit to the same multiplicity and contingency that I locate in my object of study. Authors, like books, bear the marks of their historical moment with its particular tensions and contradictions. Foucault reminds us in *The Archaeology of Knowledge* that "it is not possible for us to describe our own archive, since it is from within these rules that we speak, since it is that which gives to what we can say . . . its modes of appearance" (130). I have tried, by listening to other than canonical voices and through incorporating other than literary documents, to expand my vision. I hope to open

[23] In *Partings Welded Together*, David Musselwhite focuses on this same passage and poses an important question about it: "It is not rather the reverse? It is history that makes promises possible. . . . There are no inexorable limits. . . . The 'ruses' are all on our side: they turn our disasters into triumphs" (251). I share Musselwhite's critique; certainly, the evolution of the managing angel I chart here generates new possibilities for middle-class women. It is a triumph, however ironic.

up discussion and help break the lock on one of criticism's most stable identities: that of the domestic woman. We need to move beyond critical assessments that either celebrate or condemn this figure to more complex and even contradictory configurations of her role within Victorian culture.

To acknowledge one's historicity is to acknowledge the very conditions under which historical analysis takes place. To write, then, is to locate our present in the past and to do so in a way that may illuminate principally our own investment in versions of the past. But if we can begin to grasp this investment, we have understood something, even if only how our subjectivity is constituted.[24] Further, when ordinary women's lives are the object of our inquiry, we are exposing the ideologies that subtend such concepts as the "ordinary," the "unremarkable," the "normative," and the "natural."

The chapters that follow focus on Victorian social semiotics in a variety of texts. In its arbitrary and differential character, the signifier can be mustered by individuals and groups toward a consolidation of power through control of meaning. In this light, controlling the production of meanings yields cultural capital just as controlling the means of production realizes material capital. And the process by which social meanings are codified and capitalized emerges most clearly from an analysis that recognizes the integrity of texts in the production of specific effects.

In Chapter 2, I excavate the interacting material and mythic dimensions of Victorian women's lives, the conflicting gender and class ideologies, as they are represented in etiquette guides, management manuals, cookery books, and charitable treatises. These ephemera of mid-Victorian culture paint a picture of the middle-class homemaker that challenges conventional portraits of her as passive, helpless, and dependent. They position her as a key figure in erecting class barriers, in policing and maintaining borders, in contributing to a rhetoric that "naturalized" class difference, and in justifying and perpetuating the status quo.

[24] Jonathan Culler addresses the imbrication of theory and practice in "Literary Theory" and helpfully illuminates the issue: "Antitheory theory starts from the recognition, promoted by recent theoretical argument, that in reflecting on our assumptions, interests or purposes, language, mental operations, or subject position, we cannot render these things transparent or get outside them; but that is no reason to abandon attempts at theoretical reflection and argument, since the world of theoretical discussion is above all one in which the writings and arguments of others enable us to perceive and to modify aspects of our own position and procedures that we could not grasp through self-reflection" (213–14).

Numerous tracts of the period did, of course, attempt to circumscribe woman's sphere to the house and neighborhood, reacting to the discursive instability inherent in the domestic ideal, but these works ironically bought into the very values they were seeking to critique. In Chapter 3, I investigate the ways Queen Victoria as icon and local habitation of the middle-class angelic ideal disrupted both patriarchal and bourgeois ideologies. Then I turn to works by Sarah Ellis, Coventry Patmore, and John Ruskin, three central figures whose narratives of middle-class life helped to construct the image of the Angel in the House.

In Chapter 4, I analyze novels by Charles Dickens—*David Copperfield, Bleak House, Little Dorrit,* and *Our Mutual Friend*—in which representations of domestic establishments and their presiding "angels of competence" attempt to fuse gender and class ideologies. But the fissures opened up by the fusion illuminate the process by which domestic signifying practices constitute and regulate a field of individual possibilities. Dickens's novels culminate in mystifications of class relations and class management because the novels ultimately privilege the romance plot of a man and a woman, a plot firmly grounded within a patriarchal tradition.

In contrast, Elizabeth Gaskell's *Cranford,* one focus of Chapter 5, takes spinsters and widows as its subject and so early precludes the traditional romance plot. *Cranford* explores the male-female dialectic through contrastive economies of "vulgar" and "elegant." The former, associated with men and the production of material capital, plays off against the latter economy of women, emphasizing cultural capital and recycled resources. The implicit and explicit subversion of traditional gender roles and values enacted in the novel lays bare the mechanisms of middle-class control in the hands of the ladies of *Cranford.* I also examine Gaskell's last novel, *Wives and Daughters,* a work that turns the romance plot into a study of class politics in detailing the strategies by which a middle-class manager positions both herself and her daughters within the marriage market.

Gaskell's last novel seems to anticipate the fictions of Margaret Oliphant, in which the traditional romance plot is debunked and the rhetoric of "love" gives way to a rhetoric of "career" and a new romance of social power. In Chapter 6, I explore how Oliphant's ambitious heroines, Phoebe Junior and Lucilla Marjoribanks, assimilate male-female relationships to a bourgeois ideology that works toward a consolidation of middle-class control in their hands. The emphasis on woman as domestic manager over woman as beloved object anticipates the emergence of the "new woman" in the late nineteenth century.

In Chapters 7 and 8, I complicate and extend my central thesis by adopting a different focus on the domestic woman. In contrast to Dickens's, Gaskell's, and Oliphant's novels, in which the tension between bourgeois and patriarchal ideologies helps to destabilize the female subject, George Eliot's *Middlemarch* gives more weight to gender than class constructions. Although Eliot empowers women through moral and spiritualizing language, she simultaneously disempowers them as bourgeois managers by disconnecting them from meaningful household and social organization, masking the roles highlighted in Oliphant's contemporaneous novels. Eliminating the story of class management embodied in the social semiotics governing women's lives, Eliot inevitably reinscribes a narrative of gender difference and female disability within a patriarchal world.

Whereas Eliot's *Middlemarch* defuses the tension between gender and class by muting class constructions of female subjectivity, Hannah Cullwick's diary narrative of her life as a Victorian maidservant reveals how constitution of her subjectivity as working class alienated her from certain gender constructions. In Chapter 8, I examine Cullwick's narrative and her taboo relationship with a Victorian gentleman, Arthur Munby, who encouraged the production of her diary. This chapter pulls together several analytic strands: the relation between literary and nonliterary materials, the tension between gender and class representations of the female subject, the role of middle-class management in producing the servant; and the dynamic between the middle-class mistress and her repressed ideological Other, the domestic worker.

In the conclusion I briefly examine novels written before and after the mid-century works on which this book concentrates, to trace a genealogy of the female subject precipitated by these conflicting gender and class ideologies. I chart the emergence of the bourgeois manager in Fanny Burney's *Evelina* and Jane Austen's *Emma*. Sensation novels set the stage for the "new woman" novels concluding the century, novels that resolve the paradox of the managing angel by investing her traits in two characters: one, a reinscription of the passive, dependent angel and the other, an independent, self-reliant woman who is represented as a mannish, aggressive, proto-professional. This tendentious depiction exposes the threat of female autonomy posed by representations of competent female management. Positing the middle-class manager as a prototype for the "new woman," I illuminate retrospectively the mystified aspects of the Angel in the House and elucidate a process of change that depends as much on private life as public service, as much on those committed to protecting the status quo as on those who saw themselves as activists for change.

2

Material Angels:
Wings of Clay

Victorian etiquette manuals, management guides, and charitable treatises cannot be taken as straightforward accounts of middle-class life: these nonliterary materials did not simply reflect a "real" historical subject but helped to produce it through their discursive practices.[1] These were documents aimed specifically at enabling the middle class to consolidate its base of control through strategies of regulation and exclusion. They helped to construct an identity for a group that might otherwise seem bound together only by Thomas Carlyle's "cash nexus."[2]

[1] Pierre Bourdieu insists that the power of words is "nothing other than the *delegated power* of the spokesperson and his speech." In this conclusion he distinguishes himself from Saussure, who "treats language as an autonomous object, accepting the radical separation . . . between internal and external linguistics." Bourdieu usefully focuses on the fact that *all* language always exists within social relationships that it both reflects and creates. He speaks of the "alchemy of *representation* . . . through which the representative creates the group which creates him" (*Language and Symbolic Power* 107, 106).

[2] Michael McKeon's *Origins of the English Novel* distinguished its own focus from Ian Watt's in *The Rise of the Novel* partly on the question of an emergent middle class. McKeon questions Watt's association of the appearance of the novel with the "rise" of the "middle class." He suggests instead a need to "sophisticate" the relation between the genre and social class. Sophistication involves recognizing that "the middle class (and the category of 'class' as such) filled an explanatory need for which there had been no satisfactory alternative" (22). McKeon implies that the novel did as much to define a middle class as the middle class did to produce a novel—a process that is perhaps characteristic of the relations between genres and social classes in general. Nancy Armstrong develops a similar argument in *Desire and Domestic Fiction*. Focusing on conduct books, she looks at the ways these forms of writing "invaded, revised and contained" the British household by dividing the world according to sex. The ideal of the household, as represented by the domestic woman, allowed a "coherent idea of the middle class" to evolve before such a class existed. See also Armstrong and Tennenhouse, eds., *The Ideology of Conduct*, and Armstrong and Tennenhouse, *The Imaginary Puritan*.

In constructing the middle class, particularly the upper-middle class, these texts focus on women rather than men, implicitly acknowledging that the evolving signifiers of bourgeois identity properly belong to women.[3] Men performed their function by making the money without which the middle-class endeavor could not go forward, but money had to enter into a network of signifying practices before its social significance could be read. On that complex sign system women concentrated their attention, both producing and consolidating the bourgeoisie.

Constructing the Middle Class

A more formalized Society and Season marked the change from the eighteenth to the nineteenth century. Leonore Davidoff has commented that "in the 1830s and 1840s there was a reinterpretation of the idea of Society and the expectation for individual behaviour to gain access to that society," an expectation whose historical origins stem, in part, from the presence in England of the untitled gentry. "Tied to the nobility by marriage and similar life-styles" and to the farmers and middle classes "by family ties and farming interests," the untitled gentry played a crucial role in the English social hierarchy (*Best Circles* 22).

Lawrence Stone and Jeanne Stone's investigations in *An Open Elite?* both confirm and expand upon Davidoff's observations. The Stones conclude that "English society was given a basic fluidity of status by the vigour, wealth, and numerical strength of the 'middling sort'" who, "instead of resenting [their social superiors] . . . eagerly sought to imitate them, aspiring to gentility by copying the education, manners, and behaviour of the gentry" (408–9). In the mid-nineteenth century Frederich Engels commented about England that "this most bourgeois of all nations is apparently aiming ultimately at the possession of a bourgeois aristocracy and a bourgeois proletariat as well as a bourgeoisie" (115–16). Revising Engels, Lawrence and Jeanne Stone identify an "aristocratic bourgeoisie" produced by this process of "gentrification," a group who "adopted genteel cultural patterns of behavior" without following the economic and political practices of the upper class such as purchasing a country seat and agricultural estate (423).[4]

---

[3] Occasional etiquette texts addressed "gentlemen," but advice to men was always clear about women's precedence in the practices through which polite society was established and maintained.

[4] *The Habits of Good Society* (published between 1875 and 1878 according to the Brit-

In short, the middling classes did not ape the economic practices of upper-class life, but, afflicted by status anxiety, they set out to master its signifying practices. And although there were no "legal barriers based on privilege," this genteel society "was sliced and sliced again to extremely thin status layers, subtly separated from each other by the delicate but infinitely resistant lines of snobbery" (Stone and Stone 423). Davidoff articulates the consequences more tellingly for our understanding of women's roles. Because "formal-ised Society took the place of mobility controlled through legal clas-sification" (21), individuals sought stability in detailed decorums, which were in the hands of women.[5] At the same time, of course, women were in the hands of the etiquette books, which were help-ing to construct the very audience for whom and of whom they spoke.

Generally, with the rapid increase of wealth generated by the in-dustrial revolution and the consequent social upheavals, status be-came a fluid thing, increasingly dependent upon the manipulation of social signs. For example, two early etiquette manuals, *Hints on Etiquette* (1836) and *Spirit of Etiquette* (1837), explicitly acknowledge that in a "mercantile country like England, people are continually rising in the world" (*Hints* 10), and thus they set out to teach indi-viduals the signifiers that would allow them to claim the status that their money alone could not guarantee. *Etiquette for Ladies; or, The Principles of True Politeness* (1852) explicitly encourages its readers, alleging that "a sensible woman will endeavor to raise herself to a higher sphere than the one she occupies, and not run the hazard of retrograding by forming acquaintances below her station" (13).

Notably, these etiquette books were neither a continuing feature from eighteenth-century life nor a continuous aspect of the nine-teenth century. In his study of this genre, Michael Curtin has dis-

---

ish Library), advanced its own history of polite society: "The position of women . . . has always given the key to civilization. . . . In fact, the term 'gentleman' only comes in when women were admitted into society on a par with men. A 'gentleman' was one who could associate with ladies" (53). According to the manual, throughout the eighteenth century, women were still "inconsequential," so men gathered in clubs (54). The guide identifies three classes between "court" and "people": the noble, the "gentle," and the rich. In the nineteenth century, "these classes began to draw to-gether. The noble sought wives among the rich; the rich became gentle in a couple of generations, and the gentry became rich by marriage" (56).

[5] According to Michael McKeon, this breakdown in traditional forms originated in the eighteenth century; indeed, he claims that the emergence of the novel parallels conditions of "status inconsistency" in early modern England. Although these ten-sions may date back to the eighteenth century, they intensified in the early nine-teenth century as strategies developed to manage them.

covered that no conduct manuals were published between 1804 and 1828. Suddenly in the 1830s, numerous new volumes found print. The rise of etiquette guides thus coincides with a period in British life inaugurated by the Reform Bill, a period marked by a drive to represent new forces in British politics and economics and a compensatory desire to stabilize the system along predictable lines. In 1837, the *Quarterly* reviewed eleven etiquette books, all published within the previous two years, some in several editions (34, 40).[6] These guides, which highlighted the way "social status could be indicated through a minute control of conventional behavior," differed substantially from the earlier courtesy or conduct books.[7] The latter focused on individual standards of moral and civil conduct and had as topics "fortitude," "honesty," "fidelity," and so on—in sharp contrast to the etiquette manual's chapters on "balls," "introductions and cuts," "calls," and the like (Curtin 31–32, 130). Whereas the conduct books were aimed at individual behavior, the etiquette guides targeted the construction and consolidation of a social group.[8]

The public's hunger for these manuals intensified throughout the middle of the century, suggesting their prominent role in codifying behaviors through which mutual recognition could take place among members of the new middle classes, who marked their difference not only from the working class but also from others within

[6] Leonore Davidoff (*Best Circles* 18, 41); and Duncan Crow (47–48) also comment on the phenomenon.

[7] The etymology of "etiquette" enforces this distinction. *Manners of Modern Society* spelled it out in 1872: "Centuries ago, the word 'etiquette' conveyed to those who used it a far different signification than to us of the present day. The word—an Anglo-Norman one—originally specified the ticket tied to the necks of bags or affixed to the bundles to denote their contents. A bag or bundle thus ticketed passed unchallenged" (35). The idea of passing unchallenged, of being certified, is certainly relevant to Victorian etiquette. The manual explains that codes of manners were written or printed on cards or tickets, and thus etiquette began to take on its current meaning (35).

[8] Although Curtin's is the most exhaustive study to date, it tends to take the etiquette manuals at face value. Curtin does not address how etiquette books functioned in the construction of class and class differences. See John F. Kasson's excellent analysis of their function in forming American society of the nineteenth century and Andrew St. George's interesting study of the meaning of etiquette in England. St. George argues that "the search for rules was the cornerstone of mid-Victorian thinking" (xvii). He recognizes that "etiquette is class control exercised"; however, his focus is not on class dynamics but on the Victorians' "search for rules, thinking and feeling according to rule as a matter of instinct in any situation" (xiv, xvii). St. George does not make the genealogical distinctions I do between etiquette books and earlier conduct and courtesy manuals, and he examines only a few Victorian etiquette books. As a result, his analysis concludes with a traditional understanding of women's roles, and he positions the home in conventional ways: "The home needed to define itself against the outside" (xix).

the middle class. Many of the guides adopted a lofty tone in delineating their purpose in order to produce in their readership a high sense of cultural mission. *Etiquette for Ladies; or, The Principles of True Politeness* is typical in address, announcing that "etiquette has become so essentially necessary to the comfort and happiness (indeed . . . the very existence) of society" that no one can afford to ignore it. The redundancy of "essential" and "necessary" as well as the hyperbole of "very existence" mark the missionary zeal of these writers. This one continues: "[Etiquette] is the universal power that binds society together—an effectual barrier against the innovations of the vulgar; a rubicon, the uncouth in manner and low in speech can never hope to pass" (9). This rhetoric reveals that at least one important function of these guides was to establish as normative the notion of social barriers—the specific details mattering less than the mandate to exclude, to preserve fine distinctions of rank. For example, *Etiquette for Ladies and Gentlemen* (1862) adduces as justification for itself "protection against the intrusion of those whose abrupt manners and vulgar habits would render them disagreeable and obnoxious" (8). *Etiquette for Ladies* (1851) advances another "necessity for such rules," that is, "in large societies of men and women, . . . few people can be expected to know each other thoroughly, and all dangers of misapprehension are needful to be removed" (5).

At the same time that etiquette erects these social barriers, its rhetoric attempts to "naturalize" these boundaries and differences. *A Manual of Etiquette for Ladies; or, True Principles of Politeness* (1856) argues the propriety of social distinctions: "By some [etiquette] is regarded as essentially artificial. It is not so. . . . It is not mere tinselled covering . . . it is true and natural, arising from the sense of what is due to one's self and due to others" (5–6). The "self" and "other" are carefully positioned here in an economy of privilege that makes differences a function of nature rather than of nurture or economic opportunity.

It is a popular misconception that these etiquette manuals helped to facilitate the movement of individuals from a lower to a higher sphere in society. In fact, they appear less to have facilitated a rise in status than to have consolidated an image of the genteel middle class. These etiquette guides targeted members of "polite" society: not until the end of the century did a manual—*Cassells' Book of the Household*—address a "mass readership covering all aspects of the population" (Briggs, *Victorian Things* 218).

Two other schemes for class advancement seem more likely. First, a domestic servant occasionally could move via marriage from a position and experience in a middle-class household into the lower-middle classes. Her knowledge of the signifying practices of bourgeois life facilitated her own family's rise. F. M. L. Thompson has confirmed this phenomenon: "Working-class girls, therefore, could and did marry upwards in the social scale in significant numbers, chiefly into the lower middle class, many of them no doubt making the transition via a spell in domestic service" (95). This scheme, however, is rarely represented in literature perhaps because it confirms too fully the fear that the ranks would be contaminated by outsiders.

As a second strategy, a man successful in trade might contract a marriage with a lady. The Stones note "the relatively early acceptance of self-made men, as companions or marriage partners, by persons of genteel birth and elite status" as one paradigm for social mobility (*Open Elite* 20). This phenomenon is frequently represented in the Victorian novel, where it forms the groundwork of Louis Moore's confidence that he may wed wealthy heiress Shirley Keeldar in Brontë's *Shirley*, or Mr. Thornton's belief that he may finally win the hand of Margaret Hale in Gaskell's *North and South*, or even Pip's expectation that he will marry the genteely reared Estella in Dickens's *Great Expectations*. This pattern confirms the inviolable status of women at the same time that it accommodates the popular rags-to-riches plot of emergent capitalism. In fact, it conveniently links the hero's monetary quest to a corollary social rise.

Whereas these several novels all conclude with prospective wedding bells and thus do not pursue the social consequences of such unequal alliances, at least one Victorian novel, Margaret Oliphant's *Phoebe Junior*, represents those effects. Mr. Copperhead, a wealthy, crass businessman, has married as second wife a woman, who "though she had not the heart of a mouse . . . could play the great lady when occasion served" (76). Significantly her husband's social superior, the second Mrs. Copperhead has been bred as a lady and possesses the genteel manners that can help realize her husband's "hunger of wealth for that something above wealth" (21), his "craze for Society which so often and so sorely affects the millionaire" (20). Mr. Copperhead "somewhat despised" the progeny of his first marriage, "his elder sons who were like himself" and sets great store in the son of his second marriage: a genteel, university-educated, "perfectly useless specimen of humanity" (12). That "useless" son ultimately wins election to Parliament and so confirms the familial rise in status. The fact that a working man may marry a lady but a working woman may not marry a gentleman points to the role of bour-

geois women in establishing and representing gentility, a role whose
emergence was facilitated by the etiquette manuals, which gave priority to women in matters of calls and cuts, the means through
which social groups were formed and maintained.

Of course, noblemen did marry down, but they could afford to do
what the aspiring middle-class professional could not. Thompson
comments that "although fiction, not implausibly, records attraction
and romance across these divides, it is most unlikely that real-life
affairs of this ilk made any appreciable impression on the class and
group defences which the middle classes had erected round their
daughters and sons" (105). It is worth reiterating, pace Thompson,
that fiction, which recorded attraction but not legitimate consumma-
tion, was closely following real life; in fact, it was helping to construct that "reality."

The priorities informing middle-class marriage are articulated in
an 1856 manual *How to Woo; How to Win; and How to Get Married*,
which begins by setting out general principles.

> Let it never be forgotten, that the man who, in wedding descends
> much, in a manner *taboos* himself from the society of his equals. A peer
> may marry an actress or an opera-dancer, and the lustre of his coronet
> will act as an *open sesame* to the "at home" and the court—the dowlas of
> the wife will be expiated by the ermine of the husband. But it is differ-
> ent with a commoner in the middle ranks of life. There the ladies are
> most ultra tenacious of their rank—(the more so, perhaps, because
> some of them are aware that they hold it on a tenure not altogether
> unexceptionable), and are more strict than the Neroy King at Arms
> himself, in admitting any one to their *set* who has too suddenly clomb
> the ladder of life. The husband may keep up his bachelor acquain-
> tances, but his wife being debarred from general society, he cannot, if
> he have becoming spirit, go where she is not admitted. They cannot
> live without society, and are consequently obliged to cultivate less ex-
> clusive circles, far below the husband's rank, and in which, at one time,
> he never anticipated to move. (21–22)

A somber warning inheres in this description of a man's fate when
he marries beneath his rank: he will surely suffer a loss of caste that
he must also bequeath to his children. Much better, such guides
imply, to marry a woman who will solidify or better her husband's
social position with appropriate status display. The bourgeois narrative thus bonds gentility with monetary gain, cultural with material
capital, dictating that a man's acquisition of wealth must be matched
by his winning a genteel wife.

Although the links between Society and governmental politics are often occluded, the connection is tellingly exposed in the coincidence of the London "Season" with the sitting of Parliament, the "greatest club of all" (Davidoff, *Best Circles* 21). Dickens capitalizes on the connection in *Our Mutual Friend* when Veneering queries of Twemlow, "What do you think of my entering the House of Commons?" and Twemlow "feelingly" rejoins, "That is the best club in London" (246). In *Miss Marjoribanks*, Margaret Oliphant lays out the role of society's hostesses in furthering political careers. The eponymous heroine has returned from school to her father's home, determined to control local politics by dominating society: "To have the control of society in her hands was a great thing; but still the mere means, without any end, was not worth Lucilla's while. . . . It was this [need for an end] that made Mr Ashburton so interesting to her, and his election a matter into which she entered so warmly, for she had come to an age at which she might have gone into Parliament herself had there been no disqualification of sex, and when it was almost a necessity for her to make some use of her social influence. . . . She was a Power in Carlingford, and she knew it; but still there is little good in the existence of a Power unless it can be made use of for some worthy end" (394–95). Even as the text points to a "disqualification of sex" in national office, it affirms a compensatory qualification for social and class management at the local level. The social arbiter predicated in the etiquette guides was emerging.

Policing the Social Borders

The manuals were precise and detailed, giving exact information, particularly on the most sensitive areas governed by etiquette: introductions, calls, and cuts. The first two were mechanisms for defining and maintaining the group; the last was the mechanism for excluding undesirable individuals. Because of their central functions, all became highly elaborated (Davidoff, *Best Circles* 41). A system so fully developed—specifying the way cards were to be left, the official timetable for visiting, the duration and content of calls—obviously played a significant role in establishing and solidifying the Victorian hierarchy. *A Manual of Etiquette for Ladies* (1856) set an appropriately lofty tone in summarizing etiquette's function as establishing the "rule of conduct which is recognized by polite society . . . that law to which obedience must be rendered; the sovereign to which authority and allegiance are due" (3). Even if we are inclined to be skeptical about the possibility of persons observing such rules in daily life, the very popularity of the etiquette manuals reveals a pervasive awareness of and commitment to the class distinctions they create and reinforce.

The "call," with its elaborated rituals, became the mechanism by which social groups were formed and consolidated. Conventions of calling at the time of a woman's marriage gave her an opportunity to redesign her social list, "cutting" ineligible and undesirable acquaintances and forging more desirable bonds. *Etiquette for Ladies* (1851) stipulates that "it is generally understood if when a marriage takes place the cards of the partners are not sent to any of their previous acquaintance, the intimacy is considered at an end" (33). The bride is further instructed that when she "wishes to decline intimacy with any of her former friends, having repaid their visit, she has only politely to refuse all their subsequent invitations" (32).

Because the custom of calling functioned to define and solidify a social group, women faced a heavy burden of maintaining acquaintance through visiting.[9] As a result, the "morning" call became highly formalized. Isabella Beeton's popular *Book of Household Management* (1861), which sold sixty-thousand copies in its first year, was typically detailed, stipulating, for example, the duration and character of a call: "fifteen to twenty minutes being quite sufficient. A lady paying a visit may remove her boa or neckerchief; but neither her shawl nor bonnet" (10). Elizabeth Gaskell makes such strict guidelines the subject of wry humor in *Cranford* when a young lady is instructed "never to stay longer than a quarter of an hour." She remarks, "As everybody has this rule in their minds . . . of course no absorbing subject was ever spoken about. We kept ourselves to short sentences of small talk, and were punctual to our time" (41).

Such visits of ceremony, notes *Etiquette for Ladies* (1852), are "usually paid in the morning between the hours of one and three" (19). *Manners and Tone of Good Society* informs its readers that "calls made in the morning—that is, before one o'clock—would not come under the denomination of 'morning calls'" (23). The student of etiquette would find elucidation in *How to Behave*: "Morning, in fashionable parlance, means any time before dinner" (68–69). Ladies unable to receive visitors would have their servants announce that they were

[9] A practice of too frequent calls, however, could give one a bad reputation as a "day goblin" or as "one of those persons who, having plenty of leisure, and a great desire to hear themselves talk, make frequent inroads into their friends' houses" (*Etiquette, Social Ethics, and Dinner-Table Observances* 22). The implication is that one had to be privy to the requisite proportions of things.

"not at home," a message decoded in *Etiquette for Ladies and Gentlemen*: "These last words are not, as they are sometimes thought, a falsehood, for everyone knows they merely mean you are engaged and cannot see visitors" (19). The elaborate encodings of meanings speak eloquently of the privileged and privileging nature of this discourse.

The formulaic and ritualistic nature of the call enabled women constantly to police and maintain their social borders, keeping up "a sort of acquaintance, which, without some such arrangement, would soon fall to the ground" (*Etiquette for the Ladies: Eighty Maxims* 17). In 1872, *Manners of Modern Society* responded to criticism of the inanity of these customs by countering: "Visits of form, of which most people complain and yet to which most people submit, are absolutely necessary—being in fact the basis on which that great structure, society, mainly rests" (62). No other mechanism presented itself so clearly as a way to identify who was in and who was out. The call allowed one to override any casual contact or acquaintance. *Manners of Modern Society* continues: "You cannot invite people to your house, however often you may have met them elsewhere, until you have first called upon them in a formal manner, and they have returned your visit" (62). Because this barrier made acquaintance a highly formal matter, no interloper could easily squirrel her way into Society.

If calling conventions did not adequately perform their policing function, the "cut" was held in reserve. *Etiquette for the Ladies* (1837) opines that it is "almost unnecessary to hint that the introductions which are made at public balls and assemblies are for the night only. It is strictly in Etiquette for a lady to cut even a nobleman on the morrow" (49). Like the call, the cut was almost entirely in the hands of middle-class women. It marked a refusal to recognize an individual as part of one's set and was carried out through various mechanisms: not responding to a salutation, a bow, a card, or a call; not answering a letter or an invitation. *The Habits of Good Society* advises that "a gentleman must never cut a lady under any circumstances. An unmarried lady should never cut a married one. A servant of whatever class . . . should never cut his master; near relations should never cut one another . . . and a clergyman should never cut anybody, because it is at best an unchristian action" (280). Apparently no one else was to be deterred by the lack of Christianity in such actions. In contrast to women, men generally enjoyed more casual interactions with a wide group of individuals both in business and in clubs. But the manuals stipulate that friendships thus "casually" formed ended the moment the pater familias crossed the threshold of his home. Further, men could visit more freely than women precisely because their presence had no social significance. In *Middlemarch*, for example, Mr. Vincy is invited to dine with the Brookes, whereas "Miss Vincy . . . was of course not present; for Mr. Brooke, always objecting to go too far, would not have chosen that his nieces should meet the daughter of a Middlemarch manufacturer" (66). In Oliphant's *Phoebe Junior*, a young lady gloats to her brother: "Men may think themselves as grand as they please . . . but their visits are of no consequence; it is ladies of the family who must *call!*" (173).

As an additional guarantor of middle-class hegemony, the details of this highly formalized system of etiquette changed constantly, "to mark the knowledgeable insider from the outsider" (Davidoff 45). *Etiquette for the Ladies* (1837) opens with the acknowledgment that "the frequent and sudden changes in the observances of fashionable life, render a little manual of this sort necessary" (5–6). Thirty-five years later, *Manners of Modern Society* (1872) also adduces mutability as a reason for publishing yet another book on the subject of etiquette: "Although the broad principles of manners remain the same, yet the minutiae are continually altering and varying, and modes of speech and action which were considered the height of politeness a few years ago, would be pronounced at any rate very old-fashioned if used and exhibited in the present day" (vii). One might adapt Bourdieu's comment, "L'État, c'est moi. Or, what amounts to the same thing, the world is my representation" (106) to the Victorians: "Gentility, c'est moi. Or, what amounts to the same thing, gentility is my representation."

Dressing the Part

At the same time that the introduction, call, and cut kept strict control of the social group, dress became an increasingly complex signifying practice. Details of dress, always associated with status, took on increasing subtlety as indicators of class rank within the middle classes. Davidoff explains, "The strict demarcation by age as well as status of women and girls in the nineteenth century is indicated by the variety and complexity of their clothes as opposed to the almost uniform drab 'workman-like or business-like' look of men's clothing after the 1840s. Every cap, bow, streamer, ruffle, fringe, bustle, glove or other elaboration symbolised some status category for the female wearer" (93). *The Ladies' Science of Etiquette* (1851) particularly emphasizes fabric and headgear, but also stipulates underclothing: "The most fashionable dress for a lady on first rising from bed, is a small muslin cap, and morning gown of printed cotton. It is well that a half corset should precede the full corset, which last is used only when one is dressed; for it is bad taste for a lady not to be laced at all" (42–43). The manual further advises, "Ladies should make morning calls in an elegant and simple néglegé" (44).

The challenge for the "true" lady was to distinguish the appropriate finery for each hour of the day. The guides always caution against overdressing: "It is a mark of deficient education for a lady to appear in full dress before dinner . . . [the practice] at once betrays her deficiency of taste and judgment, exhibits her flimsy attempts at gentility" (*Manual of Etiquette for Ladies* 17–18). *Etiquette for Ladies and Gentlemen* echoes this caveat: "To appear in full dress before dinner, a time when every good wife should be attending to her domestic duties, shows a flimsy affectation and assumption of gentility" (74). Tellingly, this later guide grounds the practice of dress in the ideology of domesticity, making apparent the process of image management at work.

Distinctions of dress licensed exclusion of "vulgar" individuals from the social set. Always the emphasis rests on subtle understatement in apparel. Excessive finery becomes a trap to betray the nouveaux riches. *Etiquette for Ladies and Gentlemen* (1876) cautions, "Remember, however, that it is better to be too plainly dressed than too much dressed. Nothing has a more vulgar appearance than being too fine" (13–14). The manual continues with the following warning: "Never dress *above* your station; it is a grievous mistake and leads to great evils, besides being the proof of an utter want of taste" (15). The anonymous writer is betrayed into incoherence by conflicting ideologies.[10] If one signifies status by dress, one can never dress above one's station. How one dresses constitutes the person and class. In fact, the writer hopes to deter the arriviste by suggesting that those who dress above their station only attempt to do so, but actually expose themselves through excess finery and so do not, in fact, dress above their station at all. What the author of the manual fears is that someone might actually succeed through dress in trick-

[10] Most of these etiquette guides were published anonymously, the author listed only by her social role, which, after all, was the basis for her authority: "a lady," "a lady of fashion," "a member of the aristocracy," "an English lady and gentleman," "a mentor," and so forth.

ing the public into believing she is of a higher rank than she is. Thus, what she will have revealed is not "an utter want of taste" but an exquisite discrimination. The "great evil" arises because someone will have successfully imposed on a society that fancies sufficient its mechanisms for distinguishing rank.

The writer is led into these incoherences by a conviction that, finally, dress simply expresses the true nature of a lady. But that belief contradicts what is everywhere accepted in these elaborate discussions of apparel, that is, that dress constitutes the lady. This conflation and confusion of nature and haute couture also find expression in *Etiquette for Ladies* (1852): "The love of dress is natural to woman, and the good or bad taste they [sic] display in the selection and arrangement of it, gives you a good insight into their character" (15). Beneath their superficial aim of acquainting readers with the rituals of polite life, the manuals perform the major function of naturalizing differences of class and rank. These guides, which purport to facilitate social movement, thus work to justify and perpetuate the status quo, distinguishing particularly between upper- and lower-middle classes.

The novelists kept pace with the etiquette guides, reflecting society's preoccupation with dress as a signifier of class and rank. George Eliot's *Middlemarch* opens with dress as a social sign for Dorothea and Celia Brooke, who regard "frippery as the ambition of a huckster's daughter." Even Celia, who shows far more interest in dress than Dorothea, "wore scarcely more trimmings. . . . The pride of being ladies had something to do with it: the Brooke connections, though not exactly aristocratic, were unquestionably 'good'" (5). In *Adam Bede*, Hetty Sorrel's addiction to trinkets marks her irrevocably as lower class. Margaret Oliphant, in *Phoebe Junior*, expands on these class implications of dress. When the eponymous character, whose parents have successfully climbed the social ladder, returns to visit her shopkeeper grandparents, she finds herself negotiating a difficult social breach, concretized by her dress. One observer thinks, "How strange it was to see her . . . putting her daintily-gloved hand upon old Tozer's greasy sleeve, walking home with the shuffling old man, about whose social position no one could make the least mistake" (118). When Phoebe's grandmother wants to dress her granddaughter up and show her off to the community, she requests that Phoebe put on silk and bright colors, a lace collar, a pad, and an ostentatious brooch, to all of which requests Phoebe politely demurs, privately horrified at the implicit class transformation. "So that Phoebe's toilette, which would have been mightily admired in a

London drawing-room, could not be said to be a success [with her grandparents]" (121). A "true" lady will have internalized the principle summed up by Isabella Beeton: "It is better to be under-dressed than over-dressed" (10).

These rituals of dress were further elaborated in the paraphernalia of mourning—"in dress and its accessories, in stationery, seals, floral decorations and other insignia"—that might allow persons, upon emerging from mourning "to reshuffle their social hand by the skilful play of cards and calls" (Davidoff 55, 56). We can now fully appreciate the disdain of the ladies of Gaskell's *Cranford* when a widow appears in public "dressed in rustling black silk, so soon after her husband's death," because "bombazine would have shown a deeper sense of her loss" (108).

In a gendered politics of power, middle-class Victorian women were subservient to men; but in a class politics of power, upper-middle-class women cooperated and participated with men to achieve control, managing the cultural capital that secured their own preeminence and authority in contrast to both the working class and the lower-middle classes. Ironically, the very signifiers of powerlessness in the gendered frame of reference became eloquent signifiers of power in a class frame. As Florence Nightingale's impassioned testimony in *Cassandra* makes clear, although women sometimes suffered from the rituals of etiquette—social corsets as rigid as the physical corsets confining their bodies—nonetheless women did control these signifiers of class status. The clothes, like the customs, were constructed to distinguish lower classes and ranks from the genteel middle class. A lady's apparel, physically confining as it may have been, was also a sign of her class power because it precluded physical labor and displayed her managerial status. Of course, many middle-class women did work; one maid-of-all-work could not accomplish everything that needed to be done in a home. But ladies pretended they did no useful work (Besant 91).

The class implications of dress in Victorian England have been imperfectly grasped in our criticism to date, which has tended to emphasize the incapacitating effects of wasp waists and crinolines. One may be surprised to discover, for example, the degree to which guides and manuals decried rather than extolled the wasp waist and tiny foot, two aspects of dress much emphasized in contemporary accounts of Victorian women. *Etiquette for Ladies* (1851) urges its readers to "wear rational shoes" (17). In 1838 Samuel Smiles criticized "the aristocracy of wasp-waists" and called for arresting the practice of forcing "the little chest of the tender girl . . . within the smallest dimensions that bare existence without suffocation will admit of" (*Physical Education* 91). Phillis Browne, writing forty-two years later, sounds the same theme: "Girls who practice the suicidal habit of tight lacing know quite well what they are about; they are not foolish from ignorance. Addresses have been delivered, and diagrams have been published . . . until everyone understands that the girl who laces tightly is adopting measures that will push her heart and lungs and other organs completely out of their places, and will cause or aggravate serious disease" (*What Girls Can Do* 124). Browne at least has the sense to seek for an answer other than female perversity, and she notes that women are forced into tight lacing by the fashion industry, which designs dresses requiring the support of stays (129). Yet fashion, as I have suggested, is driven by cultural beliefs, the most telling here being that middle-class women were above menial work and were different in kind from the female servants who performed that work. A lady who had been tight laced was incapable of physical exertion; she could scarcely breathe.

The importance of dress in signifying class emerges yet more clearly when one reads the numerous pamphlets and sermons decrying fine dress in servants and urging mistresses to use their power and influence to curb this license and the class discontent it betokens. An entire pamphlet addressed to this question—*Why Do the Servants of the Nineteenth Century Dress As They Do?* (1859)—lays out the evils of servants aping their masters: "It is the love of dress that particularly marks [servants'] discontent with their station in which God has placed them, and their struggles to exchange it for another. . . . Servants should not be ashamed to appear as servants, but I very much fear that servants who dress above their station, want to appear what they are not" (21–22). The writer makes a final appeal to the "Mistresses of England": "The remedy for the evil that this little pamphlet seeks to expose, is in great measure, in your hands. . . . Let there be one simultaneous movement on the part of the mistresses of England to put down this mischievous love of dress among servants. . . . When they find that they can enter a family and dress as they like, without any command to alter the style and discontinue the nonsense, no wonder that the evil abounds and prospers" (23). Henry George Watkins makes the question of servants' dress central in his *Friendly Hints to Female Servants*:

Dress as becomes your station. The cast-off cloaths of mistresses, when worn without alteration, have occasioned great mischief, tho' the cause may not be known. A female so attired, repels him who might be a suitable partner in married life—renders herself an object of jealousy to her mistress, and only excites the attention of the seducer and destroyer. The happiness of society arises from each of us keeping in our station, and being contented with it. Among other ways of showing your wisdom, *dressing clean and neat*, but in a style very inferior to that of your mistress, is of the greatest importance. (18–19)

The strong language employed—"mischief," "repels," "seducer and destroyer"—lodged within a rhetoric of proper station, represents sartorial choice as a matter of morality rather than fashion.[11] One wonders to whom, exactly, these tracts were addressed. Many servants were unable to read and, further, lacked funds, leisure, and the inclination (one would imagine) to purchase these diatribes. Such conclusions suggest that the authors intended rather to inspirit mistresses to exercise discipline in matters of their servants' dress than to persuade servants to reform. The lines between management and labor were to be clearly drawn.[12]

Putting on the Ritz

Middle-class women were pursuing a "career of sociability" (Curtin 302), the necessary complement to a man's career of monetarily remunerated work. These were not separate, but integrated and integral careers. Indeed, the celebrated domesticity of nineteenth-century women tends to conceal the increasing domesticity of men, the expectation that a master would socialize at home in the evenings so that a couple could develop and cultivate mutual acquaintances

[11] Henry Mayhew, in *London Labour and the London Poor*, syntactically links interest in dress with immorality: "Maid-servants live well, have no care or anxiety, no character worth speaking about to lose, for the origin of most of them is obscure, are fond of dress, and under these circumstances it cannot be wondered that they are as a body immoral and unchaste" (quoted in Horn 133).

[12] Daniel Defoe was irritated that the dress of women servants did not reliably bespeak class: "I remember I was put very much to the Blush, being at a Friend's House, and by him required to salute the Ladies, and I kiss'd the chamber Jade into the bargain, for she was as well dressed as the best. Things of this Nature would be easily avoided, if Servant Maids were to wear Liveries, as our Footmen do; or obliged to go in a Dress suitable to their Station. Our Charity Children are distinguished by their Dresses, why then may not our Women Servants?" (quoted in Horn 12). By the Victorian age, a working "uniform" had evolved: "lilac, blue or pink cotton working-dresses with white aprons and caps for the mornings, and in the afternoons, at least for housemaids and parlourmaids, a formal black dress, worn with frilled apron and cap" (Horn 113). But many mistresses tried to control off-duty apparel of their servants as well.

within their social class.[13] John Stuart Mill describes this phenomenon in *The Subjection of Women*: "The improved tone of modern feeling as to the reciprocity of duty which binds the husband towards his wife—has thrown the man very much more upon home and its inmates, for his personal and social pleasures" (quoted in Briggs, *Things* 220). What I have described as a social career to match a monetary career is here represented by the phrase "reciprocity of duty," which in its very generality disguises the pragmatic aspects of the relationship as affective bonds.

Balls and elaborate dinner parties became the functions at which a husband and wife together cemented their social status. Invitations to dinner were always sent in the combined names of the lady and gentleman (*Manual of Etiquette for Ladies* 26), those to balls in the lady's name only (*Ladies' Pocket-Book of Etiquette* 57). Responses, however, in both cases were directed to the lady alone. She was the social general, the commander of field activities. The author of *Etiquette, Social Ethics, and Dinner-Table Observances*, in fact, adopts this military metaphor for the social hostess: "To order dinner well is a matter requiring great generalship" (127).

The complexities of courses coupled with the management of serving staff turned dinner parties into a crucible for the hostess. Dinner was more than a meal; it staged status. By mid-century the custom of dining at seven and sitting down to a meal already placed on the table (Diner à la Français) had given way to the Diner à la Russe. Dinner was served between eight and nine, and servants, one for each three guests, would serve diners individually. This style of dining, which required an extensive serving staff, allowed hosts to display their superior wealth and resources. If a hostess lacked sufficient servants to hand round the food, she could serve Diner à l'Anglais, "a mixture of the old method of having dishes on the table (Diner à la Française) and the new style of having them on the sideboard (à la Russe)" (Davies 139–40). But style, obviously, signified fortune.

Courses were numerous; a typical menu stipulated soup, fish, made dishes or entrées, the roast, vegetables, the game, pastry or puddings or tarts, the ice, and dessert (*Habits of Good Society* 315, also *Etiquette for Ladies and Gentlemen*). The addition of entrées

[13] Michael Curtin remarks that "the wife's duties as family emissary in the matter of calls and cards seem to have expanded through the century. The fact that it became increasingly the normal pattern for husbands and wives to spend their evenings together . . . meant that the acquaintances of each of the spouses tended also to become family acquaintances" (223).

proved a trial for many hostesses since they were to show "the skill of the cook or the taste of the dinner-giver" (Davies 143). Miss Marjoribanks, in Oliphant's novel of that name, begins her conquest of local society at the dinner table. Her resounding success there marks the first step in her triumphant sponsorship of a local candidate for election to Parliament. When a neighbor enthuses over her triumph—"I never realised before what it was to have a genius. . . . I have given dinners all my life . . . but I never could come up to anything like that"—Miss Marjoribanks placidly replies, "I don't pretend to be better than other people. It is because I have thought it all over, you know—and then I went through a course of political economy when I was at [school]" (80–81). She, in short, attributes her success at the dinner table to a knowledge of politics, a study she had insisted on having added to her curriculum while a schoolgirl. The converse, as we have seen, is also true—success in politics is due to knowledge of the dinner table—but few writers display this truth so freely as Margaret Oliphant does.

Be It Ever So Humble

Social status was marked not only on the woman's person and in her social demeanor but in her sanctum and sanctuary, the home. The Victorian home became a physical theater for staging one's social status, and architecture in the nineteenth century changed in response.

Elaborate sign systems such as etiquette, dress, and architecture reveal how Victorians bifurcated male and female; but their bifurcation of servant and master classes was more insidious because it was more thoroughly mystified. As we will see, the feminine icon of the Angel in the House is also a middle-class ideal built explicitly on a class system of difference where political and economic differences were rewritten as differences of nature. In the Victorian household, the priority accorded the class dialectic of mistress and servant led to dramatically different inscriptions of gendered subjectivities. Social ideology inscribed the lower classes as inherently less moral, less delicate, more physical, and more capable of strenuous physical work.[14] This social distinction fed several different ideological ends.

[14] Michael E. Rose argues that the middle classes saw the lower classes as qualitatively different from themselves. Distinguishing between poverty, which they regarded as a stimulus to hard work, and pauperism, "a contagious disease but also a hereditary one," they credited genetic causes over environmental ones (63). Henry

It helped rationalize female prostitution among the lower classes as a consequence of moral depravity rather than social destitution; it justified policies of religious exhortation and state punishment against crime rather than a social welfare agenda; and, more generally, it grounded class arrangements in a framework of "providential" design. This refiguration of sex and class was necessary to a domestic ideology because "the main distinguishing mark between the middle-class woman and those who were considered socially inferior was the attitude of mind which demanded that she should have at least one servant to wait on her" (Crow 49; Hall 28).

The relation of kitchen to dining room provides a bridge from the class implications of eating practices to those of architecture. Kitchen odors or smells, associated inevitably with bodily processes and needs, were taboo. As a result, the room where the food was prepared by domestic servants was at a distance from the room where the food was consumed by the bourgeois family. To prevent its smells from reaching any other part of the house, the kitchen was divided from other areas by passages and stairways, making it extremely difficult to deliver food to the dining room before it became cold. But the absolute injunction against odors prevailed over comfort and convenience.

The metonymic association of odor and the lower classes finds elaboration in Mrs. Parton's 1888 treatise *From Kitchen to Garret*: "I cannot tell how it is, but a domestic appears to me to be born into the world bereft of any sense of smell. They can never smell anything. You will go into the kitchen and discover an odour enough to appal you and you will say, 'What is this terrible smell; I wonder,' but your cook will reply, 'Smell, Mam? Oh I don't smell anything, perhaps it have drifted in at the window.' Do not for one moment think you are wrong and she is right" (quoted in Davies 71). Domestics, Mrs. Parton implies, are mired in a base materiality, a reflection of their coarser natures. Hannah Cullwick, Victorian maid-of-all-work, tells a poignant story of a constipation that leads her to request a diet of cabbage from her mistress, who fails to understand her need. "Well, I give her a hint, this way and that, but she couldn't take it; so at last I says, 'Well Ma'am, you know as cabbage is good to open the bowels.'" Her mistress's shocked response— "How can you speak like that to *me*?"—culminates in tears as the

---

Mayhew's account of London labor alleges frequent and serious misconduct by domestic servants, a conclusion more dependent on ideology than on factual evidence (*London Labour and the London Poor*, vol. 4).

poor maidservant apologizes, "I meant no harm I'm sure, only you won't let one speak to be understood" (quoted in Hiley 128). Ladies, it seems, were not to have bowels. *The Habits of Good Society* simply cautions: "Beau Brummel broke off an engagement with a young lady because he once saw her eat cabbage" (33).

The segregation of the kitchen from the rest of the household underscores gender and class distinctions evident everywhere in the architecture. Mark Girouard has noted the increasing demand for segregation and privacy of sexes and classes in Victorian houses. F. M. L. Thompson makes a similar observation that the layout of houses "encouraged their occupants to conform to a stereotype of respectability": a measure of respectability, here, as in female clothing, being that the "wife did not work or could not be seen to work apart from running the household" (176). Spaces were encoded as masculine and feminine. For example, drawing rooms were feminine spaces, which usually meant "spindly gilt or rosewood, and silk or chintz" and dining rooms were masculine spaces, dictating "massive oak or mahogany and Turkey carpets" (Girouard, *English Country House* 292). *Manners of Modern Society* (1872) distinguishes between the "grave, formal and massive" appearance of dining rooms and libraries versus the "elegant déshabille" of the drawing and morning rooms: "Tables must be placed here, there, and everywhere, and yet not be in the way" (109–10).

Men's spaces proliferated in smoking rooms, billiard rooms, and bachelor suites, a result of a "remember-there-are-ladies-present-sir" attitude (Girouard, *Victorian Country House* 34). Women's spaces extended from the drawing room to sitting rooms and boudoirs. The masters' establishment was separated from the servants' quarters, which also mirrored the separation of sexes in the arrangement of rooms. Within these multiple divisions, middle-class individuals were further separated into private rooms. Victorians increasingly valued privacy; manuals such as *How to Behave* [1865] argued that "each person in a dwelling should, if possible, have a room as sacred from intrusion as the house is to the family" (49). This dictum did not, of course, extend to the domestic servants, who were often crowded together in attic quarters.

The extent that servants are overlooked in such recommendations reveals their status as factotums in the bourgeois family. The best servant was an invisible one; aside from personal attendants, who obviously were exempt, servants were expected to time their work so that they would never meet with the family. Back staircases, hidden doorways, and secluded passageways enabled servants to escape detection as they performed their duties. Such architecture and practices fostered, one must imagine, the divorce between materiality and spirituality that characterizes the Victorian age, particularly in its representations of women. Davidoff and Hawthorn, in *A Day in the Life of a Victorian Servant*, recreate the experiences of a "tweeny," or between maid, who helps out both the cook and housemaid. In one episode, she efficiently cleans the chamber of a lady who is at breakfast, clearing away all bodily traces of the night before: "She stripped the bed, turned the mattress and then remade the bed. She emptied the soapy water from the basin on the washstand into the slop bucket, and, gritting her teeth, stooped down and reached under the bed for the chamber pot. There was a lavatory on the same floor, but there was no question of Miss Frances going along to use it at night. It was the tweeny's job to clean away the slops" (27–28). Like kitchen odors, bodily evidences were not to intrude upon refined senses.

In order to enforce a strict segregation by class, the clean lines and open spaces of the eighteenth-century house were often cut up to provide passageways and partitions: "In an age when government was organized into departments, the middle classes into professions, science into different disciplines and convicts into separate cells, country house life was neatly divided up into separate parcels" (*Victorian Country House* 28). Thus Girouard nicely pinpoints the institutional nature of the Victorian home, which a Foucauldian analysis reveals to be deeply implicated in the power arrangements of its day by serving a highly regulatory and normative function in class and gender systems. It is worthwhile quoting at length from Girouard because his description of the Victorian country house brings out the ideological implications of architecture:

> To marshal the immensely complicated accommodation of a Victorian country house in such a way that all the elements were conveniently placed and adequately lighted, that the important rooms had the right prospect and aspect, that no one saw what he shouldn't see or met those whom he shouldn't meet, was a formidable task for an architect. Half the skill lay in the correct analysis and disposition of lines of communication. . . . Within those main lines much ingenuity was shown in ensuring, for instance, that the food got to the dining room and the butler to the front door without disturbing the privacy of the family, or even meeting them in the corridors. A sizable country house could easily have six staircases. . . . Entrances could be equally complicated. . . .
>
> The Victorian country house at its best was a remarkable achievement of analysis and synthesis, a vast machine running smoothly and with

clockwork precision, a hieratic structure as complex and delicately grad-
uated as the British Constitution. But it had its dangers. Unless arranged with skill it could become a warren of small rooms, confused
corridors, dark corners and innumerable staircases. (*Victorian Country
House* 34)

Girouard's description of the country house as a "vast machine,"
operating with "clocklike precision" echoes language that might
have been employed to describe a Victorian factory, and it amalgamates the cultural capital produced in the home with the material
capital produced in the marketplace.

Representing Difference

The person who managed this complex organization was the wife.
This was as true in the larger country estates, where the man looked
after the outdoor interests, as in the modest one-servant establishments, from which the husband departed punctually for work each
morning. The wife was, in Isabella Beeton's words, like "the commander of an army" overseeing the smooth functioning of this de-
manding establishment; she was a specialist in "Household Management" (always capitalized). Beeton speaks forcefully of "proper
management" and "daily regulation," admitting that "the performance of the duties of a mistress may, to some minds, perhaps
seem to be incompatible with the enjoyment of life" (1–2). The mistress is cautioned to remember that she is "the Alpha and the
Omega in the government of her establishment, and that it is by her
conduct that its whole internal policy is regulated" (18).

Beeton underscores only what is generally accepted in the etiquette guides and household manuals, but often mystified in the
novels, tracts, and sermons: the mistress's key management role.
The Domestic Oracle (1826) early sounds a cautionary note: "Every
mistress of a family ought to be convinced that every thing depends
on her vigilance and studious care in the superintendence of her
household" (504). It is, of course, possible to read this description
and argue that women have always been urged to define their work
as "superintendence of the household," the fine-sounding phrase
masking the tedium of their menial, repetitive chores. But the Victorian age, historically distinctive in the numbers and availability of
domestic servants, meant something quite different from our contemporary notions of "homemaking." The words they chose—man-

agement, governance, superintendence, generalship—emphasize that difference.

Further, the guides and manuals went to lengths to harmonize such substantial management activity with femininity. In 1837, *Etiquette for Ladies* subsumed household management under the rubric of feminine "taste": "There is nothing so vulgar as the paltry fear of its being known that you interest yourself in your household affairs" (30). In a similar strategy, John Butcher's *Instructions in Etiquette for the Use of All* (1847) insists that management is allied with feminine excellence: "The proper arrangement and government of a household is closely connected with our . . . virtues" (60). *Etiquette for Ladies and Gentlemen* (1862) ranked "tolerable knowledge of domestic affairs" with such character traits as "religion, industry, and chastity" (43).

As the century unfolded, the role of the wife as middle-class manager was confirmed. Indeed, the bourgeoisie seemed eager to acknowledge the wife's management role to distinguish her from the idle aristocracy, for whom at least a part of these functions was usually performed by a capable housekeeper. Initial perceptions of a wife's managerial position in the bourgeois home increasingly gave way to an assertion of importance equal to that of her husband. *Guide to English Etiquette* (1844) claims that "she is, in her sphere, as important as man in his," and explains that "the whole of the internal administration is in her hands—she has the management of the children and of servants, she can make her husband's home happy or miserable, she can increase his estate by the management and frugality, or she can reduce him to beggary by her willfulness and extravagance" (72–73). It is not easy to ascertain the fidelity of the manuals to historical situations, but their detailed, specific advice, as opposed to general exhortation, points to the middle-class woman's prominence in household organization.

The bourgeois wife decided upon the household help required, drew up job descriptions, advertised, interviewed, hired, supervised, paid, and fired. Phillis Browne, in *Common-Sense Housekeeping*, lays out some pragmatic strategies for household managers seeking labor. In order to attract servants, she advises that the "best way [to advertise is] to give no particulars [especially about washing and children], but get them to apply, and then try and induce them to come" (133). Browne notes the inefficacy of her husband's proposed advertisement, which stressed the work to be done, whereas her more successful effort emphasized "liberal wages" and a "comfortable home" (133). Having hired her help, the mistress had often to train and always to supervise her staff. Phillis Browne ultimately recommends hiring a needy and unlearned girl over a more experienced one because the former will be more grateful for the job and therefore more loyal; in addition, the mistress may train her in the proper way of doing things. Browne advises, "Take care that that work is done properly and regularly; and if anything is missed or slipped, no matter how small, speak about it at once" (139). *Cassell's Book of the Household* also underscores the importance of a mistress's superintendence: "Capable servants are produced by capable mistresses, who understand how work should be done, and insist upon it being properly done; who know when it is well done, what difficulties there are arising out of the special circumstances of the case, and how much time may reasonably be spent upon the due performance of the task; and who also make it evident that they are satisfied and pleased when the work is creditably accomplished" (1:152). Such an analysis could be readily adapted to describe a successful master at a Victorian factory.[15] And Mrs. Henry Reeve's summation in 1893 could easily apply to both settings: "In every household there must be the hands to do the work, the head to guide and to control the workers." The metonyms of "hands" and "head" configure working class and bourgeoisie in harmony and mutual benefit within a healthy body politic.

The Victorian wife's role also comprehended accountancy, extending from handling the payroll to tracking expenses and expenditures. *Cassell's* firmly recommends that a husband not interfere in his wife's management strategies. Husbands are cautioned, for example, against thinking that "their position gives them a right to examine the housekeeping accounts." *Cassell's* advises that "such a practice never prevails in a well-ordered and really happy household" because "housekeepers are much more likely to keep their accounts strictly and accurately if they know they will be private," advice that concedes a wife's competence and authority (270–71). In other words, the husband cannot constitute himself as an unofficial

[15] *How to Woo; How to Win; and How to Get Married* (1856) compares household management with captaining a vessel: "While I am far from saying that a wife should be a species of drudge, or upper-servant, I would strongly urge upon all suitors, the importance of ascertaining whether the objects of their choice be given to domestic duties, so far as the management or regulation of a house is concerned. I would not ask her to compound a pudding, or ready a steak with her own hands, but I would have her to know something of the nature of such operations, in order, that she might check carelessness, or instruct ignorance in the 'help'. . . . It is a false and pitiful pride which would feel hurt by being supposed to have knowledge of such matters. The captain of a seventy-four loses nothing of his dignity, because he can tell whether the buckets be properly cleaned, or the meanest rope sufficiently tightened" (24–25).

auditor because, absent for long periods from the business, he cannot adequately supervise its operation. C. W. Haskins's book *How to Keep Household Accounts* summarizes the growing pattern of evidence in the preceding century "that domestic economy, or household management, is very largely a matter of money and money's worth, and that it marks out an important field of financial accountancy," one that, furthermore, "demand[s] of women a very fair measure of business ability" (9, 10). In this light, bourgeois women were controlling not only cultural capital but material capital and its profitable investment.

The wife's responsibility was substantial, and if she was an inefficient and careless manager, she could be bilked out of hundreds of pounds in the course of a year, especially if she permitted or was lax enough to allow servants to take payment in materials or kickbacks in lieu of or in addition to wages. For many years it was taken for granted that "certain servants had a right to certain goods belonging to their master, and these were called the perquisites" (*Cassell's* 157).[16] *Cassell's* elaborates:

> The code which regulated these appropriations was unwritten, but it was widely known and extensively followed, for all that. Thus, in large establishments the servant who paid the bills, whether housekeeper or cook, had a percentage from the tradesmen on the amount of the bills; and as a consequence, it became the interest of the servant to swell the sum expended. The old newspapers and wax candle-ends from the drawing-room were the perquisites of the butler; the lady's-maid had the left-off garments of the mistress, the valet those of the master; the cook had the dripping; the housemaid, any trimmings or trifles that were left in the bedrooms; the kitchen-maid, the kitchen grease (that is, the fat after it is rendered, together with scraps of fat left on the plates); the scullery-maid, the bones. (157–58)

In the course of a year, these items "amounted to a considerable value," and were "the fruitful cause of extravagance and dishonesty." The obvious consequence of a system of perquisites was that "the more wasteful the habits of the family, the more the servants

---

[16] The argument against perquisites (which is an argument against custom and in favor of a more "rationalized" method of doing things) recalls what E. P. Thompson describes in *The Making of the English Working Class* as the conflict between customary traditions and (supposedly) rational agricultural and industrial policies in the late eighteenth and early nineteenth centuries. The terms of the debate (e.g., the identification of "custom" with irrationality and counterproductivity), of course, represent middle-class ideology, not inevitable historical development.

gained; and it was to the interest of the servants that the master should suffer loss" (158). This legacy of the aristocracy would have quickly bankrupted many modest, middle-class households, so one of the most challenging tasks for a new mistress was to end the system of perquisites, which was "usually accepted as a matter of course where mistresses are not sufficiently experienced to forbid it" (157).[17]

Once women had succeeded at domestic accountancy and management, it is logical to conclude they felt emboldened and equipped to transfer their skills to the world outside the home. Florence Nightingale, for example, patterned the nursing profession on "a wholly familiar model of female domestic management." Anne Summers makes this argument in refuting the claims of Mary Poovey, who asserts that Nightingale's "early conceptualization [of nursing] lacks any morally reliable figure to superintend the other inmates of the hospital ward." Summers replies that this conclusion is "quite erroneous. Such a morally reliable figure was to be found in the person of head nurse, ward sister or lady superintendent drawn from a higher social class than the ordinary hospital nurses and their patients" (TLS 357). Whereas Poovey claims that Nightingale's activities undermined "the hegemony of the domestic ideals," Summers suggests that we should see her evolution of the nursing profession as a *fulfillment* of bourgeois managerial ideals. Summers's conclusions accord with my researches here. Nightingale had a viable managerial model to import to nursing: the bourgeois homemaker. However, the mystifications of the household and household labor work against our recognition of the middle-class managerial woman.

God Helps Those Who Help Themselves

Mystifications of women's management also appear in sermons on domestic duties, many of which were collected and published at mid-century. These were invariably titled "Duties of Masters, of Husbands, of Wives, of Children, of Parents, of Servants." The sermon on Duties of Masters is not counterbalanced by one on the Duties of Mistresses, a striking omission in light of the husband's rela-

[17] According to "A Practical Mistress of a Household" (1859), the perquisite system "opens the door to a larger system of robbery than many people dream of. . . . The term 'perquisite' is so comprehensive, so elastic, and accommodating, that it is made to embrace and signify almost everything in the various departments of the house" (quoted in Horn 141).

tive absence from the household and his distance from its concerns. Women, in the sermons, appear only as dutiful wives. The Reverends Frederick Chalmers and F. B. Ashley advise that "the rule of the wife's submission [to the husband] is absolute" and that women must avoid a mistress's chief temptations: "self-sufficiency and independence" (26, 40, 28). The concern that women's household management was instilling self-reliance is met by a reassertion of the master's preeminence. Those "placed by Divine Providence in the responsible position of Masters of families" are reminded to secure a "peaceful well-ordered household" through daily prayer (Garnier 44). Servants are enjoined to give obedience to masters, "inculcated in the strongest possible terms in Holy Writ" (Chalmers 51). The Reverend David Hay summarizes: a servant's treasure is "a good character," her happiness, "religion" (17, 24). The preaching directed at servants particularly insists on the divine ordination of class difference. Rev. Chalmers offers counsel: "The inequalities of human life are inevitable. In any possible form and condition of society some must serve. It is the religion of the Bible alone which has made service compatible with honour and happiness" (44). Rev. Ashley positively extols the benefits of service in decrying servants' quests for better positions: "It would be hard to find a place in which there would not be something to try you. In this world every station has its trials, but that of domestic servants least of any. Their daily wants are abundantly supplied, and they know few of the anxieties of their masters, or of the cottager" (131).

Ironically, the very individuals who were to profit from this sermon were frequently absent from the congregation, cleaning houses and preparing dinners for their masters. The Reverend Thomas Garnier recognizes that "the Sabbath dawns, but it brings to our domestic servants in too many cases, no cessation of toil. . . . How, indeed, can it be otherwise!—the late hours, at which families of the middle and upper classes are wont to rise on this day . . . —the extravagant attention which is paid to personal appearance and dress—the more than ordinary cost and care, which are lavished in making preparations for the family meal—throw insuperable impediments in the way of the attendance of their domestics at the House of God" (50–51). The distance between the rhetoric and the quotidian experience of domestic life is summed up in Phillis Browne's frank assessment: "For my own part, I must say, if I were a girl of the present day I should not like to live as servant under the majority of mistresses" (*Common-Sense Housekeeping* 137).

What emerges with clarity is that mistresses required not only menial labor of their domestics but also an attitude of obedience and subservience. Although servants grew tired under the grueling regimen of work, they plainly resented even more the fact that they were required to acknowledge and "perform" their inferior status. *Etiquette for Ladies and Gentlemen* (1862) warns mistresses "never stoop to the degradation of making companions and confidants of your servants. . . . never on any account treat them as equals; if you do you are certain to spoil them, and at the same time debase yourself" (90). *A Psychology of the Servant Problem* (1925) demystified what was at stake in the dynamic: "A mistress does not demand of her servant work only, she also demands a certain manner, a manner which shall clearly indicate her superiority and the inferiority of the woman who takes her wages; there is nothing derogatory in performing the work, but there is something hurtful to human dignity—in assuming the required attitude."[18] This is the inscription of what Bourdieu describes as "bodily hexis"—the social demand enacted on the body to enforce a "durable way of standing, speaking, walking, and thereby of feeling and thinking" (*Logic* 699–700). Preachers could sermonize about masters' duties, but, as the magazines and manuals recognized, it fell to middle-class women to manage the "Servant Difficulty." They were the ones who had daily contact with disgruntled domestic help; they were the ones who had to teach resignation, if not acceptance.

After mid-century, the problem worsened as tensions between mistress and maid, the analogue to labor unrest in the factories, became more aggravated. Unsurprisingly, the manuals address the problem as one of tact rather than one of economics and politics. *The Englishwoman's Domestic Magazine*, for example, acknowledges that the changing times demand more tact from mistresses, who used to wield their authority unquestioned: "In primitive times there was no escape. . . . Those were the times when a Mrs. Trimmer might make her household rules as strict as she pleased. . . . She could ruthlessly enforce 'no holidays'—no 'cousins'—no parasols—no smart colours—and, in short, no one of those little freaks and fancies which women, high and low, will ever set their hearts upon" (7:156). The regulatory strategies could become quite severe. One servant ob-

---

[18] *A Psychology of the Servant Problem*, quoted in Horn 171. In addition to condescension from their mistresses, servants often met with disdain from their peers, in part, no doubt, a consequence of the required attitude of subservience. See a report by C. Violet Butler, *Domestic Service: An Inquiry by the Women's Industrial Council*, compiled in 1916. There, a common grievance voiced by domestic servants is "loss of caste" (34). They complain of being "despised by our own class" (36). A lady's maid wrote: "Once a servant, you are treated as belonging to quite an inferior race" (37).

jected: "What we find most trying of all is this—to be pent up on fine days in the house . . . in dark places underground, and even the window-panes frosted for fear we should vary our weary hours by a sight of people passing in the streets" (7:157).

The mistress who complains that "servants are great plagues" is advised that "it is a greater plague to be without them," and instructed to be sure that wages are adequate and promptly paid, that working conditions are safe, that the health of domestics is not unnecessarily jeopardized, that servants are treated with respect, and that they are accorded freedom to dress as they please during their time off. In short, *Cassell's* concludes "if mistresses wish to solve the great Servant Difficulty, which is the serious domestic problem of the day, they must be willing to be just, as well as kind, to their servants, and to yield rights, as well as to claim them." If the problem is successfully handled, argues *Cassell's*, bourgeois women will have further solidified the status quo and "there is every prospect that they will have greater comfort and help in the future than ever their mothers and grandmothers had in the past" (161).

The Englishwoman's Domestic Magazine concludes in a sublime register, focusing not on the good domestics may do for the bourgeoisie but on the good the bourgeoisie is daily performing for their domestics:

> A lady with a large establishment complained to me that she had the *honours* (but not much of the *honour*) of a mistress; she supposed her servants thought her their victualler and their housekeeper . . . the care of them, hearing their complaints, discharging some, and hiring others, formed the greater part of her daily life.
>
> This difficulty I cannot help regarding as one of the all-wise laws by which Providence carries out its scheme of social improvement. The demand for domestic servants brings—and it is the only thing that ever would bring—the natives of our cottages within the sphere of higher moral influences. Every gentleman's family serves more or less as a school for the lower orders. (7:160)

The language of this tract, especially references to the "natives of our cottages," amalgamates the working classes with those peoples being colonized through Britain's imperialist ventures at this time. In the cases of both class and race, exploitation is masked. Here, mistresses are to be congratulated for providing "the humanizing influence of the domestic servitude of the present day" (7:160). This extraordinary commentary tellingly documents the power of representations in the naturalization of class, that process through which the middle class was "legitimiz[ing] itself and fully justify[ing] its existence."[19] Informed by a rhetoric of class and race, "lower orders" and "natives," this commentary also emphasizes how the fact of multiply constructed subjectivities makes it impossible to theorize gender oppression in any simple way or to deploy easily categories like praise or blame.

The central regulatory task of the Victorian angel—management of her servants—is signified in Victorian novels by housekeeping keys. Esther Summerson in *Bleak House* perpetually jingles hers; David Copperfield's mother signals her weakness by relinquishing her housekeeping keys to Miss Murdstone; and Dora Copperfield announces her failure by conceiving of the keys as a toy. Susan Grantly in Trollope's *The Warden* uses her keys as a sign of her authority, which is absolute within the household even though she bows to domestic ideology in appearing to defer to her husband. The narrator laughs at Archdeacon Grantly—"vain man!"—for his presumption in attempting to secure certain documents from his wife's knowledge: "It is probable to us that the contents of no drawer in that house were unknown to its mistress, and we think, moreover, that she was entitled to all such knowledge" (77–78). Keys, of course, keep things locked up, and all those keys to interior drawers, closets, and doors helped to secure household goods from servants, presumed to have an interest in stealing them. Henry Mayhew betrays that conviction when he comments that "there are a great number of felonies committed by servants over the metropolis. . . . Some of these females are usually not a fortnight or a month in service before a heavy burglary is committed in the house, and will remain two or three months longer to prevent suspicion."[20]

The middle-class Victorian woman, much more than the man, found herself interacting with the servant classes and regulating their behavior in the interests of middle-class control. Indeed, the same period that saw the flood of etiquette books, household manuals, and architectural changes that, for women, prescribed so carefully the decorum of social interaction from top to bottom, also saw the growing removal of men from contact with their workers. By the late eighteenth and early nineteenth centuries, middle-class men in-

---

[19] I draw here on the insights of Pierre Bourdieu: "So as to avoid being misled by the effects of the labour of *naturalization* which every group tends to produce in order to legitimize itself and fully justify its existence, one must in each case reconstruct the *historical labour* which has produced social divisions and the social vision of these divisions" (*Language and Symbolic Power* 247–48).

[20] Mayhew quoted in Horn 133.

creasingly separated their family residences from the work place.[21] This residential withdrawal was accompanied by an "increasing size and scale of the mechanised work place" so that distance between the classes also increased. It devolved upon upper- and middle-class women to bridge the widening gap (Summers 37–38).

God's in His Heaven—All's Right with the World!

Two strategies emerged to mediate class differences and to manage lower class dissent. One, as we have seen, was the regulation of the classes in the middle-class home, a strategy that I argue was masked by idealizations of the Angel in the House. The institutional practice that most concealed the gross inequities was family prayer, a custom that became increasingly popular during the 1830s. Davidoff points out that "this custom united all the elements of control . . . into one of the most significant rituals of Victorian life" (35). The entire household was summoned every day for an activity—prayer—that "reinforced the idea of community, an organic whole" (35). George Eliot's earliest fiction, "The Sad Fortunes of the Reverend Amos Barton," presents a stunning madonna in the figure of Milly Barton, who enlists undying loyalty from her maid-of-all-work, Nanny. Milly and Nanny are represented as striving together for the commonweal, an ideology cemented at the end of the day when "Nanny could now join in the short evening prayer, and all could go to bed" (Eliot 58). The institution of family prayer cooperated with the other discursive practices centered in the home to become "one of the most effective means for social control ever devised" (Davidoff 36). Manuals instructed masters and mistresses that "it is a simple duty, not only to allow [domestic servants], but to see that they do attend regularly with us in the House of God" (Ashley 101). A master is cautioned not only to "gather [his servants] around him at family prayer regularly twice a day, but to make it effective, follow it up with nurture and admonition." He is to "furnish them with suitable helps and books; and have a set time for questioning them together on their religious knowledge" (Ashley 101). *Domestic Duties: A Series of Sermons* echoes this advice, urging that "every opportunity should be seized upon by the faithful master, of instruct-

---

[21]Summers 36. See also Briggs, *Victorian Cities*, who points out that nineteenth-century cities saw an increasing de facto segregation of the classes by residential area. In earlier times the housing for the two groups had been jumbled together, workers and middle class all living in the same neighborhood (esp. 27–28, 61–62, 142–43).

ing his servants. . . . But the best and most favourable method of inculcating upon them the great truths and practical duties of our religion, is by the regular practice of family prayer" (Garnier 52–53).

Although the sermons tended to stress the master's significant role as head of the family, *The Family Preacher; or, Domestic Duties* pragmatically admits that "although the performance of family prayer is incumbent on the husband, its regular discharge depends much on the wife" (Bailey 66). It elaborates: "Much also depends on her in procuring the regular attendance of all the children and domestics to the hour of prayer. As the business of the house is under her control, those who are concerned in it will depend on her arrangements for a convenient attendance at the proper hour" (67). This advice reveals the extent to which church and family prayer could interfere with the "business" of the household, unless, of course, they were understood philosophically to subtend that "business" in significant ways.

The linking of servants with children—particularly in matters of moral instruction—is an effect of and justification for a mistress's constant surveillance and regulation of her domestic staff. In all the practical advice, there is also condescension, as in Anne Cobbett's *The English Housekeeper*: "Servants, like children, and, indeed, like all dependants [sic], may be made to be good or bad; you may, by your management, cause them to be nearly what you please" (18). Isabella Beeton's guide also makes this link in its end-of-the-day advice: "The younger members of a family should go early and at regular hours to their beds, and the domestics as soon as possible after a reasonably appointed hour . . . no servants should, on any account, be allowed to remain up after the heads of the house have retired" (17). Such policies also guaranteed that all the servants were in and accounted for at day's end. Regulatory strategies and prayer join in *Cranford* when a servant, "forbidden by the articles of her engagement, to have 'followers,'" explains away male shadows that seem to haunt the kitchen with the comment, "I don't see a creature from six o'clock tea, till Missus rings the bell for prayers at ten" (65).

The linking of servants with children facilitated the general denial of class antagonisms I mentioned in the introductory chapter. Domestic discourses and the bourgeois home served the representational function of justifying class arrangements by positing servants in the role of tutelary children to benevolent parents. Ultimately, so the logic went, those children would "grow up" to fill the parents' shoes. Functioning much as did Benjamin's folk festivals of capitalism (the great nineteenth-century exhibitions), these regulatory representations underwrote a message of social progress for the under-class without revolution.

Charity Begins at Home

The second strategy to mediate class differences also fell to women and developed as a logical extension of women's "angelic" mission—that is, philanthropy. In his *Instructions in Etiquette for the Use of All* (1847), John Butcher takes pains to make etymological con-nections between ladies and a tradition of charitable activity. He al-ludes to the former custom in which a mistress of a manor distrib-uted with her own hands a certain quantity of bread to the needy once a week: the "laff [loaf] day." Butcher continues: "Indeed, the very etymology of the work, *lady*, which has been resolved into a saxon term, composed of *loaf*, and to *serve*, signifies that dealing food to the hungry was deemed so essential a feature in her character, that the *giver of the loaf*, and the *lady*, became synonymous" (99).[22]

In the Victorian age, philanthropy took the particular form of house-to-house visiting. According to Anne Summers, although such visiting may seem "dateless and commonplace . . . this is not so" (35). Like the other practices examined here, extensive house-to-house visiting was born in the late eighteenth and early nineteenth centuries (Prochaska 100–101). Summers succinctly spells out its im-plications: "The iron fist of coercion could be supplemented or even replaced by the velvet glove of friendship. Visiting the poor in their own homes . . . help[ed] to isolate the poor from each other" (37). Summers goes on to note that middle-class women approached the poor "not merely as spiritual missionaries . . . but as managers and employers of labour in their own right. . . . Women were developing a pattern of personal relationships across class barriers at a time when men were losing the social element in relationships at work." It should not surprise us to learn that the model developed by women in the household for relations between masters and servants was extended outside it to rich and poor: "a model of the working class as economically and socially dependent, obedient, disciplined, clean and broken in to the daily methods and routines of the mid-dle-class family unit" (39). F. K. Prochaska asserts that "knowledge

[22] The *OED* gives "hlaf" or "loaf" plus the root "dig" or "knead" for the etymology of "lady," adding that the "etymology above stated is not very plausible with regard to sense." Mr. Butcher's explanation, however, seems quite plausible.

of domestic management" was "one of the secrets to successful visiting" (110), and Beeton's guide confirms this regulatory function: "Great advantages may result from visits paid to the poor . . . there will be opportunities for advising and instructing them, in a pleasant and unobtrusive manner, in cleanliness, industry, cookery, and good management" (6).

The phenomenon of visiting is described by Jane Ellice Hopkins in *An Englishwoman's Work among Working Men*, published in 1875. Hopkins, who became well known for her charitable ministrations among the working classes, confessed to her fears in undertaking the task: "I doubt whether at that time a sheeted spectre had the same unknown terrors for me as a rough in the 'too, too solid flesh'" (30). And her fears were realistically grounded; in one episode she relates, she became the intermediary between a violent, drunken man and his wife. She silenced them by banging with spoons on a tea tray, making a greater racket than they (41–42). What protected her, however, what enabled her to subdue what she calls "this lawless population of roughs" was the power of class. Hopkins recommends that the visitor not condescend to her audience, but dress as if for her own drawing room. Her silk dress, she claims, signals her "respect" for the working men. It also, of course, signifies her class inviolability as a lady, who must be accorded the same respect in rough haunts as she is in the drawing room. Class signs functioned as a protective shield, allowing women to venture into situations that might otherwise be extraordinarily dangerous to them. Victorian woman went into scenes and situations where a contemporary woman wouldn't dare set foot. Such markers functioned to protect her by naturalizing class arrangements, as each working man internalized the unbreachable distance between himself and her. Elia Burritt, who introduces Hopkin's text, summarizes the force of her influence: "Never before did they hear such a voice—never, even by accident. Not a mother's son of them ever heard the like" (8). Her voice metonymically recalls her class, which controls fully as much as the religion she preaches. Hopkins recounts the effect she has on one working man, who asks permission to see that she reaches her home in safety; he will not presume to accompany her, only follow at a respectful distance: "The man Daniel . . . asks permission to walk at a little distance from her, until she reaches her own door in safety. The spontaneous reverence for a good and true woman, latent in his uncultured nature, speaks out in chastened and delicate utterance in his voice and manner" (10). Class effects of refinement have become naturalized as the effects of goodness in a "true woman."

Anne Cobbett in *The English Housekeeper* also underscores the importance of the charitable donor's person and presence. It is not simply relief that is sought for the impoverished, but the imposition of a model of behavior. Cobbett distinguishes between relief "which is doled out from a 'Society'" and the "private mode of charity" which is "superior to the public in every way" (440). She explains that in the former, "the soup which has been obtained by presenting a ticket, is apportioned to the little hungry creatures, without their being reminded who it is that has so kindly provided it for them." In the private method, "not only must the attentions of a known individual be the most gratefully appreciated by a poor man or woman, but the child . . . cannot be expected to grow up without some of those feelings of personal respect and attachment for its benefactor, which, while they prevent the contrast of riches with poverty from becoming odious, are the strongest assurances of union between him who claims a property in the soil and him whose labour makes that property of value" (440). Cobbett is very clear-sighted about the benefits of making benevolence a question of personal debt and obligation so that it may prove the foundation for a child's acceptance of the economic status quo, his labor creating value for someone else's property.

Phillis Browne, in *What Girls Can Do: A Book for Mothers and Daughters*, cautions against encouraging young girls to undertake charitable visiting because they lack sufficient "judgment and discretion." She pragmatically advises: "Many of those who are visited would very gladly dispense with the visits, and regard the lady who makes them as an intruder. And of those who welcome the visit a large proportion do it simply for the sake of what they can get" (191). Indeed, visitors were supposed to be on the watch for those of the poor who were not truly grateful and malleable. Browne notes that "poor mothers quickly came to understand that if only they put on a look of sad submission and adopted a certain phraseology, they would quickly receive all sorts of material blessings" (159). Browne's subsequent description of visiting illustrates why the working poor would have found the process intensely intrusive. Each woman was assigned a district and urged to call at each house twice a week. The visitor would distribute coupons or "tickets," which the recipient could subsequently cash in for the necessaries of life: coal or food. The distribution of the tickets, however, was entirely at the discretion of the visitor, and she could withhold them if, after surveying the situation, she found something not to her liking. Thus, for only a modest gain, the working poor were required to submit to continual surveillance, supervision, and instruction. Naturally, the poor resented this intrusive management of their lives. One working woman rejected a coal ticket, saying that "if she could not have them reg'lar she did not care for them at all" (194). Another refused one—"such a bother"—but added she did not object to receiving three (195). Finally, another simply shut the door in the visitor's face; she was put down in the report as "exceedingly impertinent" (195). Unfortunately, however, most of the poor could not afford the license and luxury of this kind of self-assertion.

Through house-to-house visiting women became responsible for establishing "a model of class relations which suggested a remedy for present and future social ills" (Summers 41), and men began to depend upon women to manage the class question although they could not acknowledge this dependence. Summers adds, "The male writers [on philanthropy] did not think too deeply about the political dimension of women's visiting. . . . It was not admitted that women, in dispensing material assistance and using influence on behalf of the poor, could not but exercise considerable leverage upon them" (45). Further, taking this assistance into the home "made it possible to continue to focus on the family unit rather than the work place, and subordinate the issue of wages to questions of personal conduct and domestic behaviour" (55–56).

The practice of house-to-house visiting figures prominently in the Victorian novel. One of its most memorable manifestations occurs in Dickens's *Bleak House* when Mrs. Pardiggle descends on the brickmakers. Obviously, Dickens is parodying such philanthropists and positing personal benevolence against such abstract humanitarianism, Esther Summerson against Mrs. Pardiggle. Ironically, however, the brickmakers can resist Mrs. Pardiggle's high-handed attempts to take them into moral custody, whereas they are seduced by the same values when proffered with the soft voice and gentle touch of Esther. The family model that Esther holds out translates them equally firmly into the realm of middle-class domestic values and masks the economic exploitation that characterizes their situation. Likewise, in Gaskell's *North and South*, Margaret Hale's visits to the working-class Higgins family culminate in her persuading the father to accompany her home and join in their family prayer. It is hard not to read ironically the narrator's assurance that "it did . . . no harm" (41).

Folk Festivals of Capitalism

The centrality of Victorian women in the project of consolidating middle-class interests becomes clear if we recall the links I forged among the ephemera of everyday life as a source for a revisionary materialist history, the political and economic power of representations, and the regulatory effect on class of such representations. Precisely because etiquette trades in ephemera whose value is entirely representational, it can become an extraordinary force in articulating and naturalizing class difference. Whether servants were positioned generally as children and dependents or as beings at an earlier evolutionary stage, the message was as clear here as in Walter Benjamin's insights into the "folk festivals of capitalism": revolution was unnecessary. The only thing requisite for progress and development was submission to the benevolent guidance of the parent-mistress.

Nonliterary domestic discourses, such as etiquette guides and household manuals, tend to emphasize the bourgeois household manager more consistently than literary representations do, perhaps because the former carry the burden of explicitly addressing class issues, of at least acknowledging that middle-class life depends upon successful management of a servant class. Literary works— particularly domestic novels directed at middle-class audiences— have the luxury of ignoring or obscuring that fact, often burying it in the romance plot of boy meets girl, boy wins girl, boy marries girl.

In all of these constructions, class appears to be as inevitable, as "natural" a difference as gender, suggesting that one is not much more easily bridged than the other in mid-nineteenth-century England. Not surprisingly, as if in search of morphologies and anatomical structures to confirm and ground such arbitrary distinctions, the Victorians became deeply invested in the "science" of phrenology, initiated by Franz Gall in the early 1800s and widely popular as a way of reading character through the anatomical features of the skull. Gender, race, class—to the "educated" eye, all of these could be discerned in the shape of a head. Phrenology foregrounds the collaboration between "science" and cultural representations.

Class *is* a representation, inscribed on the body through characteristic postures, modes of speech, thought, and feeling. To the extent that bourgeois women produced and reproduced these representations, they contributed to a middle-class hegemony from which they also benefited. The intrication of class and gender that I examine here calls for more precision when developing any narrative of the "female subject." At the same time, in pointing to a multiply and contradictorily inscribed subjectivity, this class/gender imbrication enables us to conceptualize subjects in process and to theorize the kind of agency that enabled middle-class women to emerge into professional life.

3

England's Domestic Queen and Her Queenly Domestic Other

Mid-nineteenth-century tracts collaborated in the construction of a new image of woman: the middle-class "angel" or moral salvator, summarized famously in Coventry Patmore's verse sequence *The Angel in the House*. Yet that representation of middle-class Victorian womanhood was, in fact, riven by contradiction from its inception. In this chapter I not only examine the Angel in the House as a tendentious construction of bourgeois ideology but also explore how that construction could not be stabilized within contesting class and gender discourses. The image of the passive domestic angel, which complemented that of the active, public man, was contradicted by the bourgeois wife's pivotal supervisory role within the class system. These contradictions could not be fully bridged in the tracts, and the resulting representational gap became an opening for change.

This chapter looks at works that are intermediary between the household management manuals and the novels: the homilies, tracts, and essays of the period. These texts found a way to finesse the tensions between woman as angel and woman as manager by ascribing queenliness to the bourgeois woman.

Her Majesty's a Pretty Nice Girl

The emergence of this powerful icon, the Angel in the House, coincides with Victoria's accession to the throne of England and her embodiment of the contradictory roles of self-reliant monarch and dependent wife. She took the highest position as queen of her country in 1837; in 1840 she became both wife and mother. Popular accounts of and responses to her are riddled by this paradox of the ruler and the wife. In February of that year, Victoria proposed to Albert—according to *Punch* "a trying ordeal which she passed through with delicacy and tact"—and received both his acceptance and Lord Melbourne's congratulations: "You will be very much more comfortable . . . for a woman cannot stand alone for any time, in whatever position she may be" (*Mr. Punch's* 6). By November, she was already a mother. Any assessment of Victoria's character must address the complex interaction of the imperious, even willful queen and the devoted, even doting wife. In her reliance on Albert, in her professed inaptitude for public rule, Victoria constructed herself through emergent middle-class values; she presented herself through a scrim of domestic virtues emphasizing home, hearth, and heart. That she should, nonetheless, without disabling or disqualifying self-contradiction, take her place as head of the most powerful country in the world bespeaks her own signal role in the construction of a new feminine ideal that endorsed active public management behind a facade of private retirement.

Although it is difficult to assess fully the part played by Queen Victoria in shaping the image of the Angel in the House, she is, herself, a logical source for the image's idealism and its contradictions. It seems obvious on a first view that one effect of idealizing woman's place in the home was the corollary exclusion of women from public life; however, Victoria's person and presence argue a more complex accommodation of these apparently opposed spheres. Although women lacked a voice in government, lacked meaningful access to education and the professions, the fact of female leadership in politics was daily present in the figure of Victoria.[1]

Victoria, herself, was a paradox—both middle-class and aristocratic. Stanley Weintraub describes her through a series of oppositions: "Victoria was pleasant and unpleasant, selfish and selfless, democratic and dictatorial, heroic and passive, queenly yet middle-class at heart" (xii). Weintraub concludes his 1987 biography emphasizing the paradox of the middle-class queen: "What Victoria had left behind as legacy was the sturdy ceremonial monarchy now ratified by public affection, by a yearning for continuity and tradition, and by the middle-class values that were her own and that remain beneath the fairy-tale veneer of royalty" (643).

[1] Margaret Homans has been exploring related ideas about Queen Victoria's position in Victorian culture, but she points rather to conflicts between the images of wife and monarch and to the complex ways in which power and powerlessness were intertwined in representations of the sovereign. See "The Powers of Powerlessness" and "'To the Queen's Private Apartments.'" See also Adrienne Munich, on the tension inherent in the concept of "maternal monarch" (265).

Victoria's ascension to the throne in 1837 confirmed the emergence of a new ethic of restraint, probity, and decency. The English public had grown tired of the excesses of the sons of George III, their licentiousness and libertinism. Patricia Thompson, in her *Queen Victoria: Gender and Power*, notes that the "manners and behaviour of the last two male Hanoverian monarchs undoubtedly helped to predispose sections of the British population towards a new monarch who was young and female" (4). The historical record demonstrates a continuing erosion of moral values in Victoria's predecessors: George IV, William IV, and her own father, the Duke of Kent. They were bigamists and adulterers, exercising power irresponsibly, squandering public funds, and sponging on friends and subjects (Thompson 15). Not only Victoria's father but also his siblings had intensified the British public's alienation through their accumulation of debts, mistresses, and illegitimate children (Weintraub 69). The virginal Victoria embodied a dramatic change, and she was readily seized upon as an icon of emergent bourgeois values, despite the fact that, as Thompson points out, "if the stereotypical Victorian woman was well-mannered, self-effacing, demure and devoid of passion, Queen Victoria was so far from the stereotype as to be almost its opposite" (44). Indeed, Victoria is memorable for her distress at being forced repeatedly to bear children; she described herself as "furious" when she learned of her first pregnancy, and Albert, more maternal, was continually admonishing her to be more of a mother and less a monarch with her nine children. But the public conferred upon Victoria an image of itself which confirmed both the emergence and importance of the middle class. That self-portrait was facilitated by the "diffusion of cheap printed words and pictures [that brought] the image of the monarch and her family regularly into the consciousness of her subjects" (139). In 1867 Walter Bagehot summarized the effect of familiarizing the populace with a wifely and maternal Victoria: "A *family* on the throne is an interesting idea. It brings down the pride of sovereignty to the level of petty life."[2] Albert's death in 1861 further solidified Victoria's bourgeois image because she "refused ever again to wear the robes of state, appearing in versions of widow weeds" (141). That the queen of England became the central embodiment of middle-class familial values held great significance for the representation and role of bourgeois women.

[2] Bagehot quoted in Thompson, p. 139.

The Bourgeois Aristocrat

Although the idea of woman's salvatory potential had been around since the early 1800s, it found in the young queen a powerful local habitation and name. Here lay tangible and visible proof of a woman's power—not only her capacity for individual redemptions but also her talent for ordering and enabling the emergence of a new England. Sarah Ellis in *Women of England* (1839) makes the association: "The British throne being now graced by a female sovereign, the auspicious promise of whose early years seems to form a new era in the annals of our nation, and to inspire with brighter hopes and firmer confidence the patriot bosoms of her expectant people; it is surely not a time for the female part of the community to fall away from the high standard of moral excellence, to which they have been accustomed to look, in the formation of their domestic habits." Ellis exhorts women to "show forth the benefits arising from their more enlightened systems of education, by proving to their youthful sovereign, that whatever plan she may think it right to sanction for the moral advancement of her subjects . . . will be . . . faithfully supported in every British home by the female influence prevailing there" (59). Woman, in this scheme, become subordinate administrators of a royal "plan" for moral advancement.

Thompson's biography of Victoria explores the paradox of a female queen in a culture strongly demarcated along gender lines: "It is an odd contradiction that in the period in which the doctrine of separate spheres of activity for men and women was most actively developed and propounded, the highest public office in the land was held by a woman" (xiv–xv). Although Thompson notes the conflict inherent in the queen's person and position—Victoria "inevitably presented her subjects with impressions, images and examples which must have had considerable effects" (144)—she concludes just at the point that I want to pursue my investigations, in the complex accommodations of the public and private woman that allowed the fact of female power to exist as long as it was mystified by appropriate rhetorics of home, hearth, and heart. "If [Victoria] strengthened the moral authority of women in the family rather than making her presence in public life more immediately acceptable, there must have been many ways in which the presence of a woman at the head of the state worked at a deeper level to weaken prejudice and make change more possible in the century following her reign" (145).

Having represented herself in middle-class terms by her public devotion and deference to Albert, Victoria facilitated the corollary operation by which middle-class women were represented in regal terms and questions of a woman's "power" and its province entered the popular discourse.[3]

This process began immediately in the accommodation of the term "power" to "woman." Because Victoria was the most prominent working woman of her day and because she was pivotal in the construction of the "aristocratic bourgeoisie," we may profitably begin with two poetic representations of her role by Elizabeth Barrett Browning: "The Young Queen" and "Victoria's Tears," from her poems of 1838. "The Young Queen" opens with an epigraph, *The Queen's Declaration in Council:* "This awful responsibility is imposed upon me so suddenly, and at so early a period of my life, that I should feel myself utterly oppressed by the burden, were I not sustained by the hope that Divine Providence, which has called me to this work, will give me strength for the performance of it" (2:106). Two phrases draw our attention here—"This awful responsibility . . . imposed upon me" and "Divine Providence, which has called me to this work." In making Victoria the object of the action, the phrases underscore the queen's passive role in her queenship; the notion of "imposition" stresses her bodily, even spiritual incapacity for the weight of rulership, termed a "burden, " which the crown represents. But what buoys up—"sustains"—both body and spirit is the call of Divine Providence, which has ordained the work as her own and so guaranteed that she will be fitted to it. The notion of woman's work as providential or divine calling is embedded in this self-representation, and it both reflects and helps create an idea of work for women as distinctively different from man's monetarily remunerated labors.

Imitating Victoria's career, women's work was to be oriented to the good of human lives rather than to the goal of personal wealth. The labor of bourgeois women was understood as managerial rather than menial, rewarded by social harmony rather than remunerated with hard cash. Just as Victoria ran the nation so, too, Victorian women ran their households and communities, the class divisions facilitating their ready assumption of managerial positions even as acceptance of those positions further solidified the class divisions.

[3] The wide-ranging ideological appeal of the domestic queen can be gauged, in part, by Barbara Bodichon's adoption of Victoria as exemplum in her treatise *Women and Work*: "Queen Victoria fulfills the very arduous duties of her calling and manages also to be the active mother of many children" (quoted in Helsinger et al. 2:149).

Barrett Browning follows the epigraph to "The Young Queen" with a picture of the newly dead king, whose "shroud is yet unspread." His death testifies to "All glory's nothingness," a subtle preparation for the introduction of the "royal maiden," who "treadeth firm where *that* departed trod!" "Glory's nothingness" establishes the tone of humility that will characterize the young queen, who seems already to have anticipated the vanity of human wishes. The third stanza continues:

> The deathly scented crown
> Weighs her shining ringlets down;
> But calm she lifts her trusting face, and calleth upon God.
>
>   (2:107)

The crucifixion image of the heavy circlet underscores the reliance Victoria places on Divine Providence to teach her what her work must be.

At the same time that Victoria is depicted as an agent of Providence, she is also metaphorically inscribed as "mother" of her country. Of the young queen, seemingly bereft of guidance, Barrett Browning asks the poignant question—"Alas! can others wear / A mother's heart for her?"—affirming the importance of maternal nurture. The poet then logically expands the motif of mother to Victoria herself:

> A nation looks to thee
> For steadfast sympathy:
> Make room within thy bright clear eyes for all its gathered tears.
>
>   (2:108)

She becomes the mother of her nation:

> And so the grateful isles
> Shall give thee back their smiles,
> And as thy mother joys in thee, in them shalt *thou* rejoice.
>
>   (2:108)

The phrase "steadfast sympathy" performs the ideological task of amalgamating Victoria's work as queen of England to the ideal of motherhood. Her work is at once justified and mystified. She performs an important task in securing domestic well-being, but her success is interpreted as a function of a maternal nature.

Barrett Browning's "Victoria's Tears" continues this motif of feminine sympathy or love as a source of domestic order, a guarantor of liberty. In this poem, Barrett Browning invokes the Victorian trope of tears as visible evidence of that love. Of course, tears are also a powerful signifier of femininity. "Real women" cry because they feel deeply, because they empathize, because they're sensitive, because they're tender, because they're happy, because they're sad, because they're weak. Barrett Browning's fourth stanza points the paradoxical power of tears:

> God save thee, weeping Queen!
>   Thou shalt be well beloved!
> The tyrant's sceptre cannot move,
>   As those pure eyes have moved!
> The nature in thine eyes we see,
>   That tyrants cannot own—
> The love that guardeth liberties!
>   Strange blessing on the nation lies,
>   Whose Sovereign wept—
> Yea! wept, to wear its crown!
>   (2:109–10)

In her portrait of a weeping monarch, Barrett Browning attempts to bridge the gap in the signifier "tears" between strength of sensibility and weakness of will. Victoria's "pure eyes" move more effectively than a tyrant's scepter; the exercise of force gives way to the power of moral suasion, and "love" is installed as a more puissant guardian of "liberties" than is physical might. The ideological burden of the rhetoric is to suggest that what women accomplish is simply a reflex of their natures. At the same time, it insists on the value of a woman's work, and that work happens to be leading a great nation.[4]

The Queen Is in the Parlour

It is a striking feature of two key works of the period—Coventry Patmore's homiletic verse narrative *Angel in the House* and John Ruskin's essay "Of Queen's Gardens"—that both adopt the metaphor of "Queen" to designate the middle-class woman and rely for

[4] Focusing on the gender implications of "Victoria's Tears," Antony Harrison comments that "Browning simply transposes the domestic ideology to a much larger sphere: the kingdom becomes Victoria's household" (118).

their arguments on a notion of woman's "power" as opposed to her "sphere" or "influence."[5] Patmore's work attracts little attention today, and this author retains a place in literary histories principally for coining the term "Angel in the House," that avatar of middle-class Victorian womanhood whom Virginia Woolf immortalized by killing in "Professions for Women."[6] Patmore's moniker for his wife served as a convenient shorthand for a type generally celebrated in tracts and novels, the selfless, virtuous, pure, and spiritualized deity, who presided over hearth and home and whose presence was a refuge from the storms of commercial strife.

From the beginning of his domestic epic in four volumes—*The Betrothal* (1854), *The Espousals* (1856), *Faithful for Ever* (1860), and *The Victories of Love* (1862)—Patmore describes the female paragon as a queen with regal powers. Her power not only elevates his verse but ennobles him, much as the British sovereign ennobled Albert through her espousal of him:

> For as a Queen, who may not find
> Her peer in all the common Earth,
> Submits her meek and royal mind,
> Espousing one of subject birth,
> All burden of like gain above,
> She raised one to her noble place,
> And made my lordship of her love
> The humbling gift of her free grace.
> (1:32)

The poet's later testimony—"He notes how Queens of sweetness still / Neglect their crowns and stoop to mate"(1:47)—also echoes the royal couple. Although not of "subject birth," but a prince of Saxe-

---

[5] The metaphor of the bourgeois wife as queen was prominent not only in the tracts and essays but also in the novels, where regal images describe such heroines as Dorothea Brooke and that sublime manager Lucilla Marjoribanks.

[6] Woolf's characterization in that oft-reprinted essay has no doubt helped to solidify the one-dimensional, gendered image of the bourgeois wife as self-sacrificing victim that has come down to us today: "You who come of a younger and happier generation may not have heard of her—you may not know what I mean by the Angel in the House. I will describe her as shortly as I can. She was intensely sympathetic. She was immensely charming. She was utterly unselfish. She excelled in the difficult arts of family life. She sacrificed herself daily. If there was chicken, she took the leg; if there was a draught she sat in it—in short she was so constituted that she never had a mind or a wish of her own, but preferred to sympathize always with the minds and wishes of others. Above all—I need not say it—she was pure. Her purity was supposed to be her chief beauty—her blushes, her great grace. In those days—the last of Queen Victoria—every house had its Angel" (*Death of the Moth* 237).

Coburg-Gotha, Albert was denied both an English title and a position in the British army by Parliament, which wanted to prevent him from playing a political role in England.[7]

The point, of course, is not to turn Patmore's poem into a *roman à clef* about the royal situation but rather to discern the extent to which Patmore is employing images available in his culture and, by adopting these images, implicitly acceding to the idea that bourgeois women might assume effective public roles. Of course, he wants simultaneously to limit that public scope and interpret that imposed limitation as a privilege:

> Her privilege, not impotence,
>   Exempts her from the work of man:
> Humbling his proper excellence,
>   Jeanne d'Arc led war's obstreperous van:
> No post of policy or pride
>   Does Heaven from her holding grudge:
> Miriam and Anna prophesied,
>   In Israel Deborah was judge;
>   Countless the Christian heroines
> Who've blest the world, and still do bless . . .
>   (1:72)

But in his headlong rush to justify women's exclusion from public life as a personal privilege, Patmore runs into contradiction, a very prominent public woman: Victoria.

> And, ah, sad times gone by, denied
>   The joyfullest omen ever seen,
> The full-grown Lion's power and pride
>   Led by the soft hands of a Queen.
>   (1:73)

This picture of England, symbolized by the lion, led by "the soft hands of a Queen," underscores the tension between public and private woman, between exertion and influence. Patmore's awkward verse—the hesitations produced by the commas, the absent agent and the passive voice "denied"—testify to more than his limitations as a poet; they suggest as well his trouble managing the conflict involved in enforcing women's subservience in private life when a woman is so publicly and visibly competent to head a nation. Pat-

---

[7] Weintraub comments on the tensions generated by Parliament's refusal to accede to Victoria's wish that Albert be so recognized (134).

more ultimately reins in the implications of his metaphors and con-
fines woman's power to her capacity to ennoble a man. He concludes the first volume depicting his "queen" in subservience: "My
queen was crouching at my side, / By love unsceptred and brought
low" (1:181). In a corollary movement, he himself is elevated—"And
I submitted to the crown / No choice was left me but to wear"
(1:183).

I want to return to the underlying thread of Patmore's idyll and
focus on the tension introduced between the private and public
bourgeois woman, an uneasy accommodation. Our understanding
of contradiction in the image of Victorian woman has previously focused largely on the split between the sexual and spiritual selves.
But that split, as I noted in Chapter 2, was readily resolved by the
class division whereby women of the working class became vested
with a dangerous sexuality, and middle-class women, seemingly
sexless, became the guardians of spirituality. We can term this process either the gendering of "classed" subjectivities or the "classing"
of gendered subjectivities. The class division had the further effect
of refocusing the issue of work for women. Obviously, lower-class
women were found suited to and suitable for a range of menial
tasks—from factory and farm work, to sewing and domestic servitude. Indeed, such women had no choice but to seek remunerative
employment. The separation of classes raised the question of appropriate "work" for the middle-class woman.[8] Her exemption from the
economic imperative made it possible that she might *appear* to remain, imaginatively and symbolically, wholly outside the realm of
commerce in a "private" sphere. Stipulating separate private and
public spheres also concealed the relationship already existing between the public and the private on the level of class management
and resulted in a mystification that is partially exposed in contemporaneous descriptions of the bourgeois wife.

Sarah Ellis's *Women of England* reflects this conflict in the dialectic
between public and private. The date of this tract, just two years
after Victoria assumed the throne, suggests that it is a response to
emerging cultural constructions of the female. That function is dramatically evidenced in Ellis's exasperation over gender distinctions
imposed in the realm of bourgeois work:

It is a curious anomaly in the structure of modern society, that gentlemen may employ their hours of business in almost any degrading occupation, and, if they have but the means of supporting a respectable

---

[8] These issues are fruitfully elaborated in Helsinger et al., 2:109–64.

establishment at home, may be gentlemen still; while, if a lady does but touch any article, no matter how delicate, in the way of trade, she loses caste, and ceases to be a lady. (344–45)

Sarah Ellis is not an especially enlightened thinker of her day—her commentary tends to rehearse established truisms. Yet here she is willing to dispense with gender difference in the interests of advancing bourgeois class interests. Thus, we must at least consider the extent to which her "enlightened" opinions are a consequence of emergent trends.

A closer analysis of Ellis's book reveals ongoing tensions in the representation of woman and work that stem from conflicts between patriarchal and bourgeois ideologies. Ellis begins with an assertion that "the women of England . . . better instructed . . . in the minutiae of domestic comfort, have obtained a degree of importance in society far beyond what their unobtrusive virtues would appear to claim" (54). This statement encapsulates the paradoxical virtues of the bourgeois woman: unobtrusive yet central, unperceived yet all-seeing. It is not sufficient to the middle-class housewife that a house be "neat and clean": "It must be so ordered as to suit the tastes of all" (26). This order, successfully imposed, appears "natural," even inevitable. Warned by Ellis that "every passing event . . . has its crisis," the domestic manager is urged to "calculate with precision, or the machinery of the household comfort is arrested in its movements, and thrown into disorder" (23).

Ellis is careful to distinguish the management of the housewife from the drudgery of the domestic servant. In a significant passage, Ellis decries those "mistaken" mistresses who believe that making themselves useful involves actual menial labor: "No one can be farther than the writer of these pages from wishing to point out as objects of laudable emulation those domestic drudges, who, because of some affinity between culinary operations, and the natural tone and character of their own minds, prefer the kitchen to the drawing room,—of their own free choice, employ their whole lives in the constant bustle of providing for mere animal appetite" (41). Ellis makes clear that these are misguided energies. She laments that some people applaud this kind of application: "This class of individuals have, by a sad mistake in our nomenclature, been called *useful*, and hence, in some degree, may arise the unpopular reception which this valuable word is apt to meet with in female society" (41). Rather than risk the opprobrium associated with "useful," Ellis describes the middle-class housekeeper as "considerate," a critical signifier, which may be decoded as encompassing both benevolence and deliberation, feeling and thought. To say a mistress is "considerate" implies at once kind attention to others and due regard to her own interests. Indeed, the word "consideration" becomes Ellis's mechanism for bridging the gaps between conflicting womanly and supervisory roles.

Yet the emergence of the ideal in the works of such writers as Sarah Lewis ("Women's Mission") and Sarah Ellis suggests its other dimension: a new recognition of the public role for middle-class women. Ellis suggests a need to identify exactly whom she is addressing: "Perhaps it may be necessary to be more specific in describing the class of women to which this work relates." Why does she require specificity? Because it is implicitly understood, and accepted, that her audience will be available for a higher task than that of menial labor. Labor itself is de rigueur, but white collar, not blue collar. Ellis explains who constitutes her audience: "It is, then, strictly speaking, to those who belong to that great mass of the population of England which is connected with trade and manufactures, as well as to the wives and daughters of professional men of limited incomes; or, in order to make the application more direct, to that portion of it who are restricted to the services of from one to four domestics,—who, on the one hand, enjoy the advantages of a liberal education, and, on the other, have no pretension to family rank" (19).

Ellis has targeted a particular group of upwardly mobile middle-class individuals, who are hovering between vulgarity and gentility. The explicit rhetoric of queenliness has disappeared to reemerge, transformed, as a pragmatic acceptance of work for women, accompanied by an assessment of class trends within a burgeoning middle class that dictates the inevitable emergence and desirability of a middle-class female labor force:

A time seems to be approaching, when the middle class of society in England will have to be subdivided; and when the lower portion of this class will of necessity have to turn their attention to a different style of living, and to different modes of occupation, thought, and feeling. . . . The happiness of society, and our moral necessities, will surely, before long, suggest the importance of females of this class being fitted for something very different from drawing-room exhibitions. . . .

It seems to me indispensably necessary . . . that women in this class should be educated, not simply for ladies, but for useful and active members of society—and for this purpose, that they should also consider it no degradation to render their activity conducive to the purposes of trade. . . .

With the improvements of art, and the increase of manufactures, there must be an increased demand for mechanics and work-people of every description . . . there surely can be no reason why the second class of females should not be so trained, as to partake in the advantages resulting from this extended sphere of active and useful occupation. (343–46)

That such a conservative traditionalist as Sarah Ellis should speak with frank acceptance about lower-middle-class women in the marketplace should make us pause. For Ellis, the question does not finally involve a battle for women's rights, simply an acknowledgment of the way emergent class distinctions and class differences have made inevitable a way of thinking about bourgeois women that accepts their professional contributions to society in business and trade. The new woman who emerges at the end of the century here finds her origins in the Victorian angel as much as in the agitators for equal rights. Of course, it is also true that Ellis has preserved the more mystified prerogatives of the upper-middle-class Victorian domestic manager by articulating the "inevitability" of a schism within the middle class.

Although Ellis is candid in assessing social evolution and the role of middle-class women, she is less forthright about the skills necessary to manage a bourgeois household. The four chapters of *Women of England* that discuss household management have exactly the same title: "Domestic Habits—Consideration and Kindness." I have already elucidated the two definitions subsumed under "consideration," benevolence and deliberation, which encapsulate the tension between gender and class constructions of women. Although Ellis emphasizes the latter—and does so in such a way that it implies all of the management strategies to which I have pointed earlier in my discussion of the middle-class woman—she also keeps returning to notions of woman's special sympathy: "The considerateness I shall attempt to define is one of the highest recommendations the female character can possess; because it combines an habitual examination of our own situation and responsibilities, with a quick discernment of the character and feelings of those around us" (175). Having lodged the term within the acceptable framework of woman's general benevolence, Ellis advances by degrees to a much more radical class position. She has already introduced the idea of "habitual examination of our own situation," which implies guarding one's own interests; in the next paragraph Ellis claims that she will "consider what is due to those whom Providence has placed within the sphere of her influence" (175). "Providence," in the tracts, becomes a code word for introducing class issues, or the "servant difficulty." This encoded meaning emerges more clearly within a few pages. Ellis addresses "[want of consideration] towards those with whom we are connected by social ties, without affection—and under this head, the situation of our servants and domestics claims the greatest care" (179). In the context of servants, the idea of Providence returns: "[Servants] know and feel that their lot in the world is comparatively hard; and if they are happily free from all presumptuous questionings of the wisdom and justice of Providence in placing them where they are, they are alive to the conviction that the burden of each day is sufficient, and often more than sufficient, for their strength" (179–80). Ellis relies heavily on the static verb "to be" in this passage, using it five times in a way that underscores stylistically the unchangeability of the servant's status. Providence dictates servants' station in life, a logic that allows the mistress who keeps them in their place also to exhibit her "womanly" sympathy for them.

Ellis analogizes women's work with men's to suggest the need for proper organization to prevent chaos: "As the man engaged in business does not run hither and thither, simply to make a show of alacrity, neither does the woman engaged in higher and more important work" (176). When Ellis finally focuses on an episode demonstrating the nature of the "true English woman," those events dramatize the management activity of middle-class housewives. In summarizing the meaning of the episode, however, she reverts to the ideology of beneficent and empathetic nature, which masks the supervisory aspects of domestic life. Or, put another way, Ellis yokes a patriarchal ideology of idealized womanhood with a bourgeois ideology of class regulation in ways that simultaneously expose and disguise the role of the middle-class housewife. Ellis devotes several pages to a long narrative about the arrival and accommodation of a visitor. The narrative interest turns on lack of preparation, a failure of management that culminates in "disappointments experienced by our guest," "chagrin" for the mistress, and the "harassed and forlorn appearance of an overworked domestic" (201,202) These consequences of poor planning, the narrative implies in its dramatization, could be entirely avoided with proper organization and foresight. But the rhetoric does not make the point that this miniature society must be "managed" by the mistress to prevent antagonisms and insurrectionary impulses in the servant. Rather, at the summarizing moment, it shifts its focus to woman's essential nature: "The individual here described fails to exhibit the character of the *true English woman*, whose peculiar charm is that of diffusing happiness. . . . *She* enters, with a perception as delicate as might be supposed to belong to a ministering angel, into the peculiar feelings and tones of character influencing those around her" (202–3). By attributing problems to the failure of English feminine nature, this final passage obscures the material and political reality of domestic life, which the narrative tends to clarify. Its recourse to the image of a ministering angel entering into the feelings of those around her depicts a mistress as solicitous of her domestic servants as she is of family members. The mystifying rhetoric effects at once a justification of the status quo and a concealment of the class issues as gender ones.

The angel, or true English woman, works to make class a non-issue, relegating effects of nurture to the category of nature. And if English women exhibit their "true nature," their domestics will see the hand of Providence in determining their lot. Nonetheless, it must have been difficult at times to keep down rebellious urges, and the myth of home as a harmonious refuge from external strife and storms was daily in jeopardy from the discontent of servants. To stem such insurrection, Ellis recognizes the need to instill feelings of "confidence and affection" in the domestic staff. In short, she implicitly acknowledges that what she has to manage are, in fact, business relationships masquerading in the home as familial ones. Ellis readily admits that affective attachments are precluded rather than encouraged by the hierarchical relationship of mistress and servant and so concludes that the "tie" will not come "by nature, for no tie, except what necessarily implies authority and subjection, exists between us." She adds, "It cannot come by mutual acts of service, because the relation between us is of such a nature as to place the services almost entirely on their side." Ellis finally admits, "We cannot actually *do* much for them, because it would be out of our province, and a means of removing them out of theirs." At this impasse, Ellis has recourse to "consideration"—"we can think and feel for them" (184)—the Victorian encoding of bourgeois women's complex accommodation of class management with feminine empathy. She advises, over all, the "cheering truth of a superintending care" (194), to give the effect that a "fairy order ha[s] been at work" (196). These oxymoronic constructions might puzzle us if we paused over them: What is a fairy order?[9] But embedded in a series of rhetorical gestures that negotiate efficiently between heart and head, regard and regulation, concern and control, we are prepared to accept this con-

---

[9] Ellis's "fairy order" resonates with Rochester's eagerness to identify Jane Eyre in Charlotte Brontë's novel as a "fairy" (or as other things of that ilk, such as "elf" or "changeling") rather than as a worker in his household.

flation of what were, seemingly, dialectically opposed concepts. Thus, supervision and control become a mistress's unacknowledged and mystified agenda, which is accompanied by a rhetoric of concern whose purpose is to reinscribe bourgeois women within a domestic ideology that posits the home as refuge from the workplace it refuses to recognize that it is.

Nurture Will Out

John Ruskin's "Of Queen's Gardens" (1865) sets out a comparable argument that women (read upper-middle-class women) are peculiarly suited by their natures to become "gardeners," cultivating human plants not only at home but also abroad to remedy social ills. At the heart of Ruskin's conception is the Angel in the House, the designated "queen" of the title. Ruskin, like Patmore before him, conceptually links the two metaphors. "Of Queen's Gardens" is the second of two essays that make up the volume *Sesame and Lilies*; the first—"Of King's Treasuries"—focuses on literature. "Sesame" is "that old enchanted Arabian grain . . . which opens doors—doors, not of robbers', but of king's treasure-houses of books." "Of Queen's Gardens" is the "lily" of the title, and it takes women and education as its subject. Ruskin terms his second lecture a "sequel" to the first because the first deals with "How and What to Read," while the second proposes to ask "Why Read?"—a "far deeper" question that arose out of the first (58).

"Of Queen's Gardens" sets out an agenda for women that is at once active and passive. Woman's role, like that of the lily, is to beautify, purify, and adorn. The passive goodness that Ruskin attributes to women provides the foundation for his educational scheme for girls, which is idealistic and naive in the extreme:

Keep the modern magazine and novel out of your girl's way: turn her loose into the old library every wet day, and let her alone. She will find what is good for her; you cannot: for there is just this difference between the making of a girl's character and a boy's—you may chisel a boy into shape, as you would a rock, or hammer him into it, if he be of a better kind, as you would a piece of bronze. But you cannot hammer a girl into anything. She grows as a flower does,—she will wither without sun . . . you cannot fetter her; she must take her own fair form and way, if she take any. . . . Let her loose in the library, I say, as you do a fawn in a field. It knows the bad weeds twenty times better than you;

and the good ones too, and will eat some bitter and prickly ones, good for it, which you had not the slightest thought were good. (80–81)

In his literal and metaphoric argument from nature, Ruskin attempts to stabilize gender categories before he introduces the question of exercising power, which he interprets differently in men and women.

Ruskin acknowledges in both sexes an innate craving for power: "Deep rooted in the innermost life of the heart of man, and of the heart of woman, God set it [love of power] there, and God keeps it there" (88). This admission sets up the question "But *what* power?"—a question that informs the third section of his essay: "What is [woman's] queenly office with respect to the state?" Ruskin answers that, whereas a man's work is to secure "maintenance, progress, and defence," the "woman's duty, as a member of the commonwealth, is to assist in the ordering, in the comforting, and in the beautiful adornment of the state" (87). He explains further that woman functions as the "centre of order, the balm of distress, and the mirror of beauty"—the still center, one must imagine, of a chaotic world. The word "order" is pivotal in Ruskin's argument; the establishment of such order marks the proper application of woman's "power." Women emerge from these pictures and images as a principle of cohesion in a competitive and divisive world. When they abdicate their power, they leave "misrule and violence to work their will among men" (90): "Men, by their nature, are prone to fight; they will fight for any cause, or for none. It is for you [women] to choose their cause for them, and to forbid them when there is no cause" (91).

The male competitive principle of massive, although unfocused, energy is to be directed by the female cohesive principle of order. These are familiar and unsurprising oppositions, yet to the extent they cannot be harnessed within the framework of "natural" masculine and feminine instincts, to the extent that their rhetorical force exceeds the "natural" in this vision of bourgeois interests solidified on a national scale, they become levers for the construction of a new woman who exercises power by conferring order.

Feminist critics have been quick to point out tensions in Ruskin's position, that he advocates a more active role for women only to protect a traditional way of life. I am suggesting another tack to these conflicts. First, it seems unlikely that Ruskin would speak with such assurance of women's possible social roles unless women were already effective social arbiters, exercising social power, as I have argued they were. Indeed, Ruskin chides the woman who "abdicate[s] this majesty" of larger social ordering to "play at precedence with her next-door neighbor" (92). He implicitly acknowledges women's social career. Second, however, we also recognize that Ruskin translates women's social and political powers into symptoms of their domestic virtues and innate womanly strength. The oxymoron of "sweet ordering" is one signal of this ideological shift: "But the woman's power is for rule, not for battle,—and her intellect is not for invention or creation, but for sweet ordering, arrangement, and decision" (71). Management strategies, "ordering, arrangement, and decision," are reinterpreted as attributes of womanly character—"sweet." On the one hand, the effect of Ruskin's essay is less to argue for women's social activism than it is to insist that her social effectiveness is really just a symptom of innate womanly charm rather than practical, applied intelligence—the same kind of reformulation in which Ellis engages although Ellis is more explicit about intrinsic class tensions to be alleviated by women's sympathy. On the other hand, Ruskin has made familiar—naturalized—the association of women with notions of power and social regulation, however mystified, and so participated in the construction of a new woman.

From its inception the angelic ideal was imbricated in class distinctions. It was never, simply, a womanly ideal; it was always middle class, existing only under the condition and assumption of a supporting cast of domestic servants. The literary portrait of passive, meek, long-suffering angels must be understood as a simplified and tendentious representation of a complex phenomenon—one that cannot afford to point frankly to the class hierarchy that underwrites it and that it depends upon. This point is recognized in some analyses, yet its implications are insufficiently pursued. As the century wore on, the tension between public and private that inhered in the image was resolved by splitting off the public dimension of women's lives. This role became embodied in a contentious figure termed the "new woman." And the "angel" was reduced to a passive, static icon. This reduction has had the retrospective effect of making the image appear never to have been more than a glorification of domesticity to discourage women's active participation in the world outside the home. And the potential to institute change has been understood as the province of intentional, individual agents acting in the public sphere.

4

Charles Dickens's Angels
of Competence

The tale of Charles Dickens's increasingly unhappy marriage and his growing dissatisfaction with his wife is, perhaps, as well known as any story his novels tell. Dickens married pragmatically enough, choosing a woman who could not bewitch him and cause him to suffer as Maria Beadnell had. In selecting the daughter of a gentleman who was distinguishing himself in the arts, Dickens was no doubt anticipating his own rise and the need for a suitable helpmate. He foresaw his own ideal marriage as characterized by "warm companionship," in which he could share stories of his labors with one whose "advancement and happiness" were his goal (Johnson 95). Viewing his choice, Catherine Hogarth, through the mists of Victorian domestic ideology, Dickens no doubt anticipated that she would be "naturally" suited for the social claims that would devolve upon her as his wife. The domestic idyll that Dickens sketched hints at the social elevation to come, but it obscures altogether what— beyond sympathy and love—might be a wife's role. To be loving, good, and true—the idealized attributes of the Victorian angel— proved insufficient for the wife of the popular and energetic writer. Dickens's biographer Edgar Johnson suggests that Catherine "might well have lived happily enough if Dickens had been a busy journalist . . . with a home in some leafy London suburb." But the challenges she faced "as the wife of an enormously ambitious, volatile, and determined genius" defeated her (97).

As Dickens rose in the world, Catherine seemed increasingly out of step, her domestic incapacity a constant gall to him: "she rasped him beyond bearing" (451). Against his precision stood her clumsiness, against his energy, her lassitude, against his passion for order, her inefficiency and mismanagement. "For Dickens, who knew exactly where every article should be in every room in his house . . . whose every movement and gesture were made with precision, poor Catherine's mishaps were as irritating as if they were deliberate" (451). Her "practical incapacities" left him angered and frustrated: "It was common report in London that Dickens did most of the family shopping, 'making bargains at butchers and bakers.' The internal running of the household was in the hands of Georgina [Catherine's sister]" (451). Both Fred Kaplan and Johnson consider the possibility that Dickens "seized the control even of all domestic details from Kate's unresisting hand" or that Georgina slyly and insidiously drew into her own grasp "the reins of authority that rightfully belonged to Kate" (Johnson 452). But Johnson finds neither suggestion plausible, finding instead in Catherine's clumsiness the local manifestation of a general domestic inaptitude. In her role as social hostess, too, Catherine was a cipher, a nonentity: "So little impression did Kate make on Dickens's large circle of friends and acquaintances that during many periods she almost seems to disappear from his life" (453).

My point is not to condemn or exculpate Catherine Dickens as a household manager but to illuminate the imaginative and material investment Dickens had in his wife's skill as homemaker, in his wife's capacity to manage herself and the household to solidify their new distinction. Dickens's anguish over what he felt was Catherine's betrayal of her part in the domestic bargain finds expression in his autobiographical novel *David Copperfield*, where he ultimately kills off the first, incompetent wife, who becomes a drag on his social aspirations. It also finds expression in a certain kind of heroine who populates his texts, in whose angelic visage we can glimpse the canny eyes of a household manager. These heroines—Agnes Wickfield in *David Copperfield*, Esther Summerson in *Bleak House*, the eponymous heroine of *Little Dorrit*, and Bella Wilfer in *Our Mutual Friend*—are all loving, good, and true. More important, that angelic nature is informed by a ready resourcefulness, energy, and efficiency. If her virtue first puts the heroine in possession of the hero's love, it is only her capacity for management that secures it permanently. But perhaps it is more accurate to say that representations of her "virtue" are so entwined with depictions of the order she establishes that virtue subtly becomes defined for us as managerial skill. Dickens, like Ruskin, thus tends to put in the background traits that Sarah Ellis more consistently places in view; perhaps, again like Ruskin, he was more capable of preserving a fantasy when he did not have to fulfill the conflictual role. In describing Esther Summerson as an "angel of competence," Fred Kaplan suggests the way that

Dickens succinctly closes the signifying gap between angel and manager (302). This angel of competence is ready to accept as her husband a young, upwardly mobile, hard-working, middle-class gentleman, whose labors promise fair reward when linked with her management powers.

David Copperfield's Second Chance

David Copperfield (1849–50) depicts the struggle of just such an aspiring gentleman. The history of Dickens's hero is memorable, in part, for the domestic chaos that ensues when David marries his angel, Dora Spenlow. He is, as it were, unwarned. Having secured his desire, he expects domestic bliss to follow. Indeed, Victorian myth suggested that a woman by her nature diffused a charm and order over the home so that it became a refuge and haven from the capitalist competition of the marketplace. But David's tale both illuminates the way domestic discursive practices constitute and regulate a field of individual possibilities and reveals that household management depends less on the character of an English woman than it does on a precise set of organizational skills that also would not be inappropriate in a factory. One way to interpret David's achievement as the "hero" of his story is to measure his success at acquiring the content (or fortune) and form (status display) that will inscribe him firmly within the genteel middle class.

Indeed, David's is a story of status jeopardy. Born to a gentleman, David early learns to expect that he will become a gentleman. But his mother (whom Dora echoes) jeopardizes his status in her choice of second husband. David must claim a surrogate parent in Betsy Trotwood and adopt a new identity as "Trotwood Copperfield" in order to reclaim his middle-class status. David's subjectivity is seriously split. First, and most obviously, the "I" who speaks is not the "I" who is spoken. There exists a gap between the narrating adult subject and the youth who is the subject of narration. But, more seriously, there is a split in the narrated subject whose coherence is usually marked by a name. David/Trotwood Copperfield is both one person and two. David articulates this rupture of identity: "Thus I began my new life, in a new name, and with everything new about me. . . . A remoteness had come upon the old Blunderstone life. . . . And . . . a curtain had for ever fallen on my life at Murdstone and Grinby's" (215). Underlining the division, Dickens titles chapter 16 "I am a New Boy in more Senses than One." And David himself remarks of "the boy I was myself, when I first came there" that "that little fellow seems to be no part of me; I remember him as something left behind upon the road of life—as something I have passed, rather than have actually been—almost think of him as of some one else" (268).

David's ruminations on the self-who-is-not-himself reveal the deep, distinct, and seemingly inevitable, class divisions that structure his psyche and experience, and they early demonstrate his need for the domestic manager who can stabilize his identity as the upper-middle-class gentleman he aspires to be. They are present from the first moment he meets Little Emily, and they provide an effective barrier to his acting out his childhood and childish wish to marry her. The initial dialogue between David and Emily focuses on class. She notes that, although they are both orphans, they are different because "your father was a gentleman and your mother is a lady; and my father was a fisherman and my mother was a fisherman's daughter" (34–35). She subsequently expresses a desire to be a "lady," a wish made ominous by its association with David's prevision of her moral fall and his query: "There has been a time since . . . when I have asked myself the question, would it have been better for little Em'ly to have had the waters close above her head that morning in my sight; and when I have answered Yes, it would have been" (36). Emily's wish to be a lady anticipates her fall; the natural grace and gentility she possesses cannot institute her within the middle classes, cannot compensate for her ignorance of that class's signifying practices. Mrs. Steerforth pronounces: "I am sorry to repeat, it is impossible. Such a marriage would irretrievably blight my son's career, and ruin his prospects" (469). Her judgment that Steerforth "would disgrace himself" in such a marriage, her assertion that Emily is "far below him," is countered by Mr. Peggotty's plea to "raise her up!" But Mrs. Steerforth dismisses both the uncle and his niece with her final assessment: "She is uneducated and ignorant" (468). Rosa Dartle confirms the class bias in her dismissive comment: "They are a depraved, worthless set. I would have her whipped!" (471). The marriage of Emily and Steerforth is impossible because Emily is already inscribed within her culture's discursive practices as a Worker ("fisherman's daughter"), the ideological Other of the Angel in the House.

One measure of the distance between eighteenth- and nineteenth-century novels can be found in a comparison of Moll Flanders's fate with Emily's. Moll also expresses a childhood wish to be a lady, and she is granted her wish despite a previous fall. Moll's fortunes fluctuate, but there is a steady drive toward middle-class respectability, crowned at the conclusion of the novel by her anticipated return from America to England, married and prosperous. Emily, in contrast, is transported and remains unwed.

When Steerforth's intervention spares David an entanglement with his first, unsuitable infatuation, this "gentleman's son" appropriately directs his attention to securing a cultivated middle-class wife, who should establish him on social terra firma.[1] Of course, as we have seen, the mystifying aspects of Victorian ideology mislead David, and he selects poorly because he persists in separating Dora from the world in which he lives, in seeing her as belonging to a higher sphere: "I don't think I had any definite idea where Dora came from, or in what degree she was related to a higher order of beings; but I am quite sure I should have scouted the notion of her being simply human, like any other young lady, with indignation and contempt" (474). Dickens is one of the few authors to depict the household angel amid domestic chaos, and in that tension we see the way in which literature reproduces the ideology but also represents the material conditions that expose fault lines in it.

By way of Dora's default, *David Copperfield* allows us to glimpse the functions performed by middle-class women in furthering middle-class control through class containment and status display. David has apprehensions even before marriage and attempts to make Dora a middle-class manager through a system of education focusing on cookery texts and accounting books modeled on his aunt's. Once they actually establish a household, David confronts the full extent of Dora's managerial failure. He admits, "We should have been at [our servant's] mercy, if she had had any; but she was a remorseless woman, and had none" (635). The fault belongs to Dora, whom David lectures: "It would be better for you to remonstrate with Mary Anne." Dora begs off through incompetence, "I am such a little goose . . . and she knows I am!" But David only remarks: "I thought this sentiment so incompatible with the establish-

[1] Mary Poovey makes a related argument that domestic inaptitude and issues of sexual infidelity are linked in *David Copperfield*. She notes that Emily's moral fall is proleptically rationalized by her lower social class. Further, she argues that Emily's social class proves a "more indirect threat to the identity of the hero" than does her sexual transgression: "Class difference exists as a threat in *David Copperfield* because 'innocence' in this novel entails not only sexual ignorance, but also the indifference to class distinctions that enables David to befriend and bring together 'chuckle-headed' Ham Peggotty and the well-born Steerforth. . . . If [David] made Emily his wife, it would exclude David from the social position he 'deserves.' . . . Steerforth's presence in the novel enables Dickens to levy this admonitory lesson without contaminating David's 'freshness' by an overly self-protective consciousness of class" (98).

ment of any system of check on Mary Anne, that I frowned a little" (635). David's goal—the "establishment of . . . any check"—speaks of the containment function of household management. If the servants are not firmly kept in their places, then the entire social hierarchy is jeopardized. And, whereas members of the middle class, guided by such ideologies, wanted to deny class exploitation as long as the working classes stayed subordinate, they were quick to point out exploitation of the middle classes by the working classes under the pernicious system of perquisites.

Household management, as laid out in the guides and manuals, comprised two aspects: regulation of servants and status display. Dora's mismanagement of the domestic staff serves as an inverse lesson in several chapters on proper supervision. David refers to the "Ordeal of Servants," a summation of the couple's exploitation by those hired to serve them: "Everybody we had anything to do with seemed to cheat us. Our appearance in a shop was a signal for the damaged goods to be brought out immediately" (640). The problem, as David makes clear, is not that they incur extraordinary expenses or live extravagantly but that their resources are squandered in procuring the necessities of life, and even those disappear so readily into servant's hands that David complains: "The most wonderful fact of all was, that we never had anything in the house" (640). Dora's incompetence appears in every detail, from her inability to manage resources and track expenses to her failure to secure reliable and honest help. David ruefully laments "the washerwoman pawning the clothes . . . the chimney on fire, the parish engine, and perjury on the part of the Beadle . . . a servant with a taste for cordials" (640–41).

Dickens represents equally with Dora's failure to regulate and contain the servants the other aspect of her managerial debacle: her inability to display their status adequately, a failure elaborated in her attempt to entertain David's friend Traddles. David confesses, "I could not have wished for a prettier little wife . . . but I certainly could have wished . . . that Jip [the dog] had never been encouraged to walk about the table-cloth during dinner. I began to think there was something disorderly in his being there at all" (641). David continues his recital of this dinner, hilarious to the reader but mortifying to his own pride:

I made no allusion to the skirmishing plates upon the floor; or to the disreputable appearance of the castors, which were all at sixes and sevens, and looked drunk; or to the further blockade of Traddles by wandering vegetable dishes and jugs. I could not help wondering in my own mind, as I contemplated the boiled leg of mutton before me, previous to carving it, how it came to pass that our joints of meat were of such extraordinary shapes—and whether our butcher contracted for all the deformed sheep that came into the world. (641–42)

It is tempting to quote the entirety of David's lament over Dora's housekeeping because it so succinctly captures the labor and organization that went into successful household management. In the midst of "skirmishing plates" and "wandering vegetable dishes and jugs," David is forced to acknowledge the failure of his schemes to train Dora as a manager and to take upon himself "the toils and care of our life." Dora is left to pursue a "make-belief of housekeeping" (646, 648).

Dickens refuses one common refiguration of women's managerial work in the novel, that is, the interposition of the anonymous, all-competent housekeeper between a wife and her work. For example, Trollope's narrator in *The Warden* comments on an excellent housewife in this vein: "Mrs. Grantly, I presume, inspected her kitchen, though she had a first-rate housekeeper, with sixty pounds a year" (74). Her competence and vigilance are reinterpreted as bossy interference through the narrative addendum in the dependent clause. It is impossible to imagine a nineteenth-century novelist commenting of a male character, say the master of an estate or of a factory: "Mr. Jones, I presume, inspected his tenants' rents, though he had an excellent agent"; or, "Mr. Smith attended to his factory's productivity, though he had an excellent foreman." In the case of women, the novelist is foregrounding an ideology of passivity, dependence, and idleness. Ironically, the novelists must create the image of a working-class woman with managerial skills—the housekeeper—in order to conceal the real work performed by middle-class women as wives.

David refers to his unfortunate choice of Dora for wife as the "first mistaken impulse of an undisciplined heart" (644), language inviting a Foucauldian analysis that aligns the domestic discipline David seeks with other regulating and normalizing practices. He has already admitted that in his professional life he has the ability to subject himself to a steel discipline. He needs to find an agent similarly constituted to bring his household in line with his professional accomplishments. That agent is Agnes Wickfield, who has managed her father's household since her childhood and who is introduced into the novel, in fact, as his "little housekeeper" (222). David instantly finds the Wickfield house appealing in the order and cleanliness everywhere apparent; each room is so cosy that he imagines it could not be improved upon, until he "looked at the next one, and found it equal to it, if not better. On everything there was same air of retirement and cleanliness that marked the house outside" (223). David describes the agent who has created this perfection in terms little conducive to romance: "She had a little basket-trifle hanging at her side, with keys in it; and she looked as staid and as discreet a housekeeper as the old house could have" (223). His appreciative but cool response indicates the power of ideology over him. He has not yet learned that the competent housekeeper *is* the angel. And although the text represents fully Dora's domestic failures, implicitly challenging the ideology of the Angel in the House, it ultimately refuses to name the source of Agnes's success. It remystifies the domestic hearth angel. Agnes is "my guide and best support" (862), "the source of every worthy aspiration I had ever had; the centre of myself, the circle of my life," and "my soul" (864, 877).[2]

Although the novel terms the process "falling in love," in fact, Agnes (whose name is an anagram of "Anges," French for angel) contributes the social capital to complement the material capital of the rising gentleman. She provides the goal of David's long journey to stabilize his identity as a respectable and genteel middle-class hero: "We stood together in the same old-fashioned window at night, when the moon was shining; Agnes with her quiet eyes raised up to it; I following her glance. Long miles of road then opened out before my mind; and, toiling on, I saw a ragged way-worn boy forsaken and neglected, who should come to call even the heart now beating against mine, his own" (863). The happiness Agnes instills is written as an aspect of her nature and as a culmination of deferred romance rather than as a product of her skillful organization and control. But we have seen enough of household chaos with Dora to know that far more important than grace, sym-

---

[2] Poovey's excellent analysis of the representation of the professional writer in *David Copperfield* links the work of writing with household labor: "The two images—of effortless housekeeping and effortless writing—are interdependent at every level: not only is the Copperfields' domestic security a function of David's material success as a writer. . . but the representation of the domestic sphere as immune to the alienation of work is produced by the very writing with which it is compared" (101). Poovey is also interested in the way that middle-class women's work is mystified, noting that Agnes's duties are "signified only by her basket of keys" (101). Chris Vanden Bossche has also noted that Agnes's "actual work of housekeeping is disguised by descriptions of the basket of keys" (103).

pathy, and love are the household keys Agnes carries at her side: symbol of her authority, tool of her management, and sign of her regulatory power and control.

Esther Summerson's Bleak House II: The Sequel

Dickens's *Bleak House* (1852–53) introduces a more prominent household manager in the figure of Esther Summerson, who shares the narrative tasks with an anonymous, omniscient narrator. Although in person and in personality Esther is self-effacing, her prominence as narrator makes her perspective, her way of seeing and judging, central. The novel is built on this tension between the effaced Esther and the control exerted through her representation of events and people; she creates an all-seeing but unseen surveillance. Her own self-description could apply, ironically, to Tulkinghorn, the lawyer who seeks power through possession of family secrets, and to Bucket, the Chief of Detective Police, who gains power through unraveling secrets: "I had always rather a noticing way—not a quick way, O no!—a silent way of noticing what passed before me, and thinking I should like to understand it better" (11). And Esther shares with Bucket an insistence on "duty." Ringing her housekeeping keys and exhorting herself, "Esther, Esther, Esther! Duty, my dear!" she echoes Bucket, who hounds into respectability the Jos and Gridleys and Georges of the world: "Duty is duty, and friendship is friendship. I never want the two to clash. . . . But I have got a duty to discharge" (62, 514). The comparison is not frivolous, of course; power and control belong to those who have information and understanding, coupled with the determination to impose order on their worlds.

To discover links between the housekeeper and the detective police in Dickens's novel is to confirm the interrelationship between two forms of discipline postulated by Jacques Donzelot: contract and tutelage, the former implying voluntary consent to imposed social norms, the latter external enforcement of those norms.[3] David A. Miller's *The Novel and the Police* borrows from both Donzelot and Foucault to carry out a compelling analysis of the operations of power in *Bleak House*. Miller focuses on the tensions between repre-

---

[3] In *The Policing of Families*, Donzelot posits these two modes as complementary forms of discipline. If the family performs its duties satisfactorily, then it earns the liberty of contract; its failure incurs the tutelary mode of "external penetration" (82–95). However, Donzelot's argument has a misogynist tendency to fault women for the state's increasing intervention in the family. His argument implicitly capitulates to the patriarchal logic that "women are to blame" for the demise of the family.

sentations of institutions like Chancery and the detective police versus depictions of the family and home. He argues that the "topic of the carceral in Dickens . . . worked to secure the effect of differ- ence between, on the one hand, a confined, institutional space in which power is violently exercised on collectivized subjects, and on the other, a space of 'liberal society,' generally determined as a free, private, and individual domain and practically specified as the fam- ily" (58–59). The representational contrast that Miller identifies be- comes the basis for his own compelling analysis of the "close *imbrica- tion* of individual and social, domestic and institutional, private and public, leisure and work" (83). Miller's argument relies upon an op- positional rhetoric—inside/outside, private/public—which he attrib- utes to the novel. Ultimately, of course, Miller needs the novel to establish those oppositions so that he can demonstrate the way in which it (inadvertently) collapses them, revealing that the private is complicit in the public, the domestic in the institutional, and the liberal in the carceral. We must understand "power" in these lu- cubrations as a totalizing force, which has already anticipated and coopted resistance to its effects. But the very notion that this concept of power would destroy—belief in a realm outside of the operations of power—is itself sustained, in part, by a radical chauvinism, which can always point to women and other marginalized and dis- enfranchised groups as representations of that (illusory) "outside" of power operations. If, instead, we recognize women and the domes- tic as alternative sites of power operations in *Bleak House*, then the novel depicts not the totalizing effects of power but conflict between opposing modes of power.[4]

Miller is disturbingly unaware of gender; he speaks of the reader as "he," who through his "leisured withdrawal to the private, do- mestic sphere . . . is constituted . . . within the categories of the individual, the inward, the domestic" (82).[5] Miller elucidates the im-

---

[4] Defining a world in which external controls are replaced with self-discipline is ostensibly the goal of Miller's analysis of *Bleak House*. Yet he persists in positioning the home apart from the detective police so that he can demonstrate how the distinc- tion collapses. In Miller's account of the novel, the home and the detective police are supposed to ground distinctions between inside and outside of power, but I argue that the novel strategically calls into question that apparent distinction.

[5] Laurie Langbauer, working through the relationship of women to the romance genre, makes a similar critique of Miller: "Despite the generous complications of his argument, Miller's conclusions—that the home and family are the banal embodiment of the same indifferent disciplinary system embodied in oppressive public institu- tions—restate what Dickens's novels, and feminist readers of them, have already said: that the home is a prison" (149). Obviously, I find Langbauer's conclusion too simple, as it reproduces the binary logic of women as victim.

plications: "A drill in the rhythms of bourgeois industrial culture, the novel generates a nostalgic desire to get home (where the novel can be resumed) in the same degree as it inures its readers to the necessity of periodically renouncing home (for the world where the novel finds its justification and its truth). In reading the novel, one is made to rehearse how to live a problematic—always surrendered, but then again always recovered—privacy" (83). But what if the "reader" never leaves home? What if, in short, the reader is a middle-class Victorian woman? Why is the realm of women associated with escape, or at least its illusion? Why is the world outside the home the world "where the novel finds its justification and its truth"?

Dickens's *Bleak House*, read through the prism of gender and the middle-class manager, reveals a struggle for the terms in which meaning and identity are to be constituted. Rather than representing the family as a realm idealistically outside of an institutional and public sphere, Dickens positions the middle-class home as a competing site of power, the province of emerging cultural definitions that seek to supplant the cumbersome behemoths of Chancery and the aristocracy with the detective police and the middle-class, to displace inheritance and tradition with self-reliance and application, to replace external controls with self-discipline. And the guardians of middle-class life and the agents of that discipline are bourgeois women. Mr. Bagnet's mantra—"Discipline must be maintained"— ironically announces a man's subservient position within a culture whose order is established by women. Mr. Bagnet pronounces this mantra preliminary to enforcing his wife's authority to deliver "his" opinion on all matters: "You know me," he tells his friend George, "It's my old girl that advises. She has the head. But I never own to it before her. Discipline must be maintained" (293). She, thus, originates "their" opinions and values while he plays out his ideological role as "head" of the family. The two together enact a parodic drama of the cultural myth of dominant husband and submissive wife, while testifying to the wife's managerial authority.[6]

---

[6] Langbauer reads this episode quite differently, arguing that "*Bleak House* indeed presents Mrs. Bagnet's seeming autonomy, and even authority, as comic grotesquery, benign because clearly understood as comic, a reversal of (what the novel believes ought to be) women's actual domestic subjection" (149–50). She continues this argument, turning to Esther's narrative as exemplification: "The endlessness of Esther's narrative echoes the way women are characteristically sacrificed to the perpetual enslavement of the everyday: the monotonous and self-perpetuating drudgery performed by slaves of the home like Guster or the Marchioness" (152). But to emphasize only the patriarchal dimensions of the home and overlook the class dimensions, to link Esther's managerial tasks with Guster's menial labor, is to miss a distinction operating consistently throughout the novel. Mrs. Snagsby, who "manages" Guster, sometimes quite brutally, is a vulgar, lower-class example of the more "gentle" Esther.

Although women's authority is mystified within patriarchal ideologies, another image emerges within a bourgeois class ideology. Once we perceive the way a middle-class wife imposes discipline, we can see that the detective police are deliberately linked to the values of home and hearth for their complementary ability to impose order and coherence in the novel's fragmented, enmired world. At the center of this scheme is Esther Summerson. The London "particular"—a metaphor for Chancery—that opens the novel and greets Esther's arrival in the metropolis finds its analogue in the mire of the Jellyby household where she is lodged. Like the lawyers in Chancery, Mrs. Jellyby—one of the parodied philanthropists in the novel—engages in continual correspondences and petitions, none of which produces any resolution. Indeed, the result of her endeavors—the Borioboola-Ghan King's desire to sell everybody for rum—echoes the slavery to a system produced by Chancery.

Further, Mrs. Jellyby's domestic chaos comments obliquely on the relations between England's imperial missions and their analogue in home rule. Her mismanagement of the household anticipates the debacle of her colonizing missions overseas, and the narrative of this connection illustrates how England's domestic virtues solidify and are solidified by her far-flung colonial enterprises.[7] Thus, Esther's entry into the dirt and disorder of the Jellyby household, which she immediately sets about rectifying, anticipates the broader sweep of her colonizing endeavors. Contrasted with Mrs. Jellyby, whose "handsome eyes . . . could see nothing nearer than Africa" (28), Esther sees and evaluates everything in the household: the room "strewn with papers . . . not only very untidy, but very dirty," the slatternly dress, the unruly and unsupervised children, curtains fastened with forks, lack of hot water, broken doorknobs, torn staircarpets, smoking or extinguished fires, raw food, slatternly maids. The servants—of whom there are at least two, a maid-of-all-work and a cook—both drink and smell of it. Esther spies the cook early in the morning "coming out of a public-house, wiping her mouth" (36). Caddy Jellyby complains that "the whole house is disgraceful" (34), but neither she nor her father, rendered mute, is capable of remedying the situation. Caddy only wonders that "the very paving-stones opposite our house can have the patience to stay there, and be a witness of . . . Ma's management" (37). The order must emanate from the household's mistress; in her default, the novel implies, chaos reigns.

[7] Edward Said's *Culture and Imperialism* points to the connection between domestic arrangements and the colonial mission in an illuminating discussion of Jane Austen's *Mansfield Park* (87).

Successfully imposed domestic order is a form of middle-class colonization much more efficient and far-reaching in its effects than the loudly bruited efforts of the philanthropists. Esther quietly and systematically begins to impose order that, if pursued, will culminate in middle-class comfort and respectability for reformed individuals. Ada remarks to Esther: "You do so much, so unpretendingly! You would make a home out of even this house" (32). She efficiently releases Peepy from the prison of railings through which he has wedged his head, takes him into her own custody, subdues him, and cleans him up. In short, she sets him on the road to middle-class industry and allows us to anticipate his metamorphosis into the young man at the end of the novel, "in the Custom House, and doing extremely well" (664). Caddy, too, falls under Esther's training and management. Having secured a prospective husband, the bedraggled Miss Jellyby turns to Esther for a four-week training course in household management, three to be conducted at Bleak House and the fourth in London preparing the Jellyby house for the nuptials. They begin with dress and the acquisition of some skill in needlework, at which Caddy "improve[s] rapidly." Caddy is "very anxious 'to learn housekeeping,' as she said" (318), so Esther relates that "I showed her all my books and methods, and all my fidgety ways. You would have supposed that I was showing her some wonderful inventions, by her study of them; and if you had seen her, whenever I jingled my housekeeping keys, get up and attend me, certainly you might have thought that there never was a greater impostor than I, with a blinder follower than Caddy Jellyby" (318). The disclaimer—Esther as impostor—inevitably follows the revelation of a systematic scheme of organization. This requisite modesty about her effects contributes to the mystification of the middle-class woman's management labors. Thus, we tend not to notice that Esther, like Mrs. Jellyby, also directs affairs from a distance, because she does so, unlike Mrs. Jellyby, with little fanfare and great effectiveness. When in London, an ever vigilant Esther notes that she "was very busy indeed, all day, and wrote directions home to the servants, and wrote notes for my guardian, and dusted his books and papers, and jingled my housekeeping keys a good deal" (182).[8]

Although the novel depicts an Esther who is appropriately humble about her supervisory skills, it indirectly foregrounds those tal-

---

[8] David Musselwhite has commented on some of the class prejudices operating in the novel: "The 'poor' and the 'oppressed' seem to exist for no other reason than to be the objects of middle-class charity and the occasion for middle-class complacency" (222).

ents in portraying a number of individuals who want to appropriate her energies to their own ends. Mr. Jarndyce wants to secure them permanently by making Esther his wife. Richard and Ada imagine a ménage à trois with Esther as their "housekeeper." And those who depend on astute evaluations of organizational structures—con artists like Herbert Skimpole—have no difficulty recognizing that Esther is the person who can extricate them from their difficulties. Skimpole compliments her on her "excellent sense, and quiet habit of method and usefulness, which anybody must observe in you who has the happiness of being a quarter of an hour in your society" (56). Skimpole's reliance on Esther only confirms John Jarndyce's immediate and implicit trust in this canny keeper of the house, whom he invests with "two bunches" of housekeeping keys, "all labeled," before she has even finished unpacking her bags. A maid announces: "The large bunch is the housekeeping, and the little bunch is the cellars, miss. Any time you was pleased to appoint to-morrow morning, I was to show you the presses and things they belong to" (52). Possession of the keys installs Esther as warder of the household's belongings and automatically instills in her an attitude of suspicion toward the servants, from whom the family's goods are locked away. Despite her profession of being "lost in the magnitude of my trust," Esther appoints "half-past six" as the hour, and she is up before daylight to take mental possession of the household:

> Every part of the house was in such order, and every one was so attentive to me, that I had no trouble with my two bunches of keys: though what with trying to remember the contents of each little store-room drawer, and cupboard; and what with making notes on a slate about jams, and pickles, and preserves, and bottles, and glass, and china, and a great many other things; and what with being generally a methodical, old-maidish sort of foolish little person; I was so busy that I could not believe it was breakfast-time when I heard the bell ring. (70)

When Esther describes herself as "foolish" and a "methodical old-maidish sort," she distracts from the fact that she now knows *exactly* how much of *everything* is in the house; woe betide the servant who presides over an area in which items turn up missing. Once installed, Esther consolidates her position, denying herself leisure in order to carry out her discipline. For example, she remains at home "while Mr. Jarndyce, Ada, and Richard, took advantage of a very fine day to make a little excursion" because "it was the day of the week on which [she] paid the bills, and added up [her] books, and made all the household affairs as compact as possible" (93). Upon this managerial scene arrives the hapless and hopeful Mr. Guppy in an "entirely new suit of glossy clothes . . . a shining hat, lilac-kid gloves"—a walking signifier of lower-middle-class pretensions to bourgeois respectability. He is greeted by an Esther Summerson "full of business, examining tradesmen's books, adding up columns, paying money, filing receipts," in short, displaying the signifiers that truly put her beyond the reach of his rank (93). The comedy of Guppy's doomed proposal to Esther derives from his class pretensions.

Esther Summerson is the Florence Nightingale of bourgeois housekeepers, extending her method across the face of England. Not only does she instruct Caddy Jellyby in her system, but she also molds little Charley Necket, who had been given to her as a "gift" by Mr. Jarndyce. Working-class Charley's avowal that she will "try to be such a good maid" bears impressive fruit, as she is ultimately married to the miller, a solid lower-middle-class match of which she is justifiably "vain" (663). And Charley's sister, Emma, succeeds to her position under Esther, where she, too, will have an opportunity to develop the skills necessary for a middle-management position.

It is not simply that these young women learn to keep house; they are being installed into a particular system of values. Housekeeping is a metonymy for the principle of order and revitalization that is to stand as a counterweight to the fog and chaos of Chancery and its extensions, such as the "world of fashion" embodied in the Dedlocks. "Both the world of fashion and the Court of Chancery," says the narrator, "are things of precedent and usage; oversleeping Rip Van Winkles." Sir Leicester supports interminable Chancery suits like Jarndyce and Jarndyce: "a slow, expensive, British, constitutional kind of thing" (6, 10).

Rosa, the village girl whom Lady Dedlock has secured as lady's maid, stands at the juncture of the two contrasting systems: the noblesse oblige of the Dedlocks and the self-reliance of the new, aspiring middle classes, here embodied in Mr. Rouncewell, the ironmaster, who owns a factory. Under the Dedlock's patronage, Rosa will prosper in the "station unto which [she is] called"; she is, according to Sir Leicester, "honored with my Lady's notice and favour" (303). Mrs. Rouncewell, the ironmaster's own mother, is a product of this system, and he admits that she is "one of those examples—perhaps as good a one as there is—of love, and attachment, and fidelity in such a station, which England may well be proud of" (302). But there is an unbridgeable gap between the housekeeper as agent for a

wealthy aristocracy and the newly emerging middle-class housekeeper who manages her own more modest establishment. According
to Mr. Rouncewell, the patronage of the Dedlocks will incapacitate
Rosa for becoming the wife of his upwardly mobile, middle-class
son. He insults Sir Leicester by comparing her servitude under the
Dedlocks with employment in a factory, but both domestic service
and factory work depend on an uneducated, largely unskilled lower-
class labor force. Mr. Rouncewell proposes to give the girl a chance
by educating her for two years, so that, if she has profited by her
advantages, she will be "worthy of any station" (302). She cannot be
a servant if she is to manage servants as mistress of her own establishment.

In light of these contrasting values, George Rouncewell, the
scapegrace younger brother, must ultimately elect to take his place
with his mother at Chesney Wold rather than join his brother in the
factory. George confesses to his older sibling: "You are not used to
be officered. . . . Everything about you is in perfect order and discipline; everything about me requires to be kept so" (644). George
belongs to an older order of servitude, accepting of an external discipline; his brother identifies with an emerging middle-class, which
has internalized the disciplines necessary to replace the aristocracy
as the ruling class. It will police itself rather than be policed. At the
end of the novel the thriving Rouncewell factory and lively Rouncewell household contrast to the "dullness" of Chesney Wold, where
"Sir Leicester holds his shrunken state in the long drawing-room"
(661). Although this motionless and moribund world tenaciously
clings to its prerogatives, it seems only a matter of time before it
is exhausted by its own inertia: "Passion and pride, even to the
stranger's eye, have died away from the place in Lincolnshire, and
yielded it to dull repose" (662).

The propagation of "Bleak House" is a final, dexterous touch in
this novel. Whereas Chesney Wold is sterile and moribund, the site
of Esther Summerson's labors is so prosperous that it reproduces
itself in Bleak House II, the sequel. John Jarndyce locates in Yorkshire a "suitable little place," ostensibly for a bachelor Woodcourt,
and summons Esther to inspect it. He confesses, "When I walked
over it the day before yesterday, and it was reported ready, I found
that I was not housekeeper enough to know whether things were all
as they ought to be. So I sent off for the best little housekeeper that
could possibly be got, to come and give me her advice and opinion"
(647). Esther is, of course, that housekeeper, and everything has, of
course, been laid out exactly on the plan that Esther established in

the original Bleak House because Jarndyce knows "there could be no better plan" (648).

Although the novel points to Esther's achievements, it disguises the nature of her work because to reveal it is to introduce class issues prominently into the home-as-haven. In the novel's conclusion, Esther takes her place by Woodcourt's side, merged in the more shining qualities of her husband. She claims that the people of Yorkshire "like me for his sake, as I do everything I do in life for his sake" (665). The phrase "merged in the more shining qualities" actually described Mr. Jellyby early in the novel who was, of course, "merged . . . in the more shining qualities of his wife" (26). The irony bespeaks his own submersion, his helplessness and incapacity, in the face of household chaos. The man simply sits with his head against the wall, incapable even of speech. At the end of the novel, Allan Woodcourt's capacity for work correlates with his wife's talent for management. And the disappearance of Esther from view depends on the sleight of hand of that same skillful manager. Esther's final effacement of herself and her effects contributes to the Victorian myth of the idle angel. But that static icon is found only in the figure of Ada Clare, whose single task is to shine "in the miserable corner [of her home with Richard] like a beautiful star" (619). The many lives and houses Esther manages leave her no leisure to serve as an elegant light fixture.[9]

One final word on *Bleak House*. Mrs. Jellyby, who has reduced her own home to chaos, becomes an advocate of "the rights of women to sit in Parliament" (664). Apparently, Dickens's irony suggests, she intends to wreak havoc on the country if her folly is not stopped. The least talented housekeeper becomes the most vocal feminist. Mrs. Jellyby is joined in her efforts by women like Miss Wisk, whose "mission . . . was to show the world that woman's mission was man's mission; and that the only genuine mission, of both man and woman, was to be always moving declaratory resolutions about things in general at public meetings" (321). Miss Wisk angrily informs Esther that "such a mean mission as the domestic mission, was the very last thing to be endured" and that "the idea of woman's mission lying chiefly in the narrow sphere of Home was an

[9] Martin Danahay is interested in establishing that Esther and middle-class women, in general, do *work* in the home, despite mystifications of that fact. He claims, however, that Esther's "labor is not explicitly recognized as work in the same sense as the tasks performed by the male professionals. This lack of acknowledgment of Esther's labor results directly from the growing separation of women from work in the Victorian period" (418). Danahay reads the gaps in Esther's character "as products of the Victorian gender hierarchy of labor in which women's work could not be acknowledged overtly" (419). He does not examine class issues.

outrageous slander on the part of her Tyrant Man" (322). These pointed jibes at women who abandon their proper "mission," the home, help to persuade us that the Victorian middle-class home is a very isolated, conventional place, indeed—the repository of traditional values. They become part of the mystification.

But the home we have been examining is far from traditional—it is a primary locus for solidifying class identities and establishing a middle-class hegemony by colonizing the "natives" of England. The Victorian idealizations of home as outside of politics, as a refuge from strife, helped to facilitate its operation as a new base for struggle. Such idealizations, in which it is so easy for a public to participate because they feed into stereotypes of women, inevitably work to consolidate upper-middle-class centrality and power, separating the genteel both from the working classes, who serve them, and the lower middle classes, who emulate them.

Little Dorrit: From Bourgeois Prison to Bourgeois Palace

Dickens's *Little Dorrit* (1855–57) presents a seemingly different heroine in Amy Dorrit, "child of the Marshalsea," the debtors' prison in which she was born. As a prison for *debtors*, however, the Marshalsea is middle class at core, a world of the shabby genteel populated by individuals who embody the tenuousness of middle-class status, formerly "haves" who, through reversals, have become "have nots," yet who might, once again, reclaim their stations or win one higher. Unlike workhouses, which await those in the working class who lose their already precarious financial footing, the debtors' prison bespeaks a former affluence. In this social context, then, Mr. Dorrit may be poor, stripped of his material resources, but he remains a "gentleman," possessed of the remnants of cultural capital, unlike the unfortunate Mr. Nandy, patronized by Mr. Dorrit, who inhabits the workhouse and so earns the obloquy of "pauper."

Dickens depicts his eponymous heroine as solidly middle class at heart, her head neither bowed by her prison experiences nor turned by her ascension to aristocratic gentility at her father's sudden inheritance. She shares more values in common with the manager-heroines who precede her in earlier Dickens texts than with the world that populates the prison.[10] More obviously than her novelistic sis-

[10] George Eliot was one of the first critics to complain about Dickens's seeming divorce of personality from social circumstance, noting that the frequently false psychology of Dickens's characters encourages "the miserable fallacy that high morality and refined sentiment can grow out of harsh social conditions, ignorance, and want" ("Natural History of German Life" 271).

ters, however, Little Dorrit manages her father's life to protect his fragile sense of significance and status. And that management necessitates a clever negotiation of the issue of work. Ladies did no work, or so the etiquette manuals preached, and Mr. Dorrit clings obstinately to this dictum. Thus, Dorrit's actual labors as seamstress outside the prison walls—labors to procure luxuries for her father—must be disguised from Mr. Dorrit to salvage his illusions of familial grandeur. Because Mr. Dorrit, buoyed up by his daughter's efforts, makes a greater stand "by his forlorn gentility," then "over and above other daily cares, the Child of the Marshalsea had always upon her the care of preserving the genteel fiction that they were all idle beggars together." She must now exert herself "to keep up the ceremony and pretense of his having no idea that Amy herself went out by the day to work" (114).

In an off-center way, then, Dickens depicts a classic instance of the female worker whose work is disguised in order to preserve status. But the only person deluded is Mr. Dorrit, and perhaps laughter is the only response to his self-delusion. Yet the text advances what is a humorous pretense to a serious business in representing Little Dorrit's status management of her family. Although she labors, her tacit agreement to enter into a pretense of idle leisure signals her general inscription within middle-class values. Further, she manages the family's scarce resources to protect their "status" and also secures whatever dignity and reputation they possess by importing to their affairs her bourgeois discipline. Although the youngest, she "was the head of the fallen family; and bore, in her own heart, its anxieties and shames" (112). She brings organization and cleanliness to her father's sordid, fetid rooms. Of her own garret, the narrator remarks: "Beautifully kept, it was ugly in itself, and had little but cleanliness and air to set it off" (338). She attends to her father's wardrobe—shirts, coats, cravats, and shoes—so that he will not "set an indifferent example" (274). Her devoted suitors become a reliable source of monetary "tributes" for the Father of the Marshalsea. In addition, Little Dorrit has educated herself so that she can "read and keep accounts," "got her brother and sister sent to day-schools" (112), and procured training for herself in needlework and for her sister in dancing. She has even installed her own servant, the large, moonfaced Maggie, who functions as a kind of maid-in-waiting to run errands for the woman she calls "Little Mother."

Just as the novel both emphasizes and disguises women's work, it simultaneously exposes and obscures class pretensions. It relentlessly criticizes the falsity and superficiality of those struggling to claim a place in High Society, but the heroine's own assertion of her middle-class identity is represented as integral to her self. Little Dorrit feels alienated when forced to behave as a fine lady. The idleness imposed upon her by the inheritance of riches empties her existence of meaning: "All she saw appeared unreal . . . all a dream" (517). She discovers that "to have no work to do was strange, but not half so strange as having glided into a corner where she had no one to think for, nothing to plan and contrive, no cares of others to load herself with" (516). Little Dorrit confesses her inaptitude for her new life in a letter to Arthur Clennam: "I am so slow that I scarcely get on at all. As soon as I begin to plan, and think, and try, all my planning, thinking, and trying go in old directions, and I begin to feel careful again about the expenses of the day, and about my dear father, and about my work, and then I remember with a start that there are no such cares left, and that in itself is so new and improbable that it sets me wandering again" (522). The novel's sustained critique of the Dorrits' new leisured life depends upon a contrast between Little Dorrit's "natural" gentility and the "artificial" veneer valued by High Society. Mr. Dorrit hires a woman, Mrs. General, as a "companion, protector, Mentor and friend," to prepare his two daughters for High Society by giving them a surface, a "varnish." She is, herself, entirely surface, so successfully varnished that nothing either penetrates or escapes her: "If her eyes had no expression, it was probably because they had nothing to express. If she had few wrinkles, it was because her mind had never traced its name or any other inscription on her face" (503). She serves as a "model of accurate dressing"; her "manner was perfect, considered as a piece of machinery" (486). Varnished, proper, accurate, she is nothing more than a cog in the social machinery. She advocates choosing words not for meaning—because opinions are vulgar—but to aid in the "formation of a demeanor." She instructs Amy Dorrit that "Papa is a preferable mode of address. . . . The word Papa . . . gives a pretty form to the lips. Papa, potatoes, poultry, prunes, and prism are all very good words for the lips: especially prunes and prism" (528–29). Mrs. General represents life at its emptiest, and life at its emptiest is defined as playing at social precedence, that trivial activity for which Ruskin scarifies women in "Of Queen's Gardens" and which Dickens here identifies largely with "aristocratic" women whose idleness makes them the devil's playground.

The novel sets up Little Dorrit as a touchstone for disinterested purity in a world contaminated by self-interest and artifice. Ironically, the very behaviors that screened Mr. Dorrit from the world's contempt and were applauded by the narrator when performed by Little Dorrit are condemned when practiced by the Merdles and Gowans and Fanny Dorrits of the world. The difference: Little Dorrit's manipulations are encoded as considerations, as selfless and dutiful affection for a fallen parent. In contrast, her sister Fanny's management of her stupid husband, also meant to make the couple more socially respectable, is represented in the novel as a selfish grasping at social position. Like Mrs. Merdle, Mrs. Gowan, and Mrs. General, Fanny Dorrit is depicted as shallow, superficial, and narcissistic, a perfect foil to disinterested Amy Dorrit.

But this apparent distinction between selfish and selfless cannot adequately ground or stabilize the novel's meaning because Little Dorrit, in her perfect submission, readily adopts and endorses the callous social distinctions articulated by her father. A classic instance occurs when Dorrit, thinking she will please her father, arrives at the Marshalsea arm in arm with Mr. Nandy, the workhouse "pauper." Mr. Dorrit, horrified, condemns his youngest daughter for humiliating him: "I have done what I could to keep you select here; I have done what I could to retain you a position here. . . . I have endured everything here but humiliation. That I have happily been spared—until this day" (419). Mr. Dorrit's outraged sense of consequence and his subsequent condescension to the humble old man have led critics to identify his behavior in this scene as his worst. Certainly, Arthur Clennam, also present, "secretly pit[ies] the bowed and submissive figure" (423), who is seated at the window sill to take his tea, "with a gulf between him and the good company of about a foot in width" (424). The close quarters of the Marshalsea do not allow for significant physical distance between Mr. Nandy and the "good company," but Mr. Dorrit more than compensates for lack of physical distance by addressing the old man from the Olympian heights of his own social superiority "as if he were a gracious Keeper making a running commentary on the decline of the harmless animal he exhibited" (424). Little Dorrit, crushed by her father's condemnation of her, begs forgiveness, asks for guidance in a gesture of obeisance—"Tell me how it is, that I may not do it again!" (419)—and confesses, "What I have been so unhappy as to do, I have done in mistake" (420). Although the novel represents Little Dorrit as motivated by paternal respect, her complete capitulation to her father's selfish disdain limits her ability to provide a meaningful ground for critique.

Yet the novel persistently works to exempt Little Dorrit from complicity in this system of social snobbery, as if, having descended to its depths in poverty and ascended to its heights in wealth, she has transcended class claims. She alone is vouchsafed the understanding that the pretensions of High Society differ little from those of the Marshalsea:

> It appeared on the whole, to Little Dorrit herself, that this same society in which they lived, greatly resembled a superior sort of Marshalsea. Numbers of people seemed to come abroad, pretty much as people had come into the prison; through debt, through idleness, relationship, curiosity, and general unfitness for getting on at home. They were brought into these foreign towns in the custody of couriers and local followers, just as the debtors had been brought into the prison. They prowled about the churches and picture-galleries, much in the old, dreary, prison-yard manner. They were usually going away again tomorrow or next week, and rarely knew their own minds, and seldom did what they said they would do, or went where they said they would go: in all this again, very like the prison debtors. They paid high for poor accommodation, and disparaged a place while they pretended to like it: which was exactly the Marshalsea custom. They were envied when they went away by people left behind, feigning not to want to go: and that again was the Marshalsea habit invariably. . . . They had precisely the same incapacity for settling down to anything, as the prisoners used to have; they rather deteriorated one another, as the prisoners used to do; and they wore untidy dresses, and fell into a slouching way of life: still, always like the people in the Marshalsea. (565)

As one effect, this rich reflection on the parallels between the Continental "elegant" society and the prison inmates postulates the conventions of society as a cage that entraps and enervates. But the scope of the comparison is deliberately limited in specific ways. Although the novel sometimes ventures to suggest that all life, which must inevitably be social life, is a prison—"Far aslant across the city, over its jumbled roofs, and through the open tracery of its church towers, struck the long bright rays, bars of the prison of this lower world" (831)—generally it focuses its critique of the folly of social conventions on specific characters like the Merdles, Gowans, and Mrs. General, who ape the aristocracy.

In contrast to rhetorics of emptiness and artifice stand narrative representations that lodge Little Dorrit within an economy of the "natural." Dutiful Little Dorrit tries hard "to be varnished by Mrs. General" (556), but to her narrative credit, she fails. She is simply good and pure and true, the "angel," the "anchor" of her family

(646, 647). When she returns to the imprisoned Clennam, she reaches her apotheosis: "So faithful, tender, and unspoiled by Fortune. In the sound of her voice, in the light of her eyes, in the touch of her hands, so Angelically comforting and true!" (825).

Ironically, however, this economy of the "natural" is used to underwrite the very class distinctions it was supposedly critiquing. At the moment of Little Dorrit's apotheosis, she is witnessed by an errant but repentant Tattycoram, who had earlier rebelled against the social injustice of her lot and has now learned the error of her ways. Mr. Meagles, Tattycoram's master, points to Little Dorrit: "You see that young lady who was here just now—that little, quiet, fragile figure passing along there, Tatty? Look. The people stand out of the way to let her go by. The men—see the poor, shabby fellows—pull off their hats to her quite politely, and now she glides in at that doorway. See her, Tattycoram?" (881). Mr. Meagles drives home the lesson for a now docile Tatty: "If she had constantly thought of herself, and settled with herself that everybody visited this place upon her, turned it against her, and cast it at her, she would have led an irritable and probably an useless existence. Yet I have heard tell, Tattycoram, that her young life has been one of active resignation, goodness, and noble service" (881). Mr. Meagles's instruction explicitly contrasts Little Dorrit with a character whose presence in the novel may seem inexplicable or at least puzzling: Miss Wade. The novel represents this woman as full of vindictive rage at her discovery that she is an "orphan," less socially privileged than the girls whom she has previously considered her equals. She lashes out at the world for its "vanity and condescension" (726), poisoning her own existence as well as that of everyone who comes within her sphere. When Tattycoram meets her, she instinctively fears her because this woman seems "to come like [her] own anger, [her] own malice" (65). Miss Wade seizes upon the unhappy girl and feeds her bitterness, because Tattycoram, like Miss Wade before her, resents the special attentions that the Meagles give their own daughter, Minnie or "Pet," resents that she is "to be a little maid to Pet," resents the name they have given her "like a dog or a cat" (372), resents "her dependent position" (65). Whenever her rages come upon her, Mr. Meagles cautions her to count to "five-and-twenty, Tattycoram, five-and-twenty" (370). This prescribed remedy for her "defective" temper stems from Mr. Meagles's recognition that some of her ways will be "a little wide of ours," and he knows "what an immense deduction must be made from all the influences and experiences that have formed us—no parents, no child-brother or sister, no individuality of home, no Glass Slipper, or Fairy Godmother" (56).

In the process of excusing Tattycoram's differences in influences and experiences, the novel simultaneously naturalizes class distinctions and the behaviors that ground them. Tattycoram ultimately flees from the Meagles, and when Mr. Meagles tries to reclaim her, he is reviled by Miss Wade, who points to the social condescension in their behavior: "'Here is your patron, your master. He is willing to take you back, my dear, if you are sensible of the favour and choose to go. You can be, again, a foil to his pretty daughter, a slave to her pleasant wilfulness, and a toy in the house showing the goodness of the family. You can have your droll name again, playfully pointing you out and setting you apart, as it is right that you should be pointed out and set apart. (Your birth, you know; you must not forget your birth)'" (377). Mr. Meagles feels "inexpressible consternation in hearing his motives and actions so perverted." The novel seems to collude in his aggrieved response and so sets up a conflict with the narrator's unequivocal condemnation of Mr. Dorrit's patronage of Mr. Nandy. The repudiation there of behavior analogous to the Meagleses' produces an unresolvable tension. It is not sufficient to argue that Mr. Meagles means well, that he is genuinely good-natured. "Good nature" and such concepts contribute to the "labour of *naturalization* which every group tends to produce in order to legitimize itself and fully justify its existence."[11] Mr. Meagles is making the same distinctions between his family and Tattycoram that Mr. Dorrit draws between himself and Mr. Nandy. These are the same distinctions that Miss Wade has felt and bitterly resented, although, she, like Tattycoram, is represented as projecting her own unreasonable discontent as neglect from others.

Tattycoram's reformation dramatizes the process by which the lower classes internalize justifications for their own oppression. The critical word is "duty," the mantra by which the middle class successfully colonized the lower classes. When she ultimately rejects Miss Wade, Tattycoram credits her salvation to the example of that bitter woman: "I have had Miss Wade before me all this time, as if it was my own self grown ripe—turning everything the wrong way, and twisting all good into evil" (880). She turns from Miss Wade to Little Dorrit and the "Duty" she represents. "Duty, Tattycoram," says Mr. Meagles, "Begin it early, and do it well; and there is no antecedent to it, in any origin or station, that will tell against us with the Almighty, or with ourselves" (882). William Blake pointed the mystification of that term in "The Chimney Sweeper" in *Songs of Innocence*, when the little orphan boy, begrimed by the soot of chimneys and ignored by an indifferent society, consoles himself with

[11] Bourdieu, *Language and Symbolic Power* (248).

the reflection that "if all do their duty, they need not fear harm." Duty, to paraphrase Marx, should be the opiate of the working classes. Tattycoram, who has seen the error of her ways, seeks only to be reinstalled in her old place, and she cheerfully promises to "get better." She vows, "I'll try very hard. I won't stop at five-and twenty, sir, I'll count five-and-twenty hundred, five-and-twenty thousand!" (880). And the reader can confidently expect that such a discipline, coupled with the example of Little Dorrit, will have a strong reforming effect.

The novel ratifies class distinctions not only in the narrative of Tattycoram but also in its romance plot. When Little Dorrit falls in love with Clennam and rejects absolutely the persistent and devoted attentions of the turnkey's son, John Chivery, she is privileging gentility over vulgarity. Of course, in constantly rewriting epitaphs for his gravestone, to be inscribed after he dies for love of Little Dorrit, John Chivery appears ridiculous. But he is ridiculous in the same ways as *Bleak House*'s Mr. Guppy, who aspires after Esther Summerson's hand, or *David Copperfield*'s Uriah Heep, who in his pursuit of Agnes Wickfield is sinister as well. In all of these novels, the alternate suitor for the hand of the housekeeping angel serves to define more carefully the class to which she "inherently" or "naturally" belongs. Of course, the heroine is only following her heart; where she "loves," she marries. All of these quotation marks point to the social construction of such concepts as "love" and "nature." Fortunately, the heroine always "falls in love" with an entrepreneurial individual of the gentrified middle class, a man of some delicacy and distinction, who must, nonetheless, make his own way in the world with the help of a pragmatic and experienced household manager.

Little Dorrit thus ridicules social pretensions in their exaggerated forms—particularly as practiced by women like Mrs. Merdle, Mrs. Gowan, Fanny Dorrit, and Mrs. General—but consistently underwrites the validity of class distinctions in its portrayal of the modest heroine. What her sisters do blatantly, she accomplishes more effectively in her quiet and unobtrusive management and in the dutiful example she serves for those who would quarrel with "Providence."

Our Mutual Friend: Willful Bella Wilfer's Reformation by Housekeeping

If *David Copperfield, Bleak House,* and *Little Dorrit* present us with little housekeepers ready made—seemingly instinctive in the efficient performance of their duties—*Our Mutual Friend* (1864–65), in contrast, dwells on the formation of an aspiring middle-class home-maker and so reveals the dimensions of that process. When the novel opens, Bella Wilfer is unfitted to take her position as the wife of John Harmon. Her deficiencies in character promise misery for him rather than domestic bliss. She is as ignorant and childish as Dora Spenlow, as indulged and petted as Ada Clare, and as merce-nary and self-absorbed as Fanny Dorrit. Her husband-to-be, John Harmon, alias Rokesmith, laments bitterly: "So insolent, so trivial, so capricious, so mercenary, so careless, so hard to touch, so hard to turn." His addendum—"And yet so pretty, so pretty!" (208)—be-trays his enchantment and, thus, so smitten by her, he has no choice but to reform and transform her if he is to marry her.

Rokesmith conceptualizes this process as teaching her to love him for himself rather than for his prospective fortune, but it is repre-sented as Bella's acquisition of sufficient skills in social semiotics to ensure their place in respectable society. Her reformation and trans-formation have two manifestations. On the one hand, Bella must master the social graces of a rank higher than the one to which she is accustomed. Bella's residence with the newly wealthy Boffins will introduce her to that rank and train her in the signifying practices of her new sphere. Because she will ultimately occupy this position as John Harmon's wife, some preparation is necessary. On the other hand, Bella must become a resourceful and efficient household man-ager, a match for her discreet and industrious husband. The appren-ticeship of her marriage to humble John Rokesmith prepares for her metamorphosis into the wife of wealthy John Harmon.

Bella must, in short, become adept in the two branches of middle-class social economy I identified earlier: signifying status and man-aging a position. She takes readily to the first stage of her training, initiated under Mrs. Boffin. Not unexpectedly, Bella soon outstrips her patron, who retains some of the ludicrousness of the newly rich. Mrs. Boffin's desire to go in for fashion does not guarantee that she will fulfill all its dictates appropriately. Despite representing this woman as good and generous, the narrator enjoys a subtle laugh at her expense, noting that she wears a "walking dress of black velvet and feathers, like a mourning coach horse" (99). That ridicule of her overdressing (the great social faux pas) finds a mirror in Mr. Mil-vey's "latent smile that showed a quick enough observation of Mrs. Boffin's dress" (108). The narrator reiterates the point in introducing Mrs. Milvey, whose "open as well as . . . perceptive" face shares "her husband's latent smile" upon viewing Mrs. Boffin (104). Bella, in contrast, is "beautifully dressed" (209) and quickly assumes responsibility for preserving Mrs. Boffin's social respectability: "And thus it soon came about that Miss Bella began to set Mrs. Boffin right; and even further, that Miss Bella began to feel ill at ease, and as it were responsible, when she saw Mrs. Boffin going wrong." Bella herself is "far too quick of perception to be below the tone of her new career." The narrator questions "whether it improved her heart" but confirms that "as touching another matter of taste, its improvement of her appearance and manner, there could be no question whatever" (307).

But acquiring social savoir faire, *Our Mutual Friend* seems to suggest, is an achievement that must rank second to the primary duty in all of the Dickens novels I've examined: honing management skills. The novel quickly glides over the representation of Bella's fitness for her new sphere of social action but dwells on the area of her greater deficiency and inaptitude: household economy and supervision. According to the terms set by the novel, Bella's reformation there is enacted through "love." Love, particularly as it purifies woman, serves as panacea for a variety of social ills. In this novel, grasping for gold lies at the root of corruption, a corruption suggested through the source of wealth imaged in this novel, Harmon's dust heaps. Bella will conquer her mercenary tendencies through love and prove herself the "true golden gold at heart" (772). Bella announces early that "I love money, and want money—want it dreadfully. I hate to be poor, and we are degradingly poor, offensively poor, miserably poor, beastly poor" (37). She confesses to her father that she is a "mercenary little wretch" and she "must have money." She adds, "I feel that I can't beg it, borrow it, or steal it; and so I have resolved that I must marry it" (320).

The narrator represents Bella as "the doubly spoilt girl: spoilt first by poverty, and then by wealth" (308). The patterned opposition suggests a middling course for the errant girl: redemption through the disciplines of an upwardly mobile professional class. The motif of double spoiling proves significant in resolving the novel's complications. Bella cannot simply reject money and find satisfaction in returning to the cheerless penury of her parents' home, what Mrs. Wilfer euphemistically calls the "abode of conscious though independent Poverty" (108). Nor can she find happiness in marrying money. The novel presents an alternative in middle-class industry and efficiency. The Wilfers themselves belong to the middle class but have a tenuous hold on their position. "Rumty" Wilfer, Bella's father, works long and hard hours as secretary to the company of

Chicksey, Veneering, Stobbles. The wearing occupations of his day are extended in the wearing nature of his "domestic Bliss" (605). Mrs. Wilfer, who always stands on ceremony, has discharged her disappointment in marriage by embodying her failed aspirations in the discomforts and disorder of the house, which lacks both management and discipline. Bella's sister, Lavinia, termed "irrepressible," serves as the visible sign of insurrection in the household. Bella finds both mother and sister "very disagreeable" (315); obviously, the Wilfer household stands as a cautionary rather than exemplary model, tending toward vulgarity rather than elegance.

The novel also poses inherited wealth as something of a vulgarity through its association with the dust heaps. Thus, when Bella learns to reject the allure of "unearned" money through its apparent corruption of Mr. Boffin and learns to "love" John Rokesmith through Mr. Boffin's contempt for him, she models her own behavior on the industry of her husband-to-be. Appropriately, John Rokesmith has already appointed himself to the position of conscience for the erring girl. When Bella is in danger of finding the Boffins ridiculous, Rokesmith cautions her that "those are worthy people" (112); when she forgets her parents in her new prosperity, he reminds her of her neglect by requesting from her any "commissions for home," and adds, "I shall always be happy to execute any commands" (309). He inevitably makes the girl "penitent" (310). Her love for him bespeaks the attraction of a more disciplined, resourceful, and independent self. She disavows both the injured high dudgeon of her mother and the idle emptiness she has practiced at the Boffins' and sets about turning herself into a "Home Goddess" (374).

Dickens represents as simultaneous Bella's change of heart toward John Rokesmith *and* toward household discipline. The first signs of her reformation occur on her parents' anniversary when she takes upon herself the preparation of a celebratory meal. She announces to her mother that "you and Lavvy think magnificent me fit for nothing, but I intend to prove the contrary. I mean to be Cook today" (451). Her experience, unfortunately, does not equal her energy, and the fowls, still pink inside, must be grilled by her father. Her second sortie—preparation of a salad—is more successful, but the girl who will marry John Rokesmith still lacks adequate training for her role. She promises her father, however, and implicitly her husband-to-be that "she will marry on a hundred and fifty pounds a year. But that's at first, and even if it should never be more, the lovely woman will make it quite enough" (617).

The novel celebrates Bella's aptitude for middle-class self-discipline because, grounded in the discursive practices that consolidate class control, that discipline will permanently secure their fortune. Obviously, at this point, having won Bella on the strength of his merit and not his money, John Rokesmith could simply reveal to her his identity as wealthy John Harmon. In fact, when the Boffins and he hatched the plan to prove Bella's love for him, he promised to tell her the truth on their wedding day. But he delays, I would argue, because the novel requires that Bella prove herself worthy by becoming the competent household manager of slim resources that she has promised to be. Once she has mastered housekeeping in all its details, she can be permitted to ascend to her more elegant station. She is good at her word and enters into her duties on her wedding day, immediately following the ceremony. She takes possession of a "modest little cottage" and undertakes supervision of "a fluttering young damsel, all pink and ribbons," her serving-maid, who "unto her did deliver a bunch of keys, commanding treasures" (666–67). The hyperbolic language of "treasures" and the formal phraseology of "unto her did deliver" invite laughter as if at a child playing grown-up. So the novel obfuscates what is happening, at the moment it is most clear. These are keys, and they do secure household capital, and they install Bella in a supervisory position. Upon her first visit to her mother, Bella brags that "we have a clever little servant, who is de—cidedly pretty, and we are economical and orderly, and do everything by clockwork" (679). She has not wasted any time in establishing a system, one so successful that the narrator describes her as "fast developing a perfect genius for home" (681). But this description is followed by the mystification that "all the loves and graces seemed (her husband thought) to have taken domestic service with her, and to help her to make home engaging" (681). Organization and management are encoded as "loves and graces."

A textual tension generated by representing household management as at once trivial and serious structures the narrative at this point. The narrator continues to depict Bella in such a way that her achievements are simultaneously applauded and ridiculed. Her dress is "as daintily managed as if she managed nothing else" (681). Introducing the idea of management in the arrangement of her dress trivializes the concept when applied to Bella, but at the same time it underlines her management of much else besides clothes. When her husband has departed for work, Bella lays aside her elegant dress— "trim little wrappers and aprons would be substituted"—and "putting back her hair with both hands, as if she were making the most business-like arrangements for going dramatically distracted, would enter on the household affairs of the day" (681). Bella's pragmatic preparations for her "business" appear in the narrator's eyes as "arrangements for going dramatically distracted," a representation that continues to undercut what it affirms. Because she has only one servant, much of the household labor itself as well as its management devolves upon her. Yet the narrator makes her appear an overgrown child playing at housekeeping:

> Such weighing and mixing and chopping and grating, such dusting and washing and polishing, such snipping and weeding and trowelling and other small gardening, such making and mending and folding and airing, such diverse arrangements, and above all such severe study! For Mrs. J. R., who had never been wont to do too much at home as Miss B. W., was under the constant necessity of referring for advice and support to a sage volume entitled The Complete British Family Housewife, which she would sit consulting, with her elbows on the table and her temples on her hands, like some perplexed enchantress poring over the Black Art. (681–82)

This portrait suggests self-important busyness rather than significant business, a reinterpretation of woman's work as play, a corollary to the mystification of woman's work as "duty."

The reinterpretation of women's work as play, of discipline as love, keeps class issues submerged by highlighting gender relations and the home as refuge from commercial strife. Yet the apprenticeship that Bella's husband requires of her threatens to expose those constructions as fictions. The Boffins must witness the marriage secretly, hiding in the church-organ, because John Rokesmith/Harmon won't let them "out with [the secret of his identity] then, as was first meant" (774). He argues that "she's so unselfish and contented, that I can't afford to be rich yet" (774). He applauds the "quick wit and fine ready instinct" that enable her to make "amazing progress in her domestic efficiency" (683). When she becomes pregnant, he defers again: "She is such a cheerful, glorious housewife, that I can't afford to be rich yet. I must wait a little longer" (774). And when the baby is born, he still procrastinates: "She is so much better than she ever was, that I can't afford to be rich yet. I must wait a little longer" (798). He cannot "afford to be rich yet" because, without a disciplined helpmeet, he will soon squander his wealth. The novel represents but cannot finally assess the complex contribution of a man's wife to the middle-class venture. The superior skill she demonstrates in her new sphere retrospectively justifies the shrewd old miser's choice of Bella Wilfer as bride for his son. Although she had earlier resented that she "should have been willed away, like a horse, or a dog, or a bird" and asks if she is "for ever to be made the property of strangers" (377), she willingly enters into a domestic economy where her talents enable her to appreciate in value: "[John Rokesmith] cared, beyond all expression, for his wife, as a most precious and sweet commodity that was always looking up, and that never was worth less than all the gold in the world" (683).

Two other couples in the novel threaten to expose the economic and class base of "love": the Lammles and the Wrayburns. The Harmons find a grotesque parody of their marital partnership in the Lammles. Alfred and Sophronia Lammle have, in contrast to John and Bella, married for money. Each is deceived in the other, and their only hope of survival lies in practicing on the world the deception that they have mutually practiced. They recognize that they must "work together in furtherance of [their] own schemes" (126). That their schemes are nefarious is moot; the novel underlines in this perverse way the importance of marital partnership in securing middle-class status.

It is the impossibility of a middle-class partnership that renders unthinkable a marriage between Lizzie Hexam and Eugene Wrayburn. I alluded briefly to this relationship at the beginning, as an example of the non-narratable plot: marriage between a lower-class woman and a middle-class man. Despite Lizzie's distinction, despite the "orderly and clean" appearance of her otherwise dingy parlor (233), despite being "refined in her beauty" (518), despite becoming educated, Lizzie always speaks of herself as "so far below him and so different" (236), and of Eugene as "a gentleman far above me and my way of life" (526). He is "not of our sort" (347). And when Eugene is questioned by his friend Mortimer whether he "design[s] to capture and desert this girl," he answers "no"; equally he responds "no" when asked if he "design[s] to marry her." He concludes, "I have no design whatever" (294). His planlessness cripples him; he broods, "out of the question to marry her . . . and out of the question to leave her" (698). The impasse is overcome only when Lizzie saves his life—rescues the beaten and drowning man from the river—so that he may give her his life. Only in the extremity of his imminent death can they wed. He claims that "it would require a life . . . to pay all; more than a life" (753). She says, "I have made the marriage that I would have given all the world to dare to hope for" (753). At the end of the novel the Voice of Society pronounces on the marriage and the question it raises of "whether a young man of very fair family, good appearance, and some talent, makes a fool or a wise man of himself in marrying a female waterman, turned factory girl" (817). Podsnap replies "that [his] gorge rises against such a marriage—that it offends and disgusts [him]—that it makes [him] sick" (817–18). His wife, less hysterical, responds that "there should be an equality of station and fortune, and that a man accustomed to Society should look out for a woman accustomed to Society and capable of bearing her part in it" (818). But the pragmatism of Mrs. Podsnap's response gives way to the romanticism of Mr. Twemlow's because he has the final word: "I say . . . if such feelings on the part of this gentleman induced this gentleman to marry this lady, I think he is the greater gentleman for the action, and makes her the greater lady" (819). So the narrative colludes in the romance of this unequal marriage, just as it has colluded in calling "love" the process by which a man chooses a partner and turns her into a skillful household manager. But earlier the narrator was caustic in describing Mr. Twemlow's romantic reflections on another marriage, that of the Lammles: "For, the poor little harmless gentleman once had his fancy, like the rest of us, and she didn't answer (as she often does not), and he thinks the adorable bridesmaid is like the fancy as she was then (which she is not at all), and that if the fancy had not married some one else for money, but had married him for love, he and she would have been happy (which they wouldn't have been), and that she has a tenderness for him still (whereas her toughness is a proverb)" (118). One is tempted to paraphrase F. Scott Fitzgerald: And so we beat on, boats against the current, borne back ceaselessly into romance.

The rhetorical nostalgia and sentimentality of Dickens's novels suggest his attraction to myths of romance, but his restless ambition made it impossible for him to conceptualize marriage simply in sexual terms: the love between a man and a woman. Although his wedding-bell resolutions tend to recuperate female subjectivity within a gendered frame, class inscriptions cannot be fully effaced and are uneasily accommodated through a rhetoric of duty. Marriage was also, as Dickens only too percipiently recognized, a partnership in which economic and social capital cooperated in producing the gentleman. He required a helpmeet fit not only to love but to labor by his side. The angel who reigned in his heart had to rein in the servants at home.

Dickens's genius manifests itself in the brilliant glimpses he gives us of the pragmatic side of middle-class marriage. His novels dramatize the clash between patriarchal ideology with its gender bifurcations and bourgeois ideology with its class bifurcations. The middle-class wife, who stands on opposite sides of the gender and class divides, becomes the figure whose mystifications protect patriarchal privilege with its rhetoric of dominance and subservience, while her disciplining presence at home and colonizing effect abroad secure England as a haven for the bourgeoisie.

5

Elizabeth Gaskell's
Angels with a Twist

Elizabeth Gaskell's *Cranford* and *Wives and Daughters* share with Dickens's novels a tension between the boy-marries-girl romance plot and the corollary drive of the loving couple toward solid, middle-class respectability. The latter, bourgeois plot, however, is even more prominent. *Cranford* (1851–53) centers around women designated as "old maids," seemingly well past the point at which romance is a possibility. Yet the currents of romance swirl and eddy about them, leaving them faintly ridiculous and antiquated. This representation works as another kind of mystification of the bourgeois project, which is going forward in the ladies' capable hands and is highlighted in their skill at creating meanings and managing social interactions. *Wives and Daughters* (1864–65), in contrast, seems to return to a more traditional romance plot, but its emphasis on two marriageable young women vies with the status display and management of class conflict that structure the action. Gaskell's novels thus generate productive tensions between conventional gender-based readings of women's "limited" lives and alternative stories of their social productivity.

The different ideological emphases of Dickens and Gaskell reflect, in part, their different positions within the Victorian home. Conceiving himself primarily as a novelist who wrote at home, Dickens turned his attention to organization of his chaotic household only in exasperated acknowledgment that his rise to bourgeois respectability depended upon the twin measures of tangible income and intangible status. Gaskell, on the other hand, conceived herself as a household manager whose managerial reach extended to the construction of novels. She famously advised would-be female writers on the domestic arts as a key to successful pursuit of the creative arts.[1] Damned with faint praise by Henry James, who remarks the dependence of her art on "modest domestic facts," Gaskell has represented precisely how realities are constructed out of quotidian "feminine" details, a significance that has escaped many readers in addition to James. In this regard, Elizabeth Gaskell declares literary allegiance with Sarah Ellis, who was emboldened to write *The Women of England* by her conviction that the "apparently insignificant detail of familiar and ordinary life" bears out the "often-repeated truth—that 'trifles make the sum of human things'" (1). Truth though it may be, the notion continues to meet stubborn resistance.[2] In her book on the subject, Naomi Schor helps to explain the detail *"as negativity"* because it participates in a "larger semantic network, bounded on the one side by the *ornamental*, with its traditional connotations of effeminacy and decadence, and on the other, by the everyday, whose 'prosiness' is rooted in the domestic sphere of social life presided over by women." In short, "the detail is gendered and doubly gendered as feminine" (4). Gaskell is working to disrupt the ideological script that encodes the detail as trivial because of its association with the feminine. Her narrative procedures suggest that we should heed Michel Foucault, who recognizes behind "minute material details" the presence of "alien strategies" of power and knowledge (*Discipline* 30).

Elizabeth Gaskell's letters and novels reflect the primary importance of details as the basis for generating meanings and social order. Fundamental to Gaskell's conception of herself is the imbrication of her housekeeping and literary arts. The "Gaskell" repre-

---

[1] To a woman who had sent her a manuscript accompanied by complaints about the distractions of housekeeping, Gaskell responded with practical advice on management: "I dare say you already know how much time may be saved, by beginning any kind of work in good time, and not driving all in a hurry to the last moment. I hope (for instance) you soap & soak your dirty clothes well for some hours before beginning to wash; and that you understand the comfort of preparing a dinner & putting it on to cook *slowly*, early in the morning, as well as having *always* some kind of sewing ready arranged to your hand, so that you can take it up at any odd moment and do a few stitches. . . . Then again try *hard* to arrange your work well. That is a regular piece of headwork and taxes a woman's powers of organization; but the reward is immediate and great. . . . You have it in your own power to arrange your day's work to the very best of your ability[,] making the various household arts into real studies (& there is plenty of poetry and association about them—remember how the Greek princesses in Homer washed the clothes etc. etc. etc. etc.)" (*Letters* 694–95).

[2] As only one example, Maureen Reddy, discussing Molly Gibson's socially correct behavior, remarks: "The odd thing here is that Gaskell evidently approved of Molly's ridiculous behavior, holding it up as an example of the heroine's delicacy and refinement" (83). Patricia Beer had earlier reached a similar conclusion (120–21). One must ask on what grounds a critic decides that Molly's behavior is "ridiculous," and if that judgment depends on a tradition that encodes the detail as frivolous.

sented in and by the letters is a woman who throve amid domestic demands. Her correspondence reveals a woman deeply engaged in day-to-day life: minutiae on dress, visitors, child care, servants, accounts, and household arrangements pepper her narratives. Although Gaskell consciously grounds her labors within a rhetoric of "natural" duties as a way of authorizing whatever activities might appear outside the frame of conventional expectations, she portrays herself as a woman who worked to construct her social and domestic life even as she worked to construct her novels.[3]

The house, as base for social organization, represents not bourgeois woman's isolation but her class privilege and economic power. In an early letter, Gaskell confesses to Eliza Fox her guilty delight in getting a house: compunction that so many people cannot afford one, joy in the context it provides for her varied talents (*Letters* 108). Its purchase provokes Gaskell's speculations on her various "mes": "I have a great number, and that's the plague. One of my mes is, I do believe, a true Christian . . . another . . . is a wife and mother, and highly delighted at the delight of everyone else in the house. . . . Now that's my 'social' self I suppose. Then again I've another self with a full taste for beauty and convenience wh[ic]h is pleased on its own account" (*Letters* 108). What to many may have seemed a fragmentation of personality produced by divergent claims, Gaskell celebrates as a multiplicity of selves. Although she speaks of being plagued by her "mes," the letters present a picture of a woman comfortable with the concept of multiple selves, with the fluidity of identity and subjectivity to which her life gives rise.

The literary Gaskell, too, emerges out of the household maelstrom. Gaskell's letters brim over with domestic details, and she appears to delight particularly in corresponding with those individuals, like Charles Eliot Norton, who appreciate the representation of her "social self": "My dear Mr Norton, if I could write you short letters I should write to you much oftener; but you see I can't dash off the minute Gaskell-family-detail letters I know you like all in a minute. I am sitting here by myself in the dining room by the light of one candle,—half disturbed and half-amused by the chatter of 'the children' in the next room" (*Letters* 645). She characteristically emphasizes her physical position in the house—the center from which she directs affairs—as a strategy for ordering her letter: "Now

[3] For example, Gaskell confesses her gratitude to "Him that I am a wife and a mother and that I am so happy in the performance of those clear and defined duties." She pitied women "deprived of their natural duties as wives & mothers," who had to "look out for other duties if they wish[ed] to be at peace" (*Letters* 118, 117).

I shall go into detail. I am sitting in the dining-room, (It is a comfort to think you know our rooms and our people,) Elliott taking away breakfast things, Meta taking Julia to school, Mr Gaskell in bed with a cold . . . and I myself in a doleful mood because some Chrysanthemums I have been nursing up into bloom this past summer were carelessly left out-of-doors this past night & have been frozen to death" (*Letters* 579). For Gaskell, the discursive practices of the social self—etiquette, dress, dining, household management—constitute knowledge of an individual and for an individual. The social self, then, grounds meaning.

Indeed, Gaskell's expressed regrets at frequent interruptions of her literary labors seem more a concession to convention than a reflection of impatience with her life. Rather than bemoan her lack of literary leisure, she seems rather to revel in the reach of her organizational powers. She writes to Charles Eliot Norton:

I am sitting at the round writing table in the dining-room. . . . If I had a library like yours, all undisturbed for hours, how I would write! Mrs. Chapone's letters should be nothing to mine! I would outdo Rasselas in fiction. But you see every body comes to me perpetually. Now in this hour since breakfast I have had to decide on the following variety of important questions. Boiled beef—how long to boil? What perennials will do in Manchester smoke, & what colours our garden wants? Length of skirt for a gown? Salary of a nursery governess, & stipulations for a certain quantity of time to be left to herself.—Read letters on the state of Indian army—lent me by a very agreeable neighbour & return them, with a proper note, & as many wise remarks as would come in a hurry. Settle 20 questions of dress for the girls, who are going out for the day; & want to look nice & yet not spoil their gowns with the mud &c &c—See a lady about an MS story of hers, & give her disheartening but very good advice. Arrange about selling two poor cows for one good one,—see purchasers, & show myself up to cattle questions, keep, & prices,—and it's not 1/2 past 10 yet! (*Letters* 487–90)

This is a representation not of a frustrated, distracted individual but of a competent, energetic, practical, and successful manager. Gaskell's net effect is not to lament the lack of a library but to point to her extraordinary reach and range of accomplishments.[4]

[4]It is interesting here to contrast Gaskell's representation of domestic life with the more famous negative depiction that Florence Nightingale provided in *Cassandra*. We might account for the difference in two ways. First, Gaskell is far from "idle," and she does not share Nightingale's assessment of "useless" and time-wasting etiquette practices. Second, the difference may reflect the distinction between the mother's and daughter's positions in the household. There could be only *one* manager, and thus

Although we cannot argue Gaskell's complicity with her character, when the narrator of *Cranford* complains that her father's letter "was just a man's letter" ("I mean it was very dull, and gave no information beyond that he was well, that they had had a good deal of rain, that trade was very stagnant, and there were many disagreeable rumours afloat," 172), we may take Gaskell's own correspondence as the implicit contrast: a woman's letter, which engages the complexities of securing cultural capital opposed to a narrow focus on acquiring material capital. The woman's life, like her letter, emphasizes the plenitude of activity and multitude of social details, of which she is the regulating and organizing factor.

Gaskell argues for constructing novels along the same lines, with attention to external detail. She writes to an aspiring author, Herbert Grey: "Observe what is out of you, instead of examining what is in you. It is always an unhealthy sign when we are too conscious of any of the physical processes that go on within us; & I believe in like manner that we ought not to be too cognizant of our mental proceedings" (*Letters* 541). Without pronouncing on "whether introspection be morbid or not," she concludes that, at any rate, "it is not safe training for a novelist. . . . You are an Electric telegraph something or other" (*Letters* 541). Gaskell's understanding of novelistic reality as external and social, of the novelist as "electric telegraph," facilitates the representation of a world in which meaning is fluid and contextual, dependent upon a complex group of discursive practices. Significance emerges out of a series of quotidian encounters and subtle details. And in such a framework, there exist multiple selves, the many "mes" that Gaskell relishes as she explores both the ways in which the ideological construction of middle-class womanhood regulates possibility and the ways in which "reality" is constructed out of the patterned behaviors of middle-class women.

The Sufficient Ladies of Cranford

Cranford the novel and Cranford the place are, quite simply, worlds structured by women's signifying systems: calling and visiting, teas and dinners, domestic economies, charitable activities, and management of servants. Cranford, with its cultural capital, con-

---

daughters were often raised in idleness because they were deemed too fine to perform the functions of upper servants. Nightingale's reflections also serve as tendentious arguments for her own extraordinary career. The submerged text there is that this great nursing administrator learned and honed her talents in the home.

trasts explicitly with the neighboring city of Drumble, a world marked by expanding material capital based on factories and production, money and investments. The former appears at first glance to be stagnant, even moribund. The aging spinsters and childless widows who populate the town must eventually die. Given our conventional understanding that such lives are empty and trivial, the novel should tell a gloomy tale. Or, if it instead strikes a jocular note, it seems it must do so at the expense of the ladies. Yet those who know the novel can attest that its author finds its subjects neither risible nor morbid. They are, however, humorous; Gaskell herself confessed, "Whenever I am ailing or ill, I take *Cranford* and— I was going to say, *enjoy* it! (but that would not be pretty!) laugh over it afresh!" (*Letters* 747). That humor arises from the fullness of meaning invested in the smallest details of daily life. *Cranford* brims over with engaged life; everything matters intensely because meanings are fluid, emerging moment by moment, producing valuable cultural capital for the ladies who are society's semioticians. The only cynic in the book, Mary Smith's father, represents the commercial world of Drumble, and the economic capital he stands for seems curiously unproductive.

The critical literature on *Cranford* stresses its "charm," "delicacy," and "fragility." The novel, Peter Keating argues, presents a "rigorous exploration of a dying way of life" (10).[5] But such an analysis is too simple. Is Cranford dying? Brief reflection suggests that it is surprisingly resilient and self-sustaining. Although their way of life seems destined to die with the current crop of old ladies, in fact, it has already maintained itself through a couple of generations. Matty remembers of her girlhood: "There were many old ladies living here then; we are principally ladies now, I know; but we are not so old as the ladies used to be when I was a girl" (94). The wonderful malapropos logic of the recollection suggests that, in the case of Cranford at least, *plus ça change, plus c'est la même chose*. There have always been old ladies in Cranford; there will always be old ladies in Cranford. Even the group currently assembled ranges in age from sixtyish Miss Matty to thirtyish Mrs. Fitz-Adam, an arriviste in Cranford society. The acceptance of Fitz-Adam stems from the death of one of the staunch old guard, Miss Deborah Jenkyns: "With her, something of the clear knowledge of the strict code of gentility went out too. As Miss Pole observed, 'As most of the ladies of good family in Cranford were elderly spinsters, or widows without children,

---

[5] Keating's is a telling example of a critic reinscribing the very ideologies that the work questions.

if we did not relax a little, and become less exclusive, by-and-by we should have no society at all'" (109).

The ladies achieve remarkable success in reproducing themselves in Cranford, a kind of parthenogenesis that gives a sharper ironic point to their observation that "a man . . . is *so* in the way in the house" (39). And we already glimpse the generation to come. Mary Smith, the young narrator, passes through several seasons of nuptial eligibility during the novel without finding a husband. Indeed, she does not seem to want one. Warned by one of the spinsters, Miss Pole, that it "argued great natural credulity in a woman if she could not keep herself from being married," Mary Smith can keep her own opinion (157). She confesses, "If I had been inclined to be daunted from matrimony, it would not have been Miss Pole to do it"; then she adds, "it would have been the lot of poor Signor Brunoni and his wife" (159). Their story of privation and the death of six of their seven children stands as a cautionary tale even to those women with some "credulity."

Cranford, "in possession of the Amazons," far from being rigid and moribund, finds ways to renew itself (39). And, tellingly, the world of men, the world represented in part by the distant rumble of Drumble, is figured through images of sterility: the bankruptcy of the Town and Country Bank, the chicanery that costs Mr. Smith "upwards of a thousand pounds" in one year, and Mr. Jenkyn's public flogging of his son, Peter, which "killed" the boy's mother (201, 101). Gaskell's great triumph in *Cranford* lies in her ability to take the apparently trivial and make it productive, while reevaluating the apparently productive world of commerce and suggesting its emptiness. The novel, in this way, serves as both exemplum and elaboration of Virginia Woolf's comment in *A Room of One's Own* that

> the values of women differ very often from the values which have been made by the other sex; naturally, this is so. Yet it is the masculine values that prevail. Speaking crudely, football and sport are "important"; the worship of fashion, the buying of clothes "trivial." And these values are inevitably transferred from life to fiction. This is an important book, the critic assumes, because it deals with war. This is an insignificant book because it deals with the feelings of women in a drawing-room. A scene in a battlefield is more important than a scene in a shop—everywhere and much more subtly the difference of value persists. (76–77)

Yet, my point here comprehends much more than an examination of the differences between male and female worlds and the hierarchizing of values that inevitably occurs when we speak of separate spheres. I argue not only that Gaskell depicts a woman's world, which she informs with significance, but also that she represents reality as a construction. Woolf seems to hint at such a process in claiming that "since a novel has this correspondence to real life, its values are to some extent those of real life" (76), but she does not press the issue of "reality" itself, arguing instead for woman's vision as a correction and expansion of reality as it is dominantly presented through a male point of view. I do not want to claim, then, as in a traditional oppositional dialectic, that the women defeat the men, the feminine displaces the masculine.[6] Rather, Gaskell suggests the way in which reality itself is always contested, an expression of the values of a dominant group.

Gaskell represents, as does Dickens, the process by which middle-class women emerged as makers of meanings and shapers of class in mid-Victorian England. Gaskell's mystifications are not Dickens's, however. Nobody would think of terming Miss Matty, or Miss Pole, or Mrs. Jamieson an "Angel in the House." That epithet is reserved for blooming, blushing youth, for the virginal maiden and tender mother. For Gaskell, the mystifications of "angel" give way to the mystifications of "spinster," a term, like "angel," that implies remoteness from concerns of the "real world." The current of life flows on, but an old maid, so the cultural encoding suggests, has drifted into the backwater. Gaskell plays with these connotations, both confirming and controverting them, so that *Cranford* is at once about the transience of a way of life and about the emergence of a world whose meanings are controlled by middle-class women.

This is a world made up *of* fragments but, significantly, not a world *in* fragments. Cranford is socially cohesive and conservative. The very fragmentary, seemingly ephemeral "work" the ladies do defuses its potential threat. Yet it is enormously productive. *Cranford* is both so interesting and so telling partly because middle-class men play only a tangential role in the novel.[7] Although the ladies have all inherited monies from husbands or fathers, those funds are now entirely in their hands along with the ideological and semiotic work—women's work—of managing the class question and displaying middle-class status.

Cranford is finally a novel about economies: explicitly domestic and

---

[6] Nina Auerbach takes this position in *Communities of Women*, concluding, "In the verbal and commercial battle of nineteenth-century England, the cooperative female community defeats the warrior world that proclaims itself the real one" (87).

[7] Auerbach points to Cranford's unsettling "power to obliterate men" with its "corresponding gift of producing them at need" (*Communities* 81).

implicitly national. Economy functions in the novel in three major senses: as a system of national resource management; as the thrifty use of material resources; and in an archaic sense, as household management itself. The women's practical, conservative economies are shadowed by speculative national economies, whose unscrupulous management threatens their well-being, as in the collapse of the Town and Country Bank that bankrupts Miss Matty. The conjunction of the ladies' fixed incomes—their lack of economic productivity—with their productivity of social meanings generates a different economy in Cranford, one they term "elegant" in contrast to a vulgar money-getting-and-spending one.[8]

The principle of elegant economy enters into a chain of social signifiers but also has substantial immediate effects in allowing women to marshal scarce resources toward particular ends. The narrator articulates the economic principle at work: "I had often occasion to notice the use that was made of fragments and small opportunities in Cranford; the rose-leaves that were gathered ere they fell, to make into a pot-pourri for some one who had no garden; the little bundles of lavender-flowers sent to strew the drawers of some town-dweller, or to burn in the chamber of some invalid. Things that many would despise, and actions which it seemed scarcely worth while to perform, were all attended to in Cranford" (54). The narrator carefully saves pieces of string and wonders "how people can bring themselves to use India-rubber rings, which are a sort of deification of string" (83). Miss Matty is "chary of candles" and, in addition, saves old notes and receipts to make into candle-lighters (84). Instead of the conspicuous consumption and waste of a "vulgar" economy, the "elegant" economy bases itself on recycling resources: old dresses, fragments of flowers, pieces of string, ends of candles, old notes and receipts. It privileges exchange over consumption: the newspaper circulating among the ladies early presages the way more substantial resources will circulate among them to protect their world, their ways, and their privilege. This Cranfordian "elegant economy," though not productive of new material resources, is productive of substantial social capital and, therefore, calls into question the stability of currency as a signifier. Indeed, *Cranford* points to the very instability of money as a sign; it is just one interpretable sign among many.

The women are all relatively poor, but they manipulate cultural

[8] I should make explicit what I hope has been clear to this point, that Gaskell's terms to describe the economy, "elegant" and "vulgar," seem to anticipate the distinction Bourdieu draws between cultural or social capital and material or economic capital.

codes so adeptly and control so effectively the discursive practices that signal class—dress, dining, and the rules of etiquette that govern visiting, calls, and cuts—that they can dispense with any ostentatious display of a capitalist society tainted by the "vulgarity" of money-spending. The narrator admits, "We none of us spoke of money, because that subject savoured of commerce and trade, and though some might be poor, we were all aristocratic" (41). And she adds, "We had tacitly agreed to ignore that any with whom we associated on terms of visiting equality could ever be prevented by poverty from doing anything that they wished . . . we blinded ourselves to the vulgar fact, that we were, all of us, people of very moderate means" (42). And so they are, a condition that makes palpable the extent to which status has come to depend on a manipulation of signs. Their behaviors challenge the values of an industrial capitalism that seeks to stabilize meaning and value in productivity, profit, and use.

Instead, Gaskell represents a meaning that is always in the process of being created. The ladies all collaborate in one another's machinations, in their scripting of a middle-class scenario, as when "Mrs. Forrester . . . gave a party in her baby-house of a dwelling, and the little maiden disturbed the ladies on the sofa by a request that she might get the tea-tray out from underneath, every one took this novel proceeding as the most natural thing in the world; and talked on about household forms and ceremonies, as if we all believed that our hostess had a regular servants' hall, second table, with housekeeper and steward" (41). The ladies' behavior demonstrates that they are not naive semioticians, prey to the belief that signifiers and signifieds, signs and referents all collapse in some determinate way. They are, instead, alive to the play of the signifier, and they endlessly accommodate aberrations within their signifying practice. Perhaps the most humorous recognition of the power of these practices, albeit a tacit one, occurs when Miss Matty relates the story of her brother, Peter, and his pranks, which involve dressing up as a woman and gulling his father, a narrative that confirms the centrality of the sign: "Peter said, he was awfully frightened himself when he saw how my father took it all in, and even offered to copy out all his Napoleon Buonaparte sermons for her—him, I mean—no, her, for Peter was a lady then" (94). In Miss Matty's semiotics, if Peter signifies he is a "woman," then that is how she will represent him in her narrative.

The performance of gender that is both explicitly and implicitly acknowledged here feeds into a more general and pervasive staging of identity that focuses on class. In a similarly humorous vein, Gaskell represents the ladies' eccentric dress, which is "very independent of fashion" (40). The ladies observe, " 'What does it signify how we dress here at Cranford, where everybody knows us?' " And if they go away from home, their reason is equally cogent: " 'What does it signify how we dress here, where nobody knows us?' "(40) These antiquated ladies grasp an essential point of semiotics in understanding the arbitrariness of how things "signify." Yet, the vaunted indifference to dress is, in reality, only an indifference to the latest fashions, which the ladies cannot afford. They make do with an occasional new cap "to suit the fashion of the day," confident that the quality of their clothing, its "chaste elegance and propriety," will always denote their social position (120). That is the telling signification.[9]

The women's deployment of these signifying systems and their grasp of the realms constituted by these systems ultimately affords them remarkable latitude in arriving at social meanings; their flexibility in discursive practice declares itself in their circumvention of seeming improprieties. For example, when Captain Brown arrives in Cranford, he immediately speaks loudly and publicly about his poverty, which is a "word not to be mentioned to ears polite" (42). Such "vulgar" behavior should dictate a social cut, but "somehow, Captain Brown made himself respected in Cranford, and was called upon in spite of all resolutions to the contrary" (42). On another occasion, Captain Brown makes an egregious social blunder in "taking a poor old woman's dinner out of her hands, one very slippery Sunday" and escorting her home (49). The ladies conveniently reinterpret the semiology of the event so that they need not deny themselves the captain's pleasant company.

These last examples introduce us to the complex signifying practices of the Cranford ladies, the ways in which they are creating meaning rather than slavishly following rigid social formulas. The very conventions that seem, in the abstract, to bind them, prove enormously flexible in their practice. *Cranford* represents a female society so well versed in the semiology of class and efficient enough in economic management that it has obviated the need for men. The narrator early announces the aptitude of the ladies for all the pur-

[9] Patsy Stoneman interprets these details in a more conventional way. She claims that the "proliferation of specialized names of fabrics . . . reflects the narrowing preoccupation with dress deplored by Mary Wollstonecraft" (92). We once more come up against the trivialization of detail. It is useful, in this context, to recall Virginia Woolf's caveat against reading through an ideological grid that encodes women's preoccupation with fashion as "trivial" (*A Room of One's Own* 77).

poses of daily life: "For obtaining clear and correct knowledge of everybody's affairs in the parish; for keeping their neat maid-servants in admirable order; for kindness (somewhat dictatorial) to the poor, and real tender good offices to each other whenever they are in distress, the ladies of Cranford are quite sufficient" (39). Thus begins Gaskell's humorous revision of a domestic ideology which dictated a man's concerns and comfort as a woman's chief occupation. That same revision scouts conclusions, like those of Carol Dyhouse, that "the economic dependence of wives and daughters advertised the independence and the status of the male breadwinner" ("Middle-class Mothers and Daughters" 28). Here, obviously, the women are more than advertisements for the male. The economic independence of the Cranford women, their horror that marriage might be a contagion they could catch like a cold, allows us to appreciate Gaskell's demystification of social practices.

The ladies' small and practical gestures, their "careful economies" (193), enter into a larger system of exchange based on cooperation rather than competition. In Miss Matty's financial collapse, all the ladies pool their resources to enable her to stay in her house. Moreover, the domestic ideology of mutual interdependence (of social relations as "familial") enables Miss Matty to achieve a competitive edge in the business of selling tea. She achieves it through collaboration rather than competition: she "had trotted down to [her competitor Mr. Johnson's] shop . . . to tell him of the project that was entertained, and to inquire if it was likely to injure his business" (200). Mary Smith's father, their financial adviser, terms this idea "'great nonsense' and 'wondered how tradespeople were to get on if there was to be a continual consulting of each other's interests, which would put a stop to all competition directly'" (200). But the step answers very well, for Mr. Johnson sends all his customers to Miss Matty for their choice teas "saying that the teas he kept were of a common kind" (200–201). Miss Matty simply supersedes the competitive business ethic with a cooperative social ethic that quite successfully manages social interaction among individuals and classes; Mr. Johnson, the lower-middle-class shopkeeper is only too happy to oblige the rector's daughter, who is related to Lady Arley.

That same class solidarity also facilitates intraclass bonding when the ladies need to protect one of their own. When Miss Matty goes bankrupt, the community colludes in stratagems to enable her to open a shop selling tea "without materially losing caste" (184). Mrs. Jamieson, the social arbiter, decrees that "whereas a married woman takes her husband's rank by the strict laws of precedence, an unmarried woman retains the station her father occupied" (199). This decision contradicts an earlier conclusion that Miss Jessie Brown, impoverished by the death of her father, Captain Brown, betrays a lack of proper feeling in proposing to go into a shop. "Some people," one lady argues, "hav[e] no idea of their rank as a captain's daughter" (59). In another, analogous episode, the community is scandalized that a lady would even speak, in polite company, of having shopkeepers as relatives. Yet Miss Matty opens a shop and thrives socially as well as economically.

Matty's success calls into question conventional ideas of the home and women's role within it, and thus contributes to the subversion of domestic ideology that bespeaks women's naïveté, innocence, and ignorance. Miss Matty has run a tight financial ship at home, settling and balancing her accounts every Monday (118). She confesses to Mary Smith: "I never was ambitious . . . but I thought I could manage a house (my mother used to call me her right hand)" (158). And when her bank collapses, she is able to calculate to the pence her loss of income: "one hundred and forty-nine pounds thirteen shillings and fourpence a year" (179). The exactness speaks for itself. Mary Smith and Miss Matty have the last word. In response to her father's comment that Miss Matty's "simplicity might be very well in Cranford, but would never do in the world," Mary notes, "And I fancy the world must be very bad, for with all my father's suspicion of every one with whom he has dealings, and in spite of all his many precautions, he lost upwards of a thousand pounds by roguery only last year" (201).

I suggested earlier that it has been easy for critics to miss the ideological subversion that occurs in *Cranford* when gender and class are read simultaneously. Such critics often stress, therefore, the ways in which male characters "when they do appear in the shapes of Captain Brown, Holbrook, Peter, and to a lesser extent Signor Brunoni . . . bring with them, by their very awareness of a wider world and larger values of life, a serious challenge to Cranford's existence" (Keating 24). This is precisely the conclusion the text works against. Why, we might ask with Virginia Woolf, are men's values always "larger"? What is larger about the provincialism of Holbrook, who stubbornly holds to his yeoman habits and disdains all refinement? What is larger about the hand-to-mouth existence of Signor Brunoni, whose wanderings have led to the deaths of all but one of his children? What is larger about Captain Brown, who has scandalously pronounced his poverty in a loud voice to the ladies of Cranford but doesn't manage even a whisper of it to Lord Mulverer, whose life he has saved and who might help relieve his distress? Mr. Smith, with all his practical wisdom, has nothing to do but facilitate the plans that women have already originated. And Peter? "Peter was a lady then." According to critic Peter Keating, Peter Jenkyns, in dressing as his elder sister and pretending to nurse a baby, "strikes instinctively at the repressive life around him" (25). But, properly considered, Peter is more comfortable with women than men, and his prank is just a good joke. And the only person profoundly disturbed by it and the unstable meanings it suggests is Reverend Jenkyns, the rector, who tore off the feminine clothes and "before all the people . . . lifted up his cane, and flogged Peter" in an attempt to end the play of signifiers (96), an action that ultimately defeats him and spells the decline of patriarchal rule in Cranford.

Not only does *Cranford* question the proposition of a "larger world" inhabited and dominated by men, but it also troubles gender categories. When Reverend Jenkyns strips off Peter's clothes, the narrator does not describe what is underneath. The text never names Peter's body, which is an absent signifier. Thus, this scene also emblematizes the way in which the novel denies biology and the body as telling signifiers within the ladies' discursive practices.[10] Peter, who prefers dressing as a woman, announces thereby his identity and position within society, just as his sister Deborah, with her "helmet" cap, declares herself her father's logical heir.

Peter, who loves performing identities, also takes on racial difference. When he finally returns to Cranford from India, many years after he has fled the patriarchal tyranny of his father, he does so in the guise of Aga Jenkyns. The ladies think of him as the "arrival from India" who tells "more wonderful stories than Sinbad the Sailor" (211). "So very Oriental," Peter once again appropriates the status of an Other to destabilize cultural encodings. He enters smoothly into the ladies' elegant economy, facilitating the social interactions and cooperation upon which it depends.

In this regard Peter is a positive and revisionary figure in the novel. But there is another dimension to his narrative positioning. In a commentary on traditional patriarchal practice, Luce Irigaray has suggested that men trade in women to facilitate their homosocial

[10] Dennis Allen has given sustained attention to the confusion of gender in *Cranford*, a confusion that stems from a refusal to name the body. He argues that Gaskell's construction of gender differences relies on a biology she is "reluctant to express." She handles the threat posed by biology through the Virgin Mary motif, where motherhood is the "ideal of a biology without sexuality," a cultural fiction that renders the vulgar facts of the body acceptable to culture by redefining them to exclude the sexual (77–78).

bonding: "Wives, daughters, and sisters have value only in that they serve as the possibility of, and potential benefit in, relations among men. The use of and traffic in women subtend and uphold the reign of masculine hom(m)o-sexuality" (172). When Peter teases his now aged sister about playing her cards very badly in letting his friend Holbrook slip through her fingers, he implies that he might once have carried out such a role in Matty's life. He laughs that she "wanted [her] brother to be a good go-between" (213). But *Cranford* refuses the story of women exchanged, like other commodities, for the "smooth workings of man's relations with himself, of relations among men" (Irigaray 172) and substitutes the alternative economy I have explored here. When Peter returns, he is himself positioned as the figure that facilitates *female* bonding, yet within an economy that does not degrade *him* as commodified object. Irigaray questions about women: *"But what if these 'commodities' refused to go to 'market'? What if they maintained 'another' kind of commerce, among themselves?"* (196). She postulates that "use and exchange would be indistinguishable. The greatest value would be at the same time the least kept in reserve" (197). Irigaray's closing words to "Commodities among Themselves" read as an apt coda to the struggle between the worlds of Drumble, with its "laborious accumulation of capital," and Cranford, with its recycled resources: "As for all the strategies and savings, the appropriations tantamount to theft and rape, the laborious accumulation of capital, how ironic all that would be" (197).

Yet the harmonious conclusion of *Cranford*, which I here postulate, depends entirely upon the mystification of labor: both household work and childbirth. Production and reproduction are class issues in the novel. As persistently as the text denies the body of Peter and his sexuality, it just as pertinaciously insists on the body and its functions as a class signifier. Miss Matty refuses to suck an orange in public because the activity evokes a suckling child. She cannot eat peas with the utensils available because the action would be indelicate. She is so entirely ignorant of biology that she fails to perceive her maid's pregnancy and accepts unquestioningly the seemingly "miraculous" arrival of a baby, which the narrator encodes as a "little bundle of flannel" (204). Against Miss Matty's effaced, refined body stands the flesh of her maidservant Martha, her sexuality writ large through her pregnancy.

The novel opens with the observation that "in the first place, Cranford is in possession of the Amazons; all the holders of houses, above a certain rent, are women. If a married couple come to settle in the town, somehow the gentleman disappears" (39). Ironically, the number of middle-class men seems in inverse ratio to the number of men in the lower classes, so the task of class management—the "servant difficulty"—devolves entirely on women:

> This subject of servants was a standing grievance, and I could not wonder much at it; for if gentlemen were scarce, and almost unheard of in the "genteel society" of Cranford, they or their counterparts—handsome young men—abounded in the lower classes. The pretty neat servant-maids had their choice of desirable "followers," and their mistresses . . . might well feel a little anxious, lest the heads of their comely maids should be turned by the joiner, or the butcher, or the gardener; who were obliged, by their callings, to come to the house; and who, as ill-luck would have it, were generally handsome and unmarried. (64–65)

The "ill luck" of handsome and unmarried lower-class men gives rise to a number of regulatory strategies and rules governing "followers." "Gentle" Miss Matty, for example, initially forbids her maid-of-all-work any followers whatsoever, a policy laid down during the reign of her more austere sister. Her first frisky maid, Fanny, practices deception and concealment; Mary Smith confesses that "a vision of a man seemed to haunt the kitchen" (65). And Fanny plays on her mistress's "weakness in order to bewilder her, and to make her feel more in the power of her clever servant" (67). Fanny's tenure, however, is brief: "It so fell out that Fanny had to leave" (65). This explanation tells us nothing and everything. Its brevity, its elliptical nature, is fleshed out by our sense that her disrespect and dishonesty disqualify her for holding the situation.

Fanny's replacement is "a rough, honest-looking country-girl, who had only lived in a farm place before" (65), and even though the new servant, Martha, is "terribly deficient" in knowledge of household routines and needs careful instruction, the ladies prefer to train her and mold her to their values rather than work with someone more competent but less respectful of class prerogatives.[11] Martha is both honest and properly grateful that "missus is very kind, and there's plenty to eat and drink, and no more work but what I can do easily" (79). Her loyalty is rewarded when Miss Matty, reminded of her own disappointed love, relents on her policy regarding suitors and decides to allow Martha one follower, who

[11] This was a strategy recommended by the household management manuals, particularly Phillis Browne's.

may visit one day a week. In her capacity as servant, Martha is being drilled in the routines of middle-class life, disciplining her preference for men and regulating her sexual appetites to "once a
week."

In internalizing middle-class values this domestic servant is seemingly closing the gap between herself and her mistress; yet, representations of the body reinscribe their class positions. Earlier in the
novel, Miss Matty and Mary Smith had tried to instruct Martha in
how to serve a dinner for ladies and gentlemen. When her teachers
tell her to serve ladies first at table, Martha leaves them both "uncomfortable and shocked" when she responds that "I'll do it as you
tell me, ma'am . . . but I like lads best" (68). Her robust sexuality
functions, in part, to highlight the ladies' prudery. Yet, at the same
time, her frank acknowledgment of bodily needs—food and drink
and sex—marks her as lower class; the biological imperatives signify
her social position and naturalize the difference between her mistress and herself. Thus, the internalized values function largely in a
regulatory rather than in an equalizing way.

The gap between labor and management is further reinforced by
the represented synergy between Martha and Miss Matty. Indeed, if
one more depends on the other, the text suggests that labor requires
management, rather than the other way around. In a significant dis-
placement, when Miss Matty loses her fortune, Martha is depicted
as more devastated by the prospect of leaving her "kind" mistress
than her mistress is by the prospect of sacrificing her competent servant. In this way, Martha is represented as requiring the very conditions that contribute to her class oppression. The social discipline is
so successful that Martha remains unswerving in her loyalty to her
mistress and hurries her surprised suitor, Jem Hearn, into marriage
so that she and he can continue to provide a home for the spinster.
His excellent joiner's wages of "three-and-sixpence a-day" contribute to the wherewithal to keep the lady's establishment going. Before he has even moved in, Jem promises that "Martha would do
her best to make you comfortable; and I'd keep out of your way as
much as I could, which I reckon would be the best kindness such an
awkward chap as me could do" (189). When Miss Matty's fortunes
are restored by the return of Peter, the community assumes that
Martha and Jem will now move out of the mistress's house. But
"Miss Matty would not hear of this" (213). In fact, she holds tenaciously to her position: "As long as Martha would remain with Miss
Matty, Miss Matty was only too thankful to have her about her."
And Jem has succeeded so completely in his promise to "keep out of

[her] way" that Miss Matty finds him "a very pleasant man to have in the house, for she never saw him from week's end to week's end" (214). He, like the middle-class gentlemen of Cranford, conveniently disappears, his presence marked only by the daughter Martha bears to fill the arms of a mistress, the erasure of whose body naturalizes the difference between them. Miss Matty happily anticipates the "probable children": "If they would all turn out such little darlings as her god-daughter Matilda, she should not mind the number, if Martha didn't. Besides the next one was to be called Deborah" (214). A happy circumstance indeed; the lot of management—the child is to be a girl named Deborah—falls to Miss Matty while the labor of childbirth falls to Martha. One has the mental work, the other the menial labor, a reinscription of the "head" and "hands" dialectic. It certainly is an ideal set-up for the bourgeoisie; it almost seems "Providential," especially when the mistress gets all the ethical credit for balking social opinion to preserve intact her little "family." Class difference has all but disappeared from before our eyes.

If Dickens's novels indulge in the romance of terming the desire for a household manager "love," Gaskell's *Cranford* colludes in the romance of interclass commonweal, the notion celebrated in the manuals that Providence so ordained domestic service to allow the lower classes to benefit from the middle-class models even as the middle class profited from lower-class labor. Nonetheless, one never forgets who is serving whom. However convenient it may be to close the class gap from time to time, it can always be reasserted, as we see when Miss Betty Barker entertains her friends with the help of her maidservant, Peggy. The narrator says: "When Peggy came in, tottering under the weight of the tea-tray, I noticed that Miss Barker was sadly afraid lest Peggy should not keep her distance sufficiently. She and her mistress were on very familiar terms in their every-day intercourse, and Peggy wanted now to make several little confidences to her, which Miss Barker was on thorns to hear; but which she thought it her duty, as a lady, to repress" (111). This is not to argue that the class structure allows no movement. Perhaps little Matilda Hearn will successfully internalize middle-class values and so facilitate her own rise in class status.

Gaskell, in fact, does represent class mobility, albeit as a limited, conservative process. The many etiquette practices, as I noted earlier, were directed not at the working classes, who needed to be managed in a household but did not threaten the upper middle classes. Rather, they were aimed at the lower middle classes, the tradespeople and shopkeepers, who aspired to gentility, having already purchased the house and hired the servants that lifted them into the middle class generally. The Miss Barkers in *Cranford* are themselves an example of successful social climbing. The eldest began as a maid to Mrs. Jamieson, one of the ladies with whom she now visits as an equal. She and her sister enjoyed a significant rise in status with the purchase of a selective millinery shop. Their strict policies—"they would not sell their caps and ribbons to any one without a pedigree" (105) (that is, they snub their former companions)—have made them both valued among the elite of Cranford and capable of dressing with sufficient elegance to take their place among them. Thus, those who can become disciplined to the routines, rhythms, and refinements of middle-class life may find the path to gentility open before them, especially if they help to bar the gates behind. For the ladies are always at the gate to ensure that the established forms are fulfilled and the distinctions carefully preserved.

The social practices of the ladies produce a strong class solidarity that facilitates numerous offices of kindness to the poor. Charity begins, however, at a remove of two steps down the social ladder. The narrator remarks that the Miss Barkers "aped their betters in having 'nothing to do' with the class immediately below theirs" (106). This policy helps explain the unexampled goodness of the ladies to their maids, where no danger of class confusion exists, and the absolute distance maintained between them and the wives of local shopkeepers and farmers, members of the prosperous merchant and yeoman classes that often surpass theirs monetarily.

Gaskell's *Cranford* is written against the grain of traditional ideology that positions "old maids" on the margins of productive activity. In its understanding of the ways in which women's discursive practices and their quotidian details constitute society and its meanings, it constructs another reality, another truth that counters that of women's marginality, passivity, and dependence. At the same time, *Cranford* points both forcefully and subtly to the way that the "Providential" logic of class exploitation is daily rearticulated in the home by those very women who—so Victorian mythology tells us—are seemingly most removed from the class question.

The novel's multiple figurations of female subjects as cultural capitalists managing human and monetary resources produce complex, even conflictual, responses. To describe this world and its inhabitants through such commonly employed adjectives as "fragile," "delicate," and "charming" is to participate in the very mystifications that the novel subtly exposes.

Wives and Daughters in Social Circulation

Gaskell fully understood the implications of a domestic economy run by women and its role in the world at large. And her protestations in *Mary Barton* that she does not grasp political economy should be taken with a grain of salt.[12] As her contemporaries pointed out, Gaskell was an apt pupil, if not an expert. She grasped the complex interplay among masters, workers, and production. Further, she grasped what the political economists failed to see: the way women's domestic economy—process-oriented and focused on control of social signs and signifiers—intersected with a political and product-oriented economy, focused on controlling the means of production. She articulates the relationship between use or exchange value and representational value. Her last novel, *Wives and Daughters*, sets forth a brilliant depiction of the domestic economy at work.

The title suggests that we must see women in their relationship to men, as wives or as daughters, but that initial emphasis is subverted by a shift of focus to the ways men rely on women.[13] The novel concentrates on the discursive practices of middle-class domestic life. At its center is a "socially ambiguous" figure, Dr. Gibson; that is, as a doctor, neither is he bound by society's rules, nor can he use them as others might for social advantage. As Leonore Davidoff explains, "non-participants [in society]—like servants—could not introduce or cut. Nor, it is interesting to note, could functionaries like

[12] "I know nothing of Political Economy, or the theories of trade. I have tried to write truthfully; and if my accounts agree or clash with any system, the agreement or disagreement is unintentional" (38). It is striking that Gaskell pits "theory" against her "truth." One is tempted to interpret her disclaimer ironically because a theory that does not reflect truth is useless.

[13] Margaret Homans points out, "Before she started writing *Wives and Daughters*, Gaskell proposed to her publisher, George Smith, a long story (to head a collection of stories) to be called 'Two Mothers . . .'" (251). Homans notes the appropriateness of both titles to the manuscript of Gaskell's last novel, the actual title emphasizing the "circulation of daughters as wives," the other pointing to "the relation that is prior to the circulation." This Lacanian interpretation, focusing on Molly as a split subject, reads many events negatively that are positive and productive in my materialist framework. This tension is inevitable, and I wish to use the conflict here to point out the way in which psychoanalytic perspectives tend to reinscribe women's position as Other within patriarchy, even as they try to disrupt that reinscription through a reinterpretation of the mother-daughter bond. A cultural materialist perspective suggests several possible scripts. Whereas one might argue that Molly is simply being put into social circulation as a commodity-wife, issues of control and power are complicated when we turn from a gendered perspective to one that examines the ways gender is inflected by class, class by gender. Ironically, psychoanalytic approaches often feed into Victorian ideology by reading all women's experience of oppression as similar. They play into the bourgeois mystification of the priority of gender difference over all others.

clergymen, doctors or governesses" (*Best Circles* 42). Indeed, doctors were neither fish nor fowl. Davidoff comments on the social hierarchy of parties: "The ambiguous doctor and other neighbours would be allowed the semi-privacy of lawns and tennis courts while still being denied the inner sanctum of the drawing room" (67). Thus, we can readily intuit that what happens to the doctor's daughter—whether she improves her social lot or not—falls to the doctor's wife, her mother. Here we discover the inherent drama of Gaskell's final novel, which presents two charming and marriageable girls—one the daughter, Molly, the other the stepdaughter, Cynthia, of the Hollingford town doctor. The doctor acquires his stepdaughter in the course of the novel by wedding a Mrs. Kirkpatrick, a second marriage for both. Dr. Gibson's new wife has been compared to Jane Austen's Mrs. Bennet, but the comparison is only superficially apt.[14] Both women are presented as vain, foolish, shallow, and self-interested, easily vexed when thwarted in their wishes. Like Mrs. Bennet, Mrs. Gibson is ambitious for her daughters, but, unlike Mrs. Bennet, she actually succeeds in furthering their interests. This difference is an enormous one, and it reveals how the social importance of the middle-class mother and wife, the semiotician of the middle class, has been consolidated in the fluid and shifting society of Victorian England.

When critics "read" Mrs. Gibson, they often dismiss her, as Patsy Stoneman does, as a "neat satire" of "human deficiency" (173). Laurence Lerner pinpoints in her the "little clevernesses of a mind that lacks the imagination really to understand that she has done wrong" (26). Even feminist critics have found only a negative value in her portrayal: that is, she reveals the "deficiencies of female education and dependency on men" (Stoneman 176).[15] But Gaskell's triumph of presentation, her demystification of domestic ideology, depends on simultaneously inscribing Mrs. Gibson within two different scripts—the patriarchal and bourgeois—and foregrounding their contradictions. In conventional gender terms, as wife and mother, Mrs. Gibson appears insensitive and selfish. In class terms, as

[14] Stoneman makes this particular comparison (173).

[15] These assessments are part of a general critical tendency to interpret Mrs. Gibson negatively, as a monster stepmother: unaffectionate and overly concerned with "appearances" rather than "reality." But, I reiterate, these critics reproduce the ideological scripts that the novel problematizes. It is striking to see the critical interpretive agreement on Mrs. Gibson. Although by any social standards her daughters make spectacular marriages, the critics define Mrs. Gibson as a failed mother. In order to reach this conclusion, a critic must divorce the patriarchal from the bourgeois narrative and so simplify the complex, unfolding tale of female subject formation.

household and status manager, she demonstrates fine discrimination and familial loyalty. Her masterful negotiations of signifying practices—etiquette (including introductions, visiting, calls, and cuts), dining rituals, household decor, and dress—make her a key player in the socially prestigious marriages of Molly and Cynthia, marriages that install them permanently within the upper middle class and remove them from the ambiguous status of doctor's daughters and potential governesses.

Although Gaskell has been regularly faulted by critics for privileging social codes over "deeper values," for confusing appearances with "reality," her strategies, in fact, critique the idealist metaphysics that inform such concepts as truth and reality.[16] Gaskell's subtle tactics align concepts of nature, inherent goodness, and virtue with patriarchal oppression of women. Although *Wives and Daughters* superficially celebrates the mutual devotion of the doctor and his daughter, the dangers in Molly's unhealthy idealization of her father and the degree to which he has failed her emerge in the tension between conceptions of "natural" virtue and "artificial"—or social—cultivation. Fearful of spoiling his daughter, the doctor has set forth an educational plan that is primarily proscriptive, and Molly remains intellectually and socially backward. Dr. Gibson has secured a governess for Molly largely as a chaperone to protect her from the attentions of his male apprentices. This governess, Miss Eyre, has these instructions: "Don't teach Molly too much; she must sew, and read, and write, and do her sums; but . . . I'm not sure that reading or writing is necessary. Many a good woman gets married with only a cross instead of her name" (65). Miss Eyre, intimidated by the doctor and financially dependent upon him, endeavors to carry out his wishes and "taught Molly to read and write, but tried honestly to keep her back in every other branch of education" (65). This disastrous course is countered solely by Molly's own energetic struggles against it, and the narrator relates that "it was only by fighting and struggling hard, that bit by bit Molly persuaded her father to let her have French and drawing lessons" (65). Mr. Gibson's intentions for his daughter remain somewhat obscure because his policies virtually guarantee that she will be unfitted to maintain herself after his death, and he is contemptuous of the first young man who presents

---

[16] For example, Maureen Reddy faults Mrs. Gibson for "not realizing that system of social codes ought to be based upon deeper values" (78). Inevitably, then, she has to convict Gaskell of the same "limitation": "[Gaskell] seems to endorse women's suppression of their feelings and strict adherence to a constraining code of manners" (83). Such details are "constraining" only when read within an idealist metaphysics that, as Schor points out, is threatened with dismantlement by valorization of the detail (3–4).

himself as a suitor. Mr. Coxe, who aspires to win Molly's hand, serves as apprentice to Mr. Gibson and, with surgical training and an inheritance in store, he would seemingly be a highly eligible match for the doctor's daughter, especially since she has been educated by a governess who "only took rank as a shopkeeper's daughter" (66). Rather than allow Mr. Coxe to communicate with Molly, however, Mr. Gibson sends her out of harm's way.

The submerged logic of this episode reads: rigorous education of women is like social grooming, a falsification of nature. The attitude Mr. Gibson holds resembles Ruskin's in "Of Queen's Gardens," but, if anything, it is less liberal. Molly is not even to have the liberty of Ruskin's girl let "loose in the library" like a "fawn in a field." But Mr. Gibson shares with Ruskin a deep suspicion of women's "play[ing] at precedence with her next-door neighbour." Early in the novel, it is clear that although he reads the backwardness of his daughter as a sign of her natural goodness, that sign has only a very limited social currency. Proud of his daughter's social clumsiness, Gibson admits that "she is a little ignoramus, and has had no . . . no training in etiquette" (88). Her taste in clothes is atrocious, and Mrs. Hamley, the local squire's wife, is persuaded that Molly will not prove a dangerous distraction for her sons because, as she tells her husband, "she's not at all the sort of girl young men of their age would take to. We like her because we see what she really is; but lads of one and two and twenty want all the accessories of a young woman. . . . Such things as becoming dress, style of manner" (112). The novel, however, dismantles such conventional distinctions between what she "really is" and how she appears. Appearances shape lives; valorizing a natural goodness in individuals helps to keep them in their "natural" social place. And Dr. Gibson, who has entrusted Molly's dress to "his old servant Betty," whose taste he esteems "as the more correct, because the more simple" (43), is collaborating in this social project, which, of course, helps keep women in *their* "place." Molly is good, but dismissable. This seemingly small episode of the importunate Mr. Coxe sets up the complications that will drive the narrative. In Gaskell's humorous revision of Jane Austen, it is a truth universally acknowledged that a widower in possession of a marriageable daughter must be in want of a wife. He seeks a kind of chaperone for his daughter to protect her from the wolves circling the patriarchal stronghold, but in the novel's poetic justice, he gets a woman who is a master of the social discourses he despises. She challenges *his* values through the consummate success of her own.

Contempt for details leaves individuals vulnerable to the social power operations that work through status display and class regulation. Dr. Gibson's failure to prepare Molly for any fate other than that of a small-town apothecary's wife is mirrored in the chaos and confusion that afflict his household at his servants' whims. The link between the corollary strategies of household management—status display and class regulation—emerges most clearly in Dr. Gibson's inability to control his servants, who subject him to their spites and punish him with discomfort, disorder, and social disgrace. When he dismisses a young servant, enlisted as go-between by Mr. Coxe, he is vulnerable to the remaining servants' pique. When Dr. Gibson invites Lord Hollingford to dine with him—the normal class barriers between the two men erased by their common scientific interests— "it was just at the time when the cook was sulking at Bethia's dismissal," and she punishes him by being "unpunctual and careless" (134). The luncheon proves a disaster: "At last dinner was ready, but the poor host saw the want of nicety—almost the want of cleanliness, in all its accompaniments—dingy plate, dull-looking glass, a table-cloth that, if not absolutely dirty, was anything but fresh in its splashed and rumpled condition, and compared it in his own mind with the dainty delicacy with which even a loaf of brown bread was served up at his guest's home" (134). Dr. Gibson apologizes that he does not have "a regulated household which would enable [him] to command the small portions of time [he] can spend there," but Lord Hollingford advises that he find "a sensible, agreeable woman of thirty or so . . . to manage your home" (134–35). Science may enable the lord to overlook certain discomforts, but he makes clear that Gibson's own professional interests will advance if he regulates his household. And, although Dr. Gibson may invite Lord Hollingford to dine at his house, he has a precarious position at the Towers, the home of Hollingford's parents, Lord and Lady Cumnor. There, he attends strictly as a functionary—the local doctor; thus, he goes "in by the back-way to the house; the 'House' on this side, the 'Towers' at the front" (40).

The issue here is strictly social, but Gaskell indulges in the rhetoric of romance in a way that exposes it as a fiction concocted by individuals to mask more utilitarian motives. That is, Dr. Gibson's need for a household supervisor is interpreted as desire for a wife, a companion for his quiet hours, someone to love. The entanglement of social convenience with personal desire reveals "love" as a construction, especially because the question of a "suitable" partner is foremost. In emphasizing social matters in this way, Gaskell is much

more blunt than Dickens, who swerved away at key points to reinforce a romance of "love." The doctor experiences no small difficulty
in identifying someone of his rank who is eligible, a problem expressed colloquially as "a case of 'first catch your hare.' Where was
the 'sensible and agreeable woman of thirty or so'" that he is to
marry? He reflects on the social difficulty: "Among his country patients there were two classes pretty distinctly marked: farmers,
whose children were unrefined and uneducated; squires, whose
daughters would, indeed, think the world was coming to a pretty
pass, if they were to marry a country surgeon" (135). Hyacinth Clare
Kirkpatrick, formerly the Cumnors' governess, widow of a curate
and gentleman, fits the bill, and, although Dr. Gibson eagerly submits to the romance of "falling in love," the novel remains clear-
sighted about the way love is harnessed to the work of solidifying
social bonds and social status; sexual desire is thus generally
mapped out on a social grid. Although disabused of his love for his
new wife, Dr. Gibson can always assure himself of the "advantages
to be gained to his daughter from the step he had just taken" (143),
partially disguising from himself the advantages that *he* has realized.

Gaskell's deft representation of this bourgeois narrative of upward
mobility through cultural capital thus exposes as mystification
Dickens's rhetoric of love and spiritual uplift. Mrs. Gibson is not a
ministering angel, a spiritual guide, a sympathetic, charming, self-
sacrificing goddess. Nor does "love" survive the nuptial vows. Mrs.
Gibson is a social mentor who makes the doctor and his daughter
figures to be reckoned with socially, and that, as Elizabeth Gaskell
forces us to recognize, is the goal occluded by Victorian mystifications of middle-class women.

The romance of falling in love is thus continually shadowed by a
narrative depicting the clever deployment of cultural capital. Mrs.
Gibson's management strategies begin with her reluctant and resistant stepdaughter, and the novel again plays with the idea of a
"natural" as opposed to a "cultivated," or artificial, self. But *Wives
and Daughters* systematically dismantles this opposition, which is oppressive to women, as Molly's supposed naturalness is represented
as just another, inferior, form of cultivation. Before her stepmother's
arrival, Molly's appearance has been, at best, "quaint." It is not simply that Betty's tastes are simple; Molly's own unformed sense of
fashion is appalling. When she must choose a new gown to visit the
local squire's home, the narrator reveals that "Miss Rose's [the
dressmaker's] ready-made resources and Molly's taste combined,
did not arrive at a very great success" (92). She chooses a "gay-

coloured flimsy plaid silk," which the narrator characterizes as a "terrible, over-smart plaid gown" (92, 118). When asked by Molly what she should wear on a particular occasion, the squire's wife privately thinks, "anything but that horrid plaid silk" (160), and urges Molly to dress in her last year's muslin, so that she looks "a little quaint, it is true, but thoroughly ladylike, if she was old-fashioned" (160). Roger Hamley, the squire's younger son, assesses Molly as "a badly-dressed, and rather awkward girl" (119). The heart will not be enraptured when the eye is offended. Lady Cumnor early predicts that "Clare" (the designation for their former servant, which reminds her of her place) "may make something" of Molly (164), and her talent for human management promises well. Lady Harriet, Lady Cumnor's daughter and Clare's former pupil, confesses to Molly that "I used to think I managed [Clare], till one day an uncomfortable suspicion arose that all the time she had been managing me" (195). The former governess rapidly assesses Molly's deficiencies and shortly after becoming Mrs. Gibson "had already fidgeted Molly into a new amount of care about the manner in which she put on her clothes, arranged her hair, and was gloved and shod" (216). Even before the marriage, she commissions "a very smart dressmaker" from the county town to sew a dress "which was both so simple and so elegant as at once to charm Molly," who is "almost startled" at the "improvement in her appearance" (187). Her dear old friends, the Miss Brownings, are so surprised that they confess they "shouldn't have known" her (187). And the squire's fastidious older son, who has previously ignored Molly, immediately notes that "her appearance was extremely improved" (216). That Molly ultimately marries the squire's younger son testifies to Mrs. Gibson's success in putting her stepdaughter into social circulation. The narrator seems to pinpoint Mrs. Gibson's folly in such comments as: "Cynthia and Molly looked their best, which was all the duty Mrs. Gibson absolutely required of them" (306). But while the text appears to collude to some extent in an ideology that debases women's interest in fashion as frivolous, it is subversive in showing how preoccupation with dress leads to social advancement because sexual attraction is inscribed on the body through social signs.

The contrast between Molly and Cynthia helps establish the value of Cynthia's cultivation, which, ironically, counterbalances notions of natural goodness put into circulation through representations of Molly. Both Cynthia and her mother, the narrator claims, possess an inherent "genius for millinery and dress," which enables them to settle "a great many knotty points of contrivance and taste" in their appearance, achieving magnificent results with limited resources

(476). The novel makes clear that Cynthia's impeccable taste in dress forms the foundation of her "charm," which promises to secure for her an eligible husband, once she can appear in higher circles. Cynthia's charms, the narrator remarks, are perhaps "incompatible with very high principle," a subversive debunking of the angelic ideal. And Roger falls in love first not with the "real" angel, Molly, but with the apparent one, Cynthia, she of exquisite taste. Indeed, Roger never loves Molly until she has acquired her stepsister's charms. Together, Cynthia and Mrs. Gibson give Molly social currency. A young woman's social advancement depends on her millinery tastes and talents, as Cynthia fully appreciates in refusing to visit her elegant relatives without new clothes. She argues, "It would not do to go there in a state of shabbiness, for . . . I remember, my aunt was very particular about dress; and now that Margaret and Helen are grown up, and they visit so much—pray don't say anything more about it, for I know it would not do." (470). Dr. Gibson accepts the validity of her arguments and the desirability of her keeping up the acquaintance, so he finally offers her ten pounds to outfit herself. His money and her management combine to produce the desired effect: Cynthia's prestigious marriage.

While the novel stresses the dramatic changes in Molly under new management, it also asserts the more general social transformations effected by Mrs. Gibson, a repositioning of the family within Hollingford society. At the same time that Mrs. Gibson is putting her daughter and stepdaughter into social circulation, she is attending to much neglected household affairs, whipping up the entire establishment to a higher social standard, a process that begins with a renovation of household discipline.

Gaskell's representation of those renovations challenges Victorian sentimental pieties of the happy, bonded family of servants and management. When the servants grumble about the work their new mistress demands of them, she summarily dismisses them—even Betty, Molly's nurse and surrogate mother, who has been with the family for sixteen years. We share Molly's point of view and distress over the dismissal, aggravated by the honeyed expression of Mrs. Gibson's regret: "But, sweet one, you seem to forget that I cannot go against my principle [never to take an apology from a servant who has given notice], however much I may be sorry for Betty. She should not have given way to ill temper, as I said before; although I never liked her, and considered her a most inefficient servant, thoroughly spoilt by having had no mistress for so long, I should have borne with her" (212). Mrs. Gibson will not tolerate the kind of purposeful neglect practiced by the servants when they want to "mark their displeasure" (210) with the family. Nor will she allow Molly to perform menial tasks when "there are servants to do it" (236). As a result, the organization of the house improves, the hierarchy is reasserted, and the insolence and carelessness disappear. Gaskell's depictions bring to the fore what is disguised in other texts, that is, the process by which the middle class served its own ends, justifying and legitimizing its controls to perpetuate its existence. The bourgeois manager reasserts middle-class ideals to the ultimate benefit of the middle-class family.

Gaskell also debunks Victorian domestic ideology in depicting the reach and extent of Mrs. Gibson's reforms, which encompass even her resistant husband. The social historian Carol Dyhouse argues in support of Victorian mythology when she claims the existence of a "social expectation that a wife should be solicitous for her husband's needs. . . . Even in the lower-middle-class home meals would tend to be taken at times which fitted around the routine of the man's work" ("Mothers and Daughters" 33). Gaskell's representations challenge that ideology when Mrs. Gibson overturns long-established pleasures and customs in her husband's life, disrupting his schedule when that schedule upsets her manipulations of the discursive practices that will win them social standing. In short, her social business "rather diminished [his] domestic comfort" (213), a truth rarely represented so directly in Victorian fiction, where ostensibly the angel is feathering a nest with only the master's comfort in mind. Mrs. Gibson entirely rearranges her husband's schedule, forcing him to give up a noon dinner for a "six o'clock dinner" to prevent the aromas of "hot, savoury-smelling dishes from the kitchen . . . when high-born ladies, with noses of aristocratic refinement, might be calling" (213). Mrs. Gibson also forbids her husband his favorite diet of bread and cheese because, as she says, "really I cannot allow cheese to come beyond the kitchen" (214).[17] Further, when the cook objects to late dinners and the newly popular entrées, she departs, and Mrs. Gibson institutes a more fashionable cuisine, so that Mr. Gibson has "to satisfy his healthy English appetite on badly-made omelettes, rissoles, vol-au-vents, croquets, and timbales" (214). Of course, all of these changes are accompanied by Mrs. Gibson's fulsome protestations that she has only her husband's wishes at heart, her concession to Victorian sentimentality.

Mrs. Gibson ultimately enforces a high standard of bourgeois dis-

[17] No manual I discovered explained the objection to cheese. *Etiquette for Ladies and Gentlemen* [1876] gives this guidance: "Ladies scarcely ever eat cheese after dinner. If eaten, remember it should be with *a fork*, not with a knife" (35).

cipline, lacing her family into a straitjacket of social custom to achieve significant results. When Molly chafes against having to go through every ceremony "in the same stately manner for two as for twenty," so that dinner "took up at least an hour" and includes dessert—"although Molly knew full well, and her stepmother knew full well, and Maria knew full well, that neither Mrs. Gibson nor Molly touched dessert" (548)—her stepmother remonstrates: " 'It's no extravagance, for we need not eat it—I never do. But it looks well, and makes Maria understand what is required in the daily life of every family of position' " (549). And in the end the social disciplines that seem pointedly futile to Molly and her father triumphantly justify Mrs. Gibson. First, the gossiping townspeople remark on the social elevation the Gibsons have enjoyed under the regimes of the new mistress, who is "quite the lady herself; dines late . . . and everything in style" (553). The townspeople agree: "Very different style to what Bob Gibson, her husband, was used to when first he came here . . . we called him Bob Gibson then, but none on us dare Bob him now; I'd as soon think o' calling him sweep!" (554). Second, Lady Harriet—sister to Lord Hollingford—makes a morning call on Mrs. Gibson and decides to stay for luncheon. In sharp contrast to the tardy and unappetizing fare that Dr. Gibson had earlier offered her brother, Mrs. Gibson has anticipated the possible guest and has arranged for a lovely meal, which so impresses Lady Harriet that she was "more and more convinced that Clare had done very well for herself" (404–5). The elegance and taste of this repast confirm a series of impressions in Lady Harriet's mind that the Gibsons are a family worth troubling about, and the positive consequences for Molly are enormous.

The episodes in which Mrs. Gibson figures are both amusing and distressing; the way her character is complexly figured through conflicting gender and social expectations stresses the pressure of social codes, that complex system of signifiers which Mrs. Gibson reads so well, to force at least grudging admiration from those in her world. Although he grumbles about his wife's lack of integrity, Dr. Gibson admits:

> So the prestige was tacitly sold and paid for; but neither buyer nor seller defined the nature of the bargain. On the whole, it was well that Mr Gibson spent so much of his time from home. He sometimes thought so himself when he heard his wife's plaintive fret or pretty babble over totally indifferent things, and perceived of how flimsy a nature were all her fine sentiments. . . . Still, . . . he forced himself to

> dwell on the positive advantages that had accrued to him and his through his marriage. He had obtained an unexceptionable chaperone, if not a tender mother, for his little girl; a skilful manager of his previous disorderly household; a woman who was graceful and pleasant to look at for the head of his table. (364–65)

This is not an entirely fair assessment, since it refuses to recognize that her "fine sentiments" are not flimsy in their effects. But it does begin to appreciate her productivity within his household. There sits Mrs. Gibson in state, a master of the semiotics of status, fully constituted by the discursive practices of her society, unaccompanied by any mystifying rhetoric of sensitivity, sympathy, and sainthood. It is a measure only of persisting mystifications of patriarchal ideology that Mr. Gibson cannot but regret that his wife is not more saintly and selfless, less shallow and selfish.

In sum, the premium Mrs. Gibson places upon appearances may elicit the reader's laughter or censure, depending upon the particular context foregrounded, but the novel consistently depicts her efforts and emphases as socially productive rather than destructive. This is part of the text's substantial revision of cherished ideas, such as that substance counts for more than surface. In fact, as Gaskell demonstrates here, appearances are productive of substantial effects, and those who know how to manage the social signifiers are individuals to be reckoned with. For example, Mrs. Gibson may seem to reach a nadir when Squire Hamley rides into Hollingford to request that Molly immediately accompany him home to attend to his ailing wife, who has had one of her "bad fits of illness" (222). Molly is preparing to go, bolstered by her father's permission, when Mrs. Gibson scotches the whole plan because Molly forgot that she was to go out with her stepmother that night, "to visit people . . . with whom I am quite unacquainted" (222). Despite earnest entreaties, Mrs. Gibson insists "an engagement is an engagement" and Molly is "bound to accompany me, in my husband's absence" (223). Although, initially, the narrator seems to pinpoint Mrs. Gibson's folly in placing a meaningless social visit and social forms over meaningful attentions to a suffering individual, ultimately the text does not collude in this assessment. No death or dramatic event intervenes in Molly's absence. In fact, Mrs. Hamley is always ailing; the delay of one day has no consequences whatsoever, and Molly spends several days with the invalid. Furthermore, Mrs. Gibson helps put Squire Hamley in his place; the squire is only too willing to appropriate Molly when he or his wife feels the need for some daughterly affection, but he repeatedly insults Dr. Gibson by insisting that his sons must look higher than the doctor's daughter when seeking wives. Mrs. Gibson helps claim a social importance for Molly that will partially counteract the squire's implicit estimate of her as a servant at his beck and call. Even after the humiliation of his eldest son's marrying a French Catholic nursery maid—whom he calls that "French baggage of a servant" (613)—even after Molly has served both him and his wife devotedly, he stills remarks to her that she is "beneath what [he] ever thought to see [his sons] marry" (689). Gaskell's representations of both squire and doctor's daughter underline the productivity of the signifier. And, in spite of the squire's sense of consequence, Lady Harriet opines that elegant, intelligent Molly Gibson, whom Mrs. Gibson has put into social circulation, would make an excellent wife for Roger Hamley.

One of the novel's concluding episodes confirms both the productivity of social signifying practices and Mrs. Gibson's positive effect in Molly's life. Molly, who has been ill, is invited by Lady Harriet to recuperate for a few days at the Towers while the rest of her family travels to London for Cynthia's wedding. This visit recalls her only previous experiences at the Towers before her father's remarriage, and structurally it serves as a point of reference in evaluating Molly's changes. On the first visit, Molly was poorly dressed and awkward, her own undeveloped taste and manner aggravated by the vulgarity of her advisers. One guest characterizes her as "wild and strange" (53). She feels like a "careless intruder" (53) and balks at the task of thanking her hostess, who identifies her as "the daughter of our medical man at Hollingford" (54). Lady Cumnor dismisses Molly as one of the townspeople to whom she condescends once a year for helping her in the charity school she sponsors. The school helps perpetuate the class system by ensuring a steady stream of domestic servants for the Towers; the "girls are taught to sew beautifully, to be capital housemaids, and pretty fair cooks, and above all, to dress neatly in a kind of charity uniform devised by the ladies of Cumnor Towers;—white caps, white tippets, check aprons, blue gowns, and ready curtseys, and 'please, ma'ams', being *de rigueur*" (37–38). And in Lady Cumnor's view, Molly is not far from that rank. In sum, Molly confides to her father, "I was never so unhappy in all my life, as I have been all this long afternoon" (59). At this point, she has been effectively "schooled" by the Cumnors to stay in her place.

Molly's second visit with the Cumnors is an entirely different matter because of Mrs. Gibson's social discipline and its good effects.

Completely prepared, Molly captivates the society at the Towers. Even critical Lady Cumnor is "pleased by Molly's manners and appearance" (669). When dressed for dinner, Molly "scarcely knew the elegant reflection [in the glass] to be that of herself" (670), and when she goes to bed, "she was constrained to admit that staying at the Towers as a visitor was rather pleasant than otherwise" (671). Molly's subsequent effort "to reconcile old impressions with new ones" will depend on her own grasp of society's signifying practices of class. The Towers is unchanged, but her elegant dress and refined manners are productive of a different effect. She is now, to general acclaim, a "very pretty, lady-like, and graceful girl" (671). Mrs. Gibson gratifyingly pronounces on Molly's further improvements when she returns from Cynthia's wedding and is "impressed with her [stepdaughter's] increased grace" (677). She says, "'Ah, Molly . . . it's really wonderful to see what a little good society will do for a girl. . . . There is something quite different about you—a *je ne sçais quoi*—that would tell me at once that you have been mingling with the aristocracy'" (677–78).

Again, we see the way in which sexual desire itself is always mapped within a social grid, and feminine beauty is inscribed onto the body through signifiers of social status. The lady that Molly has now become attracts the romantic interest of the squire's son, who, at this point in their long acquaintance, finally learns to "love" her. Roger Hamley, whom Molly has long loved, is visiting the Towers at the same time and "hardly recognized her, although he acknowledged her identity" (672). This disruption in his conception of Molly's "identity" paves the way for his desire of her: "He began to feel that admiring deference which most young men experience when conversing with a very pretty girl: a sort of desire to obtain her good opinion in a manner very different to his old familiar friendliness" (672). Molly possesses the same sterling virtues she has always had, but now she looks like a Victorian angel, that is, a refined lady. Lady Harriet callously pinpoints the role of class in perception when discussing Mr. Preston's appearance: "I never think of whether a land-agent is handsome or not. They don't belong to the class of people whose appearance I notice" (128). No one has better grasped that truth than Mrs. Gibson, who exploits her command of the society's signifying practices to settle her daughters into upper-middle-class life. And not only has she enriched their lives monetarily; they also now move in circles that the novel represents as more sophisticated, talented, and educated, so that Dr. Gibson finds his own sphere greatly enlarged by the stimulating contacts of London society. He is as much a beneficiary of his wife as is his daughter, but he prefers to cultivate the myth that he suffers from her foolish innovations and pointless vanities, a view that the novel rhetorically supports but structurally subverts. In fact, Mrs. Gibson has skillfully employed cultural capital to accumulate superior material resources, which further enhance the family's cultural capital, marking a permanent rise in status. No longer teetering between lower and upper middle class, the Gibsons take their place among the gentility at the novel's conclusion.

Morality, like sexual desire and sexuality, is also inscribed and interpreted within a social text. Gaskell undertakes a substantial examination of social signifiers and women's centrality in one of the novel's central complications: Cynthia's entanglement with the Cumnor's land agent. As a girl of sixteen, Cynthia has been betrayed by youth and inexperience into contracting a secret engagement with Mr. Preston. Although she subsequently wishes to break from the relationship, he refuses to release her and uses some letters she wrote to blackmail her. When Molly intervenes and tries to extricate her stepsister by retrieving those letters, she is observed by the townspeople, who conclude that she is carrying on a clandestine relationship with him. They communally castigate her specifically in class terms. Mrs. Goodenough avers "she might as well be a scullery-maid at oncest" (552), while Mrs. Dawes claims that "Molly and Mr. Preston were keeping company just as if she was a maid-servant and he was a gardener" (561). Despite his outrage at the gossip and his conviction of Molly's innocence, Dr. Gibson is powerless to stem the rumors; he only warns her darkly "how slight a thing may blacken a girl's reputation for life" (569).

Dr. Gibson's powerlessness is contrasted with the power of a lady, the Cumnors' daughter Harriet. Molly is finally rescued from her suffering by Lady Harriet, who uses her prerogatives as social superior in the town to redeem the girl. Having determined that the gossip is groundless, Lady Harriet clears her reputation through the rituals of "full etiquette" (585). First, she calls on the girl, then parades the "unconscious Molly" through "all the length of the principal street of the town, loitered at Grinstead's for half-an-hour, and wound up by Lady Harriet's calling on the Miss Brownings, who, to her regret, were not at home" (584). She then leaves her own card with Molly's name penciled underneath, in spite of naive Molly's protests that she "never leave[s] cards; I have not got any, and on the Miss Brownings, of all people; why, I am in and out whenever I like." But Lady Harriet pursues her plan that "today you shall do everything properly, and according to full etiquette," congratulating herself at the conclusion that "we've done a good day's work!" And she continues addressing the now-absent Molly: "Hollingford is not the place I take it to be, if it doesn't veer round in Miss Gibson's favour after my today's trotting of that child about" (585). Molly is completely redeemed. Of course, one might argue that Molly's innocence is important. Cynthia, however, is not innocent. More important are appearances. The girl branded a scullery maid for apparent indiscretions is both exonerated and elevated by the patronage of Lady Harriet. The community never possesses the "truth." It is guided entirely by the semiotics practiced by the ladies; therein lies its truth. Morality is articulated through sociality.

The functioning of this domestic economy has implications, too, for the national economy through their intersection in politics. That particular imbrication is not emphasized in the text; rather, it emerges like the negative of a positive image. But accession to the powerful centers of political influence in London—Cynthia through government, Molly through the new scientific disciplines—shadows the fates of Cynthia and Molly as they move toward socially desirable marriages. This intrication of class and politics has one telling but brief representation in the novel when the Cumnors, accompanied by a duchess, attend a local public ball, ostensibly as a gesture of goodwill, actually as a campaign tactic. Lady Harriet, ever alert to social signs, circulates through the crowd of tradespeople and shopkeepers. She takes the measure of their disappointment in the duchess's dowdiness. She quietly goads her brother into performing the part of a lord: "You don't know how these good people here have been hurt and disappointed with our being so late, and with the duchess's ridiculous simplicity of dress." She answers his incomprehension with the retort: "Oh, don't be so wise and stupid; don't you see, we're a show and a spectacle—it's like having a pantomime with harlequin and columbine in plain clothes." When he still professes not to understand the significance of their class "performance," she simply urges, "Then take it upon trust. . . . We must try and make it up to them; for one thing, because I can't bear our vassals to look dissatisfied and disloyal, and then there's the election in June" (337). Lady Harriet recognizes two things that escape her brother: by performing class status they preserve class prerogatives and by preserving class prerogatives they ensure their continued control of national policy through election to Parliament.

It is easy for the reader to succumb to the romance with which the plot of *Wives and Daughters* concludes, as if it were only a simple and natural matter for the young people to fall in love. Alternatively, one may resist the romance plot only to succumb to the now-fashionable critique of that romance, the fact that it culminates generally in the sacrifice of rare and substantive creatures in marriage—particularly, here, in the spectacle of a commodified Molly Gibson. Indeed, it has become common for feminists to read Victorian narratives of courtship and marriage as stories of sacrifice of talented women in patriarchy. But that gendered script diminishes the narrative of multiply constructed female subjectivity which Gaskell has crafted. The textual crosscurrents of *Wives and Daughters* invite us to evaluate the productivity of sociality in the development of women. A Molly Gibson married to wealthy, intelligent Roger Hamley, moving in sophisticated and scientific circles in London and abroad, will be a different and more fulfilled person than Molly Gibson, wife of a small-town apothecary, Mr. Coxe. A Cynthia Kirkpatrick married to Mr. Henderson, with "a handsome private fortune," will enjoy an identity quite other from that of Cynthia Kirkpatrick wed to an insignificant land agent, Mr. Preston. Class tells; it is the telling signifier in this world.

The same truth holds in Gaskell's other novels, such as *Mary Barton*, which represents the other side of the class coin. The working-class Mary, who has experienced the freedoms of Manchester and Liverpool streets, must learn that she truly "loves" a man of her own class, Jem Wilson, instead of the wealthy son of the factory owner. The rhetoric of love justifies the wisdom of Providence in so placing individuals. And the romance plot is revealed to be less about boy meets girl than it is about the right boy meeting the right girl. And those who know how to make it right, like Mrs. Gibson, have might.

Gaskell mixes this message of socially managed mobility into the romance plot, allowing certain illusions to be partially preserved in terms such as "love." Margaret Oliphant, one of her successors, was less interested in the illusions of romance. She represents the social managerial role of women as it extends from the home to the community, and the principal love affair for her heroines lies in their romance with a career.

6

Margaret Oliphant's
Parliamentary Angels

Margaret Oliphant's novels continue Gaskell's privileging of the domestic detail as a basis for cultural meanings, and further, they emphasize what is only a leitmotif in Gaskell: the idea of identity as performed, the ways in which individuals are inevitably constituted out of discursive practices whose very purpose is to distinguish the self from other. The idea informing etiquette and other domestic discourses—the significance of the sign—makes inevitable an increasing commitment to the self as a complex sign.

The idea of a self continually produced from signs destabilizes categories drawn from nature and makes identity performative rather than essential, a conclusion to which Oliphant seems to have been temperamentally as well as philosophically drawn. She pronounced in her *Autobiography* that "I have never, I am glad to say, been 'a student of human nature' or any such odious thing" (79). Ironically, however, if readers today think of Margaret Oliphant at all, they often associate her with conservative, even reactionary beliefs, a reputation that rests largely on a few pieces she wrote for *Blackwood's*, particularly one critical of the morality of Thomas Hardy's later novels.[1] Most readers know of her only secondhand, having no actual acquaintance with the novels or autobiography. To encounter her work directly, then, has a salutary effect. In her autobiography, for example, what appears to have been a temperamental distaste for feminism in its declamatory modes gives way to a practical feminism, enacted in her support of her own family as well as of her

---

[1] Oliphant condemns Hardy's claim of "pure woman" for Tess because a pure woman "is not betrayed into fine living and fine clothes as the mistress of her seducer by any stress of poverty or misery" (139). Of *Jude the Obscure* she wrote that "nothing so coarsely indecent as the whole history of Jude in his relations with his wife Arabella has ever been put into English print" (138).

brothers and their broods. Her own experiences gave her a pragmatic appreciation of women's capacity to manage, an appreciation that culminated in her support for "a Married Women's Property Act, a mother's right to the custody of her children, women doctors, and university education for girls" (Williams 108). Oliphant's immersion in the complex mechanics of daily life and subjection to the pressures of material circumstances made her impatient with generalizations and philosophical posturing. She can only wonder if she would "have done better if [she] has been kept, like [George Eliot], in a mental greenhouse and taken care of" (5). Instead, she "always had to think of other people, and to plan everything. . . . To keep [her] household and make a number of people comfortable, at the cost of incessant work" (6–7). She, like Jane Austen, wrote in the family drawing room "where all the (feminine) life of the house [went] on"; she doubted that she "ever had two hours undisturbed (except at night, when everybody [was] in bed) during [her] whole literary life" (24).

The impression that emerges from a reading of Margaret Oliphant's autobiography is thus of a woman both perplexed and amused by her contemporaries' passion for self-examination, dependent, of course, upon a stable, evolving self to be examined. She wrote her own memoir late in life, more with the idea of bequeathing it to her children than to the world, and their deaths, which punctuate the narrative, leave her questioning her motive in continuing. Oliphant has little to say about her own art, dismissing it as it was dismissed by a public, which early accused her of "working too fast, and producing too much" (44). She claims, "I have written because it gave me pleasure, because it came natural to me, because it was like talking or breathing, besides the big fact that it was necessary for me to work for my children" (4). This last motive, which Oliphant asserts was "not the first motive," nonetheless made it necessary that she pursue some "trade," and writing suited her. Beyond that, she resisted self-examination.

The Victorian attraction to autobiography finally conquered even Margaret Oliphant's resistance, however, and she admits she was "tempted to begin writing by George Eliot's life" (4). Anthony Trollope had a share in that prompting as well, and Oliphant confides that his "talk about the characters in his books astonished me beyond measure, . . . I am totally incapable of talking about anything I have ever done in that way" (4). Seeking a reason for his confession, Oliphant suggests that "as he was a thoroughly sensible genuine man, I suppose he was quite sincere in what he says of them,—or was it that he was driven into a fashion of self-explanation which belongs to the time" (4). Her astute recognition that a "sincere" impulse for public confessions may have been motivated by the Victorian age betrays her understanding of the extent to which our "inner" imperatives are hostage to social values and beliefs. The only thing that can move her to laughter after the deaths of her two sons is "reading the life of Mr Symonds"; she finds it humorous to "think of the strange difference between this prosaic little narrative, all about the facts of a life so simple as mine, and his elaborate self-discussions" (80). In her autobiography, then, she eschews the confessional-philosophical mode and sticks to the "trivial" details of quotidian life.

Oliphant makes it her autobiographical goal to "try to remember more trivial things, the incidents that sometimes amuse me when I look back upon them, not merely the thread of my life" (65). As one example she relates an episode in which she and Miss Blackwood, "one of the elders of the Blackwood family," deliberately baited and ridiculed an unsuspecting male author:

> Miss Blackwood had asked him to dine with us alone, and he came, and we flattered him to the top of his bent, she half sincerely . . . and I, I fear, backing her up in pure fun, for I was no particular admirer [sic] of Aytoun, who was then an ugly man in middle age, with the air of being one of the old lights, but without either warmth or radiancy. We got him between us to the pitch of flattered fatuity which all women recognise, when a man looks like the famous scene painter, "I am so sick, I am so clevare"; his eyes bemused and his features blunted with a sort of bewildered beatitude, till suddenly he burst forth without any warning with "Come hither, Evan Cameron"—and repeated the poem to us, Miss Blackwood, ecstatic, keeping a sort of time with flourishes of her hand, and I, I am afraid, overwhelmed with secret laughter. I am not sure that he did not come to himself with a horrified sense of imbecility before he reached the end. (72)

Her ability to make Aytoun perform the idiot, to take on a normative gender role within discourse—that's what amuses Oliphant. George Eliot could never have been so cruel—more's the pity. For, it is precisely that asperse, irreverent eye, the appreciation of the "trivial," the way that individuals enter into an economy of the sign, that allows Oliphant to pierce the mists of romance that cling to representations of men and women and to novel plots structured around marriage.

Margaret Oliphant distances herself not only from George Eliot but also from that avatar of passionate representations Charlotte

Brontë, admitting, "I don't suppose my powers are equal to hers—my work to myself looks perfectly pale and colourless beside hers" (67). However, she continues, "yet I have had far more experience and, I think, a fuller conception of life. I have learned to take perhaps more a man's view of mortal affairs,—to feel that the love between men and women, the marrying and giving in marriage, occupy in fact so small a portion of either existence or thought" (67). Oliphant's novels—particularly two from the "Chronicles of Carlingford" on which I will concentrate here—represent what does, in her estimation, occupy a large portion of existence and thought: the close interrelationship of domestic and political life facilitated by Victorian social semiotics. *Miss Marjoribanks* (1866) and *Phoebe Junior* (1876) set forth the careers of young women bent on employing their talents in social semiotics to achieve power. Q. D. Leavis is credited with rediscovering *Miss Marjoribanks* in the 1960s, and she wrote that "[Oliphant's] Lucilla has long seemed to me a triumphant intermediary between their [Austen's] Emma and [Eliot's] Dorothea, and, incidentally, more entertaining, more impressive and more likeable than either"(135).[2] This tribute testifies to the special brilliance of Oliphant's novel. Lucilla does resemble Emma Woodhouse in "meddling" in people's lives, with the definitive difference that Oliphant represents her intervention as productive and positive. Part of that difference in presentation results, I suspect, simply from the emergence of the bourgeois domestic manager in the previous half century, a figure whom Emma anticipates. But, ironically, Oliphant's refusal to "punish" her heroine has led to condemnations from critics whose values are challenged by Oliphant's portrayals. In an early feminist analysis of women's fiction, Patricia Stubbs concludes that "*Miss Marjoribanks* is trivial in a way that *Emma* is not, and it is so because of the author's attitude, endorsing as she does Lucilla's exploitation of her traditional female role" (41). To reach this conclusion is both to fail to see the ways in which the "traditional female role" is being demystified by an ironic presentation of its performance and to participate in the ideology of triviality that the novel is critiquing.

Oliphant's depiction of her heroines' opportunistic negotiations of

[2] Leavis's 1969 introduction to the Chatto and Windus edition of *Miss Marjoribanks*, reprinted in her *Collected Essays*, remains the most sophisticated treatment to date of Oliphant's novel. The critical tendency is to assess Oliphant exactly as did her contemporaries. Leavis, in contrast, pinpoints the "same acute and unsentimental critical mind that had produced *Emma* in the Regency period," and she describes Lucilla as a "Victorian anti-heroine" (136). She summarizes, "We have reason to conclude that Mrs Oliphant's purpose in writing this novel was to campaign against false Victorian values where women are concerned" (150).

social discourses has produced dismay in critics both early and late, harkening back to her publisher John Blackwood's initial critique of *Miss Marjoribanks*, with whose early numbers he was extremely pleased. He wrote to Oliphant that this novel was challenging for the right to join the great books, and he warned her to modify her "hardness of tone." She simply responded, "You make me nervous when you talk about the first rank of novelists"—especially, no doubt, because his comment carried with it a request that she alter her representation of the protagonist. Oliphant, however, persisted in her artistic vision, arguing: "As for what you say of hardness of tone, I am afraid it was scarcely to be avoided. . . . I have a weakness for Lucilla, and to bring a sudden change upon her character and break her down into tenderness would be like one of Dickens's maudlin repentances. . . . Miss M[arjoribanks] must be one and indivisible, and I am pretty sure my plan is right."[3] Later critics follow Blackwood's lead. For example, of Phoebe Beecham, Merryn Williams has said that she "behaves in a way which most novel-readers would have found unpleasant" (85).[4] The heroines are too self-consciously manipulative and self-interested; they recognize and exploit the power conferred by mastery of the semiotics of social life. Marriage is represented as a means to an end, never an end its itself. It must supply the proper "field that was necessary for . . . ambition" (114). Lucilla Marjoribanks, for example, refuses to waste her prime on a husband. She devotes ten years—from age nineteen to twenty-nine—to the reorganization of Carlingford society and is regarded enviously by one of the local wives, who acknowledges that "it would be very foolish of Miss Marjoribanks to marry, and forfeit all her advantages, and take somebody else's anxieties upon her shoulders" (374). Phoebe, too, insists that marriage provide her with political opportunities. But Oliphant revises much more than the romance plot, and the negative comments are also responding to her demystification of the angelic ideal, her ironic staging of the feminine roles of dutiful daughter and ingenue, and her unrelenting focus on women's work that stresses the interpenetration of the political and the domestic, the way men's actions are informed by

---

[3] Quoted in Leavis, p. 155.

[4] Williams, whose biography is the most thorough and sympathetic account written of Oliphant's life and works, has difficulty moving beyond critical truisms in her assessments of the novels. She accounts for that "hardness of tone" by noting that *Miss Marjoribanks* describes situations that are "disturbing and painful, and although there is a believable happy ending, the author is obviously well aware of the darker aspect of life" (81). However, that characterization would seem to apply to most other Victorian novels, which have escaped Blackwood's condemnation.

women's discursive practices. What is more troubling to her audiences, they highlight the way that those discourses allow the heroines to manipulate situations to their advantage.

Finally, in an even more striking ideological revision, Oliphant dramatizes the way in which women bond within local sociopolitical spheres to facilitate class agendas, and marriageable men function as pawns or tokens through which class allegiances are defined and solidified by women. We glimpsed this practice in Gaskell's *Cranford* when Peter became the mechanism for restoring social harmony among the women. This pattern of female sociosexual desire counters patterns of "male homosocial desire" that Eve Sedgwick has identified as dominant in the Victorian novel. My perspective on multiply constituted female subjects, highlighting the way class is implicated with gender in the construction of subjectivity, makes it difficult to speak simply of "men promoting men's interests" (Sedgwick's definition of patriarchy) or even of women promoting women's interests. A sociosexual script stresses the way in which desire is articulated through social formations and emphasizes here the way in which the middle class promotes middle-class interests through sexual alliances, women often trafficking in men to solidify social bonds.[5]

Challenging, as they do, so many Victorian sacred cows—romance, angels, feminine duty, innocence, passivity, and the separation of home and state—we must ask if Oliphant's novels have been consigned to obscurity, if not oblivion, for that very challenge, a position that reads canons as repositories of a culture's professed values and self-representations. Oliphant's vision of reality, however faithful to quotidian affairs, pierced the myths that were sedulously guarded in other depictions of Victorian life. And the very source of her insight, the frenetic yet pragmatic life she lived as breadwinner trying to preserve the middle-class status of her family,

[5] Although Sedgwick scrupulously calls attention to the ways "sexual meaning is inextricable from social meaning—in the English case, from class," in practice her argument gives priority to sexual meanings *over* social ones, partly because she is committed to reading "male homosocial desire" and does not pursue the possibilities suggested by the female sociosexual desire I postulate. Sedgwick urges that we study the ways "the meanings of 'masculinity' and 'femininity' themselves are produced within a context of class difference, are ascribed for political reasons to classes by themselves and by other classes, and have different functions, manifestations, values, and consequences according to class" (214–15). We should be able to revise her formulation to help discourage affording primacy to one term over the other. I suggest that we look, instead, at how the meanings of "middle" and "lower" class themselves are produced within a context of sexual difference; how each sex for political reasons ascribes these meanings to itself and to the opposite sex; and how these meanings have different functions, manifestations, values, and consequences according to sex.

became the basis for stigmatizing her achievement: she wrote too much and too quickly.[6] Oliphant had to settle for a place outside the Pantheon of Greats, recognizing that the Carlingford series *"almost made me one of the popularities of literature. Almost, never quite"* (*Autobiography* 70).

Lucilla Marjoribanks's Social Campaigns

Miss Marjoribanks opens with a death, but a death portrayed as an opportunity for social reorganization rather than as personal tragedy. This depiction is all the more shocking because the two individuals engaged in a preliminary power struggle are the husband and daughter. The woman who was wife and mother has so little currency and importance in the lives of her family members that at her death Dr. Marjoribanks experiences only a "painful heaviness . . . when he became aware how little real sorrow was in his mind, and how small an actual loss was this loss of his wife" (28). She passes out of the world, leaving "little trace that she had ever been there" (28). Later she is described as "fad[ing] out of her useless life" (67). The daughter's response, although appropriately tearful, is represented as "enlightened by novels and popular philosophy" (25). Lucilla, in short, enacts the appropriate feminine response to maternal death. The narrator's comment that her feelings are "sufficiently real in their way" (27) points to the way reality is constructed out of conventional behaviors, a regime of the norm. This brief representation of the Victorian "angel" as nonentity—"the pretty creature whom Dr Marjoribanks had married . . . had vanished into thin air years and years ago"—punctures popular myths of her redemptive and sanctifying presence in the home (28). Of far more concern to both father and daughter than the loss of a wife and mother is the future balance of power in the household. The etiquette manuals' advice that mourning rituals might offer individuals the opportunity to "reshuffle their social hand" (Davidoff 56) takes a sardonic twist

---

[6] Because Margaret Oliphant was writing to support her family, she had to pay attention to her novels' commercial reception. Unsurprisingly, in view of its challenge to Victorian pieties of home, hearth, and heart, *Miss Marjoribanks* was not highly successful with the reading public or later critics. As Leavis remarks, "The Oliphant tone was calculated to grate on Victorian sensibility." She adds, "If the public of the mid-sixties had signified enthusiasm for *Miss Marjoribanks,* no doubt she might have continued to produce interesting fiction that satisfied her own critical judgement" (156). When her novels did not sell, Oliphant turned to sensationalism to seduce audiences.

when Lucilla seizes upon her mother's death as an occasion "to have her mourning made *long*, which had been the desire of her heart" (30). Having taken on the sign and signature of womanhood, the daughter is determined to take over her father's household as well and mounts her campaign through the rhetoric of duty. Although her father bests her in this first contest, returning her to school for an additional three years, Lucilla capitalizes on the situation by undertaking a course in political economy, the better to prepare for her reign to come. She has requested the course "to help [her] manage everything" (33), and the narrator remarks that "since the day when she began to read political economy . . . Lucilla had exercised a certain influence upon the school itself" (36). At that point, when she perceives that shared meanings and beliefs form the groundwork of political action, she grasps the larger realm opening up to her and is prepared "for an illustrious and glorious reign at home" (40).

Whereas in Dickens's novels the rhetoric of duty disguised the pursuit of class interests, Oliphant's novels emphasize the way in which it encourages audiences to misrecognize the bourgeois agendas under way. Lucilla has hoarded the clichés of her culture like candy, and she serves them back to a gullible public, arguing "the duty of an only child to devote herself to her father's comfort, and become the sunshine of his life." The narrator's remark—"as so many young persons of her age have been known to become in literature"—pinpoints the conventional ploy that Lucilla will use so effectively (26). To those who challenge her position, she piously and promptly responds that her "only ambition," her "great aim," her "object in life" is to be a "comfort to papa," to "dear papa," to "poor papa." This personal mantra silences her critics, who fail to grasp her staging of the role of dutiful daughter and who understand less perfectly than she does how to manipulate images to one's advantage. Lucilla insinuates her own purposes under the guise of domestic duty, and her bewildered audience capitulates. She leaves in her wake a "mystified" cook, Nancy (who cannot fathom the logic of Lucilla's remark, "I want you to know that the object of my life is to be a comfort to poor papa; and now let us think what we had better have for dinner"); a suspicious beneficiary Barbara Lake ("puzzling to make out how the discovery of a fine contralto, and the possibility of getting up unlimited duets, could further Lucilla in the great aim of her life, which was to be a comfort to her dear papa"), and a bewildered and despondent lover, Tom (who, "like most other people, was utterly incapable of fathoming the grand conception which inspired Miss Marjoribanks. When she told him that it was the object of her life to be a comfort to papa, he believed it to a certain extent" [52, 58, 73]). Lucilla's father briefly resists her rule, but she preempts his place at head of the table and as head of the house the better to minister to his "comfort." Having deftly withdrawn the "reins of state . . . from his unconscious hands" (50), she proceeds from conquest of household to conquest of local society, laying down the rhetoric of duty like paving stones to facilitate her progress.[7]

Miss Marjoribanks, like *Phoebe Junior* to follow, dramatizes the process by which a young woman seizes control of local society through a dexterous manipulation of domestic discursive practices and a clever staging of class and femininity. At the time of Lucilla Marjoribanks's anticipated return to Carlingford, the narrator assures us that "affairs were in an utterly chaotic state" (41). Although Grange Lane "was inhabited . . . by the best families in Carlingford . . . without organisation, what good does it do to have a number of people together?" (42). The narrator adds, "You might have gone over Grange Lane, house by house, finding a great deal of capital material, but without encountering a single individual capable of making anything out of it," nobody capable of "making a harmonious whole out of the scraps and fragments of society" (43). The narrator terms this a "lamentable condition," but "all that was wanting to Carlingford was a master-hand to blend these different elements" (43). Of course, that master hand belongs to Miss Marjoribanks, who "possessed by nature some of the finest qualities of a ruler" (39).

The text's martial metaphors trouble the placid surface of Victorian domestic ideology. Lucilla articulates her goal as "to revolutionise society," and the narrator's rhetoric supports a conception of this heroine as a revolutionary or heroic general, a man for the hour, "the real agent of . . . change" (44): "To be sure, it was not a man this time, but Miss Marjoribanks; but the atmosphere thrilled and trembled to the advent of the new luminary all the same" (44). The phrase "to be sure, it was not a man this time" subtly suggests a gender interchangeability within the category of "real agent of [social] change." The significant point is not that she is a man or a

---

[7] In Chapter 7, I more broadly compare George Eliot with Margaret Oliphant but want to remark here Oliphant's demystification of the concept of feminine duty, so prominent in Eliot's work. Nietzsche (*Portable Nietzsche* 515) mocks Eliot for being, in his words, so typically English—dispensing with God and religion, but not with Duty (the equivalent opiate of the people, to paraphrase Marx). Oliphant gives us "duty" recycled, used to subvert the values it usually supports.

woman but that she is *the* class agent. Lucilla establishes "quarters" and a "base of communication," begins a "campaign," goes on "reconnaissance" missions, takes up "strategic position[s]" (53, 98). The narrator depicts her as "a revolutionary of the highest class," compares her to "great generals" or "accomplished warrior[s]" and applauds the "boldness," the "victorious career," the "consummate ability of the young revolutionary" (100, 53, 54, 67, 68). What are the implications of the narrator's applying words like "bold" to Lucilla's venturing outside of her social class, or characterizing a dinner party as informed by "genius," or locating "a mind made to rule" in her singing only a couple of ballads for the first dinner party, or describing as a "bold coup" the polite dispatch of a young woman who is making a spectacle of herself? Unlike the effect of the mock heroic where the foolish pretensions of a contemporary figure are exposed by being measured against the grandeur of a heroic past, this technique unsettles common assumptions and makes conventional distinctions appear facile. By describing a young girl of nineteen setting out to control local society as if she were a Napoleon or Wellington on the eve of battle, a Danton or Robespierre on the verge of revolution, the narrator links social belief with control of social policy. Miss Marjoribanks does not need weapons; she has a system of signs.

The domestic discursive practices of middle-class Victorian life are exposed as neither socially disinterested nor politically impartial. Lucilla carefully sets the stage for her reign by attending with punctilious exactness to each of those signifying realms through which she will establish control and preeminence in Carlingford: architectural design, dining rituals, dress, and etiquette. First, of course, she must have control of her household and the servants in it. Thus, from the moment of her considerate arrival on the 5:30 train, she is working to conciliate the woman designated as her "prime minister": Nancy, the Marjoribanks' cook and housekeeper. Rather than resent Nancy's authority in the formerly mistressless household, a futile sexual competition, Lucilla graciously consults and so disarms her: "I don't mean to let down your reputation. . . . Now we are two women to manage everything, we ought to do still better" (52). In thus forging an apparent interclass alliance with her cook, Lucilla successfully recruits her talents for larger social conquests. Nancy, who is "totally unprepared for this manner of dethronement . . . gave in." The "young sovereign" subsequently attends to all aspects of the household, enunciating as one of her principles "that things are never rightly done if the lady of the house does not pay proper attention" (92).

The rhetoric of sovereignty that peppers the narrative links local and national politics. It recalls Queen Victoria, who, like Miss Marjoribanks, began her reign in her late teens. The entangled discourses of queenliness and middle-class domestic management that I explored in Chapter 3 find their logical exemplification in Oliphant's novel, where Lucilla, the "queen of Carlingford," orders—in both senses of commands and organizes—the subjects of her realm. Late in the novel, when her father dies and Lucilla goes into mourning, the parallels between England's and Carlingford's queens become even more explicit. The narrator comments on the insurrectionary impulses of Lucilla's subjects, who yearn for liberty from her long-standing sway: "As long as she remained in Grange Lane, even though retired and in crape, the constitutional monarch was still present among her subjects; and nobody could usurp her place or show that utter indifference to her regulations which some revolutionaries had dreamed of. Such an idea would have gone direct in the face of the British Constitution" (421). While ostensibly a humorous allusion to Victoria's prolonged mourning for Albert, the passage also underscores the way a politics of social regulation subtends national and international policies, facilitating class and racial supervision.

Pierre Bourdieu elucidates the connection between political effectiveness and social semiotics: "Politics is the site *par excellence* of symbolic effectiveness, an activity which works through signs capable of producing social entities and, above all, groups" (*Language and Symbolic Power* 249–50). He explains: "Specifically political action is possible because agents, who are part of the social world, have a (more or less adequate) knowledge of this world and because one can act on the social world by acting on their knowledge of this world. . . . More precisely, [political action] aims to make and unmake groups" (127). Household, community, and national management are intertwined agendas as represented by Oliphant. The initial conquests that guarantee control over her household enable Miss Marjoribanks to enact the measures that will bring the entire society under her sway. She evolves a coordinated plan that encompasses the several discursive practices within her sphere. Her grand scheme includes Thursday dinner parties followed by "Evenings," not parties, in the drawing room, at which the appropriate dress for ladies is a "white dress, high." The stipulated apparel signals the pragmatic design of these gatherings. They are not dances, at which a low-cut dress would be appropriate, but social gatherings where Lucilla will consolidate her influence. "The white dress, high, which she had brought in to fashion in Carlingford," becomes a kind of campaign uniform bespeaking sociality over sexuality, her self-interested commitment to social reorganization and her indifference to personal coquetry. Each dimension receives Lucilla's careful attention and proves instrumental to the effect of the whole. The established ritual of Thursday dinners and "Evenings" positions the Marjoribanks household as the social center of Carlingford. And local politics, which answer to the social standing of the leading citizens, come increasingly under Lucilla's sway. The compliment of Mr. Cavendish after her first successful Evening anticipates the greatness to come: "As for your conception of social politics, it is masterly. . . . Heaven be praised! . . . I think you ought to be Prime Minister" (111). The "social politics" dramatized here by Margaret Oliphant are seldom represented in the Victorian novel and nowhere else so explicitly. But this representation provides a bridge we have been missing between social upheavals that marked the beginning of the century and a consolidated image of the genteel middle class that had emerged by mid-century.

Miss Marjoribanks works as a novel through a careful accumulation of domestic detail that is made to yield its larger social and political implications. For example, the strategic care with which Lucilla plans meals extends to the design of the drawing room, the scene of some of her most important campaigns. She organizes it in such a way that it both represents her, that is, reminds guests of their benefactor, and enables her to assemble or segregate groups. When Lucilla initially surveys the "big, dull, faded, respectable drawing-room," it strikes her as a "waste and howling wilderness" (48). The narrator's humorous exaggeration underscores the pivotal function of the ladies' drawing room in establishing social order in a chaotic, competitive world. She superintends the choice and placement of each piece of furniture, solemnly assuring her family that "as for furniture and things, they matter a great deal, I assure you, to people's happiness" (92). And she is exasperated to find her cousin proposing marriage to her at the very moment her presence is wanted in the drawing room to supervise the renovations. In answer to his complaints that she is "trifling" with him, she responds, "It is you who are trifling . . . especially when you know I have really something of importance to do" (94).

In this humorous encounter between Miss Marjoribanks and a young suitor, Oliphant revises the marriage plot that dominated the nineteenth-century novel. Uninterested in marriage, her protagonist directs her substantial talents toward a career as Carlingford's social general. When narrow-minded individuals disparage Lucilla's efforts, the narrator, half in fun, half in earnest, remarks that "this public-spirited young woman . . . only shared the fate of all the great benefactors of the world" (104). For Oliphant *is* having good fun in representing this young revolutionary who refuses to accede to convention and calmly defeats social expectations, not only those of Carlingford but those of unsuspecting readers who have been fed a steady diet of passive angels timorously awaiting a lover's call.

The romance plot is not the only victim sacrificed here; so, too is the Victorian ingenue, the performance of which role is only one in Miss Marjoribanks's arsenal of strategic impersonations. This performance, like that of the dutiful daughter, is staged to consolidate her power. On two major occasions she brings it out of her repertoire. First, early in her social reorganization, she faces a challenge to her authority from the local divine, Reverend Bury, who has decided she is too young and inexperienced to have governance of her father's house. He proposes to encumber her with a matron and chaperone in the person of an impecunious widow, Mrs. Mortimer. Lucilla, of course, does not intend to suffer any abridgment of her powers and cleverly thwarts the rector's plan through her own manipulation of codes of etiquette. She quickly sizes up her adversary and his intention and unleashes upon him, as she will later upon the archdeacon, her impersonation of the ingenue. Pretending to misunderstand his intention of providing her with a chaperone, she imputes to him the indelicate intention of proposing Mrs. Mortimer as wife for her father. Then, "staging" her innocence to discomfit him, she asks "with a look of artless surprise," "Do you mean you have found some one for him to marry?" (86). She does not hesitate "as a weaker woman might have done, out of consideration for anybody's feelings" (86). Fully into her role, she "kept up the air of amazement and consternation," "bending her earnest gaze on Mr Bury's face" to add, "It is very dreadful for me that am so young to go against *you* . . . but if it is *that*, I cannot be expected to take any part in it—it would not be natural" (86). The category of the "natural" in Oliphant's novels is often appropriated by her heroines as part of the feminine drama they are staging, so that the natural becomes simply what is conventionally familiar and expected. The rector, "a man caught in a trap," blushes "to the roots of his gray hair" while the poor embarrassed widow faints. Although Lucilla regrets the need to hurt Mrs. Mortimer, she pragmatically accepts that "there are cases in which it is absolutely necessary to have a victim" (86). She, of course, is determined never to play the victim.

Luce Irigaray's concept of mimicry helps to explain the effect of those scenes in which Lucilla stages her impersonation of the ingenue. Irigaray says that one "must assume the feminine role deliberately. Which means already to convert a form of subordination into an affirmation, and thus to begin to thwart it. . . . To play with mimesis is thus, for a woman, to try to recover the place of her exploitation by discourse, without allowing herself to be simply reduced to it" (*This Sex* 76). Lucilla Marjoribanks's imitation of the ingenue is represented as sufficiently stylized that the men are not only duped but also uneasily aware that they have been duped, that is, that they are forced to take on their roles in her performance; Mr. Bury is caught in "this little *entr'acte*, which was not in his programme" (87). The net effect is precisely what Irigaray postulates: "to make 'visible' . . . what was supposed to remain invisible" (76). Lucilla's audiences recognize both the performance and the role being imitated. But the effect of her mimicry is not the one Irigaray seeks—destruction of the discursive mechanism. In part, because the men are forced to play to the performance, the image can continue to circulate in discourse. The parody, however, is not simply recuperated because it has been productive of new power alignments in the novel and of heightened awareness both in the textual audience and in the readerly audience that gender roles are performed rather than "natural." This destabilization of gender opens to view the multiple discourses through which subjectivity is constructed.

Oliphant's second representation of Lucilla performing the ingenue stresses larger political and personal stakes. The single greatest beneficiary of Lucilla's efforts is a man whose intelligence and talents seem to destine him for Parliament. This is, after all, a novel about wielding political power through shaping social organization. Lucilla's quick discernment has informed her that this Mr. Cavendish, who early identified her talents as those proper to a Prime Minister, will produce a sound return on her investment in him. Guilty of certain indiscretions in the past, Mr. Cavendish faces exposure. In her first great social work, Lucilla dramatically rescues him and secures as well the happiness of several other individuals implicated in his fate. Mr. Cavendish's crimes are venial ones, but they threaten to ruin him socially, to jeopardize his sister's relationship to her husband, and to sever forever a couple in love. The happiness of many lives is threatened by his exposure as a social pretender, a humble Mr. Kavan who has appropriated the Cavendish name and the prestige of that moniker when he inherited a large fortune. Lucilla's authority also hangs in the balance; that she might have countenanced an "adventurer" in "best society" would ""destroy public confidence for ever in the social leaders" (172, 171). Further, such a revelation would damage Lucilla's "work itself . . . of turning the chaotic elements of society in Carlingford into one grand unity," a work "which was progressing in the face of all kinds of social difficulties" (176).

Oliphant's representation of Lucilla Marjoribanks as a person whose own aims are deeply entangled with her idea of the general good of society underscores not simply Lucilla's vanity but rather the way domestic practices are implicated in the community's political life. That is, Lucilla is not simply a Rosamond Vincy manqué for whom the "best" is that which suits her the best. What suits Miss Marjoribanks is that which ensures the perpetuation of her own privilege and that of others like her, the gentrified middle class. Mr. Cavendish must be saved because he is a man of talent, who will solidify the middle-class power base in his town and his country. Social consensus has already decreed him the logical successor to Parliament when the current aged MP dies. The man who waits to denounce him, Archdeacon Beverley, believes that the young woman he once loved—the very Mrs. Mortimer who has already figured prominently in Lucilla's schemes—has been cheated out of her inheritance by Cavendish; his anger over the lady's refusal to prosecute or complain has led to a breach between them. At the same time, Mr. Cavendish's sister has married into Carlingford society on the force of their reputed relations. Her husband, Mr. Woodburn, undeceived about her origins, would possess "a cruel and overwhelming power over her . . . that he was not at all too generous or delicate to make use of" (305). The narrator heightens the sense of the threat facing Mrs. Woodburn with a vivid metaphor: "In such a case she would be bound to the rock, like a kind of hapless Andromeda, to be pecked at by all the birds and blown at by all the winds, not to speak of the devouring monster from whom no hero could ever deliver her" (305). The metaphor, which in another context might be overblown and melodramatic, here feeds into a system of images that describe loss of caste as, what it after all is represented to be, a destruction of identity or a loss of life.[8]

[8] Readers will recall that even that brave radical Jane Eyre, when invited by Mr. Lloyd to consider leaving the tortures at Gateshead to take up residence with some of her poorer relatives, responds negatively: "I could not see how poor people had the means of being kind; and then to learn to speak like them, to adopt their manners, to be uneducated, to grow up like one of the poor women I saw sometimes nursing their children or washing their clothes at the cottage doors of the village of Gateshead: no, I was not heroic enough to purchase liberty at the price of caste" (20).

The novel, then, is constructed to highlight the consolidation of middle-class interests in Carlingford. Not only will Mr. Cavendish and his sister suffer from exposure, but the cruelty of such an act will drive a permanent wedge between Mr. Beverley and Mrs. Mortimer. His arrogant insistence upon redress in a case where she claims she had no expectations and no resentment early led to their separation. Lucilla Marjoribanks alone possesses the power to arrest the exposure of Mr. Cavendish and heal the breach between the alienated lovers, and she accomplishes these ends, as she has earlier goals, through a clever mimicry of the ingenue. Lucilla sets the stage for a confrontation at her social forum, the Thursday evening dinner and gathering, to which she also explicitly invites both Mr. Cavendish and his adversary, Mr. Beverley, as well as Mrs. Woodburn and Mrs. Mortimer. From the beginning, Lucilla has recognized that "if she but lost her head for a moment and lost command of affairs, everything might have been lost" (167–68). She acknowledges that she had "never yet had any piece of social business on so important a scale to manage" (228), but the narrator points out that the archdeacon "did not know whom he had to deal with, nor that he was not the first man whom Miss Marjoribanks had reduced to his proper place" (234). Lucilla writes to Cavendish to "have full confidence in me and a little in yourself" (288). As Lucilla prepares for battle, the narrator portrays her as "looking to the joints of her harness, and feeling the edge of her weapons" (271). She is "on the eve of a crisis which would be the greatest failure or the greatest success of her public life" (304). Of course, hers is a battle of signifiers and control over social meanings. When the "moment of trial" arrives during her dinner party, Lucilla takes command, fixing her eye "upon the Archdeacon's face," ready for the instant he perceives "his favourite adventurer" among the dinner guests, "surrounded by every kind of regard and consideration, full in the light of the lamp" (307). At that second, "Lucilla [rises] to the height of the position" and forestalls his denunciation with soup and social confidences. With "pretty pause[s]" and "confiding eyes," in a "flutter of happy confusion," she intimates the existence of an engagement between herself and Mr. Cavendish. "She laughed as she spoke, a kind of laugh which is only appropriate to one subject, and which is as good, any day, as a confession; and the flush was so obliging as to return at that moment to her ingenuous countenance." Lucilla enhances her performance by "clasp[ing] her hands together, just for a moment . . . with an eloquent meaning which it was impossible to mistake" (308). The archdeacon, unsure "whether it was true—or whether he was being made a fool of more completely than ever man before was" is as fully trapped by the performance as the Reverend Bury was before him (308). He is forced to swallow his pride and his dinner with chagrin: "It was a terrible position for the Broad-Churchman. After such a tacit confession he could not spring from his seat and hurl the impostor out of the room, as in the first place he had a mind to do. . . . He could not publicly expose the man who had just received this mark of confidence from his young hostess, who knew everything" (308–9). He finds himself so completely checked that he experiences "one of the greatest trials of Christian patience and fortitude which the Archdeacon, who was not great, as he himself would have said, in the passive virtues, had undergone in all the course of his life" (309).

The kinds of control that come readily to Lucilla through manipulation of discursive practices evade the men, who never fully grasp these practices and their complex possibilities. The archdeacon only feels "the tables altogether turned upon him, and [is] confounded, and [does] not know what it could mean" (310). He has not conjured with the "restraints of society": "he dared not follow his natural impulses, nor even do what he felt to be his duty, for fear of Miss Marjoribanks" (312). He expostulates with "concealed ferocity" on women: "And these are the creatures made in the image of God! . . . the future wives and mothers of England. It is enough to make the devils laugh and the angels weep!" (313). But he is powerless to do more because he is incapable of grasping the play of signifiers that informs Lucilla's strategies. He is stuck, fulminating on women's innate evil and invoking conventional gender categories that ensure that Lucilla, a more sophisticated semiotician, will continue to defeat him. When he finally encounters Mr. Cavendish, his anger is rapidly defused, and he finds himself sufficiently confused by the presence of pretty Mrs. Mortimer (who has been instructed how to dress for the evening by Lucilla) that he ends up proposing to her once again. And, naturally, Lucilla "made the arrangements for Mrs. Mortimer's marriage, and took charge of everything" (322). All of Carlingford acknowledges that "it was owing to her goodness that the widow had been taken care of and provided for, and saved up for the Archdeacon" (322). But Lucilla, who has controlled everything, "felt an instinctive certainty in her mind that *now* Mr Beverley would never be bishop of Carlingford" (323). When Lucilla herself had earlier contemplated marrying Archdeacon Beverley, she did so in the expectation that *his* possible eminence as bishop of Carlingford would give appropriate scope for *her* social and political schemes. This "instinctive certainty" that no such fate now awaits him has force because it belongs to the person, Lucilla Marjoribanks, who will, in fact, decide if Carlingford should become a bishopric and, if so, who should be installed as bishop.

The notion of staged performances I have engaged here not only echoes mimicry as defined by Irigaray but also resonates with ideas developed by Judith Butler in *Gender Trouble* and her more recent *Bodies That Matter*. Butler usefully distinguishes between this kind of staged gender performance and a more subtle notion of "performativity," which she both links to and distinguishes from the process by which subjects are constructed and bodies materialized. Butler wants to correct any previous implications from *Gender Trouble* that performativity might be understood "as a singular or deliberate 'act,'" by which "a subject brings into being what she/he names" (*Bodies* 2), in short, that "one woke in the morning, perused the closet . . . for the gender of choice, donned that gender for the day, and then restored the gender to its place at night" (x). In *Bodies That Matter*, Butler clarifies performativity as "the reiterative power of discourse to produce the phenomena that it regulates and contains" (2). She claims that "the 'performative' dimension of construction is precisely the forced reiteration of norms" (94). Butler pointedly insists that although "'performance' is not a simple act," rather a "ritualized production," it is *not* determined fully in advance (95).[9] As if proleptically to exemplify this concept, Oliphant's text emphasizes the productive stylization of Lucilla Marjoribanks's normative behavior. With no irony whatsoever, Lucilla announces, "I always make it a point to give in to the prejudices of society. That is how I have always been so successful" (72). She is utterly humorless and succeeds precisely because she takes herself so *seriously*, because she so fully inhabits convention or, rather, is so fully inhabited by it. She confesses that she has "never . . . had a sense of humor" and is constantly misunderstood by her father, who reads a clever and deliberate subversion in her behavior. Lucilla's seriousness has the effect of naturalizing the very actedness of her roles. And her repeated citations of such norms as female duty destabilize them precisely because no citation or repetition of a norm can ever be identical;

---

[9] Butler works through Lacanian psychoanalysis to theorize this concept of production as constituted but not fully determined. She also brings to bear Foucault's understanding of the process of signification: "A prohibitive law, by underscoring a given practice in discourse, produces the occasion for a public contest that may inadvertantly enable, refigure, and proliferate the very social phenomenon it seeks to restrict" (Butler 109). Finally, she incorporates Jacques Derrida's work on citationality. In *Limited, Inc.*, Derrida explains that no citation or repetition of the norm is ever identical; there is always a difference.

there is always a difference. Lucilla's subversion depends, then, not on her own intention but on this enabling power of the normative, a process intensified by the subject's articulation through conflicting class and gender positions. These signifiers converge, Butler theorizes, at a "crossroads that is not a subject, but, rather, the unfulfillable demand to rework convergent signifiers in and through each other," enacting a destabilization that facilitates resignification (117). In the process, manifestations of the late Victorian "new woman" begin to emerge.

It is this same fidelity to a world of signs that allows Oliphant to depict a female sociosexual desire in which women often use men to cement class bonds, a subversion of the usual novelistic patterning of male homosocial desire, or male trafficking in women to solidify male bonds, identified by Eve Sedgwick in *Between Men*. The novel seems to epitomize this pattern in Lucilla's reflection that "to be sure the men did not even find out what it was that awoke the ladies' attention; but then, in delicate matters of social politics, one never expects to be understood by *them*" (122). Oliphant's text presents Miss Marjoribanks's life in two phases, or "fyttes," the first dramatizing "the course of organising society," the second depicting her struggles ten years later "with nearly the entire social organisation of Carlingford depending upon her" (338). Both phases are marked by Lucilla's consolidation of power through control of social semiotics and clever manipulation of sociosexual bonds. If she had initially thought she might use Archdeacon Beverley and a possible bishopric as a route to heightened influence, she ultimately turns to parliamentary elections, ensuring the election of "her man," Mr. Ashburton, to the House of Commons, just as certainly as she determines Mr. Cavendish's defeat.

In the process Oliphant dramatizes more forcibly the play of signs, the entanglement of social and political practices, and the articulation of sociosexual desire. Lucilla enters the election as de facto manager of Mr. Ashburton's campaign. As Margaret Oliphant realized long before the age of television, successful electioneering consists of image management. While the other candidates in the field write speeches arguing fine points of public policy, Miss Marjoribanks persuades Mr. Ashburton to tear up his position papers and to rely on images and recognizable tokens. She has the instincts of a politician, telling her candidate not to worry about "opinions": "the thing was to have a good *man*" (346). She announces forthrightly, "Mr. Ashburton, it is you who must be the man" (345). She cautions him, "What does it matter about opinions? . . . Don't go and make speeches about opinions. If you begin with that, there is no end to it. . . . But if you just say distinctly that you are the best man—" (346). Mr. Ashburton's first impulse is to dismiss Lucilla as "only an ignorant woman," but as she continues arguing, the "meaning of his fair adviser, as he called her, began to dawn" upon him. "He began to prick up his mental ears, so to speak, and see that it was not womanish ignorance, but an actual suggestion. For, after all, so long as he was the Man for Carlingford, all the rest was of little importance" (347). Lucilla supplements his political identity as "the best man" with an arresting image—a cockade of the colors she has made her own in Carlingford. The colors, of course, work through association, allowing him to draw upon her power in Carlingford. She completes her election strategy with a campaign organization that targets influential voters and plays on her own social ties with key women. Although Ashburton first greets her suggestions with an "explosion of amusement," thinking "what a fool she was, or what a fool he was to think of taking a woman into his counsels," he is quickly persuaded that "Miss Marjoribanks was very clever" (348–49). Dr. Marjoribanks's own regret at this time, his feeling of "how great a loss it was to society and to herself that Lucilla was not 'the boy,'" simply stands as another testimony to her political brilliance (400).

But the text itself does not collude in this retrospective sexual nostalgia; to think in this way is to afford gender singular primacy in the construction of subjectivity, a position Oliphant has complicated throughout. The narrator remarks, "She might have gone into Parliament herself had there been no disqualification of sex," a comment that seemingly invites us to indulge in the traditional lament that women do not have the opportunities men have (394). The text, however, subverts that ideological move to sharpen its focus on the way strategies of social management effectively produce political control. The only nostalgia Lucilla feels is class-based not gender-based, the regret that she lacks the entrepreneurial freedom of pursuing a trade available to lower-class women and men.[10] When her father dies and her capable maidservant proposes leaving her to set up business innkeeping, Lucilla experiences a spasm of envy, recognizing that she "would have been very glad if she could have taken a little business too" (425). She reflects that "it was life the housemaid was about to enter on—active life of her own, with an object

[10] Readers of Austen's *Pride and Prejudice* will recall the horror with which the Bingley sisters remark that Elizabeth and Jane's uncle, Mr. Gardiner, is in trade and lives within sight of his warehouses.

and meaning" (426). But these reflections arise only at an ebb in Miss Marjoribanks's full life. She simply has had to make her mark in middle-class terms rather than in trade. Her business recalls that of a politician moving bills through Parliament or a prominent official in a colonial administration at the height of the empire.

Social management is at the heart of Oliphant's novel. No one knows better than Miss Marjoribanks how to create a semblance of unity out of disparate class elements, how to "make and unmake groups," in Bourdieu's definition of political action. And no one understands better the difference between the vulgar and the refined and how to police the borders between them, how to guarantee that the images that collect around individuals serve to keep them in their "place." This ability is manifested when Lucilla resourcefully enlists the talents of Barbara Lake, daughter of the drawing master in Carlingford, for her Thursday Evenings; Barbara possesses the contralto that suits perfectly with her own soprano and so electrifies the assembly. But Lucilla does not suffer vulgar Barbara Lake to participate in the society as an equal. When Barbara retaliates for Lucilla's condescension and seduces Mr. Cavendish, who has been paying marked attentions to the queen of Carlingford, Miss Marjoribanks simply drops them both into social purgatory. Although Miss Marjoribanks can save Mr. Cavendish from Archdeacon Beverley, she finally cannot rescue him from himself, and she relinquishes him with the arrogant regret that "no fate higher than Barbara was possible for the unfortunate man" who has compromised both himself and her (296). Lucilla ultimately colludes in the judgment of Grange Lane that Barbara Lake from Grove Street is "not even a lady," that she is a "vulgar antagonist" (128, 132). After Mr. Cavendish's indiscretions with the stormy contralto, Miss Marjoribanks "was too well aware of her duty to her friends, and to her position in society, to have given her consent to his marriage with anybody's daughter in Grange Lane" (297). Mr. Cavendish is powerless against her judgment.

This sequence of events, like the election, vividly enacts female sociosexual desire, in which interfemale social allegiances work to protect middle-class interests and men tend to become pawns manipulated by women like Lucilla to consolidate bourgeois power. Mr. Cavendish's indiscretions with Barbara ultimately elicit Miss Marjoribanks's profound regret that "such a man, who had been capable of appreciating her self, . . . having known her . . . should decline upon Barbara!" "Decline upon" rather than "incline to": the difference speaks volumes. In the attraction he feels for Barbara,

Cavendish finally betrays his lower-middle-class origins, elucidating how desire comes to be articulated within particular class formations. It is Barbara's similarly class-inscribed body—with its heaving bosom and flushing cheeks, the site of violent moods and jealous rages, impetuous whims and vindictive triumphs—that seduces him instead of Lucilla's more placid surface, which testifies to her genteel refinement. Although Mr. Cavendish flees Carlingford and the attraction of Barbara Lake, he cannot escape the class inscriptions of his masculinity and the ultimate exposure of his body's social grossness. Ten years' time finds his male body "inconceivably gone off" (389), the fate Lucilla has always anticipated for her female body at twenty-nine. Constructed as she is, however, through genteel class discourses, she is, if anything, "rather better looking than otherwise"; even to Mr. Cavendish's critical eye, she "absolutely had not gone off" (392). He attributes her undiminished bloom to a "feminine incapacity for going too far," an amusing ascription of femininity to the class-inflected body. In contrast, Lucilla remarks of Mr. Cavendish that "the outlines of his fine figure had changed considerably, and his face was a little red, and he had the look of a man whose circumstances, spiritual and temporal, would not quite bear a rigid examination" (385). His changes echo Barbara Lake's: "She had expanded all over. . . . Her eyes were blacker and more brilliant in a way, but they were eyes which owned an indescribable amount of usage; and her cheeks, too, wore the deep roses of old, deepened and fixed by wear and tear" (443). In a telling scene of self-recognition, a mirror confirmation of his own identity, Mr. Cavendish finds himself "somehow consoled and justified" in regarding Barbara: "[She] *had* gone off, like himself. . . . She, too, had been in the wars, and had not come out scathless" (443–44). The sexual encodings of class intensify. Seeing Barbara again, Mr. Cavendish finds himself poised between Pleasure, which "wooed him on one side, while Duty, with still small voice, called him at the other" (442). He chooses, of course, Barbara and Pleasure. This is how the bourgeoisie encodes the class-inflection of sexuality: to be seduced by Barbara's body represents attraction to indulgent pleasure, by Lucilla's, the capacity for disciplined duty. The narrative colludes throughout in this kind of social evaluation and approval of a socio-sexual trafficking that reinforces the sociopolitical bonds.

This is a narrative in which class and gender are so inextricably involved in each other's formation that it becomes impossible to theorize the terms separately. Oliphant deepens the impact by representing not only the lower middle class, from which Barbara Lake is drawn, but also the poor. The latter have only a marginal presence in the novel, one that underscores their need for social supervision and so justifies the intervention of the managerial woman. Early in her Carlingford career, Lucilla encounters a beggar with her six children in Grange Lane, and she refuses her money "for that was contrary to those principles of political economy which she had studied." She did, however, "[stop] and [ask] her name, and where she lived, and promised to inquire into her case. 'If you are honest and want to work, I will try to find you something to do'" (75). The six children are a figuration for the woman's excessive indulgence in "pleasure" and her corollary disinclination to work as "duty." The narrator's comment that the offer of employment "was a threat appalling enough to keep her free from any further molestation" (75) shares in the middle-class prejudice that informs Lucilla's own response. Somebody has to manage the poor, and Lucilla comfortably designates herself as that person: "The poor . . . could not help being the better for what one did for them. They might continue to be as stupid as ever, and ungrateful, and all that; but if they were warm and comfortable, instead of cold and hungry, it would always make a difference" (485). Lucilla's arrogant complacency makes unclear the object of the narrator's irony: "What would be the good of a spirit full of boundless activity and benevolent impulses if there was nobody to help?—what would be the use of self-devotion if the race in general stood in no need of charitable ministrations? Lucilla had been of use to her fellow-creatures all her life; and though she was about to relinquish one branch of usefulness, that was not to say that she should be prevented from entering into another" (488).

Miss Marjoribanks will be "useful" within an economy that allows her to trade unsentimentally in other lives to consolidate her material and social capital and that of the middle class generally. Her marriage to her cousin Tom at the novel's conclusion spells not a diminishment of her social power but its increase and new direction. She persuades him to purchase Marchbank, a country estate coveted by her father, who had "explained to the ignorant that this was the correct pronunciation of his own name" (486). The breathtaking logic arrests Tom at once; he would be "Marjoribanks of Marchbank." For Lucilla, the position answers well. She will remain Lucilla Marjoribanks, and she will find a new career in reorganizing the community attached to Marchbank, "where every kind of village nuisance was to be found" (488). Lucilla has been disappointed by the ingratitude of Carlingford society for her efforts. At the conclusion of the novel, the managerial skills honed in Grange Lane will be imported to the country, where Lucilla will bypass questions of gratitude and ingratitude. She complacently reiterates her new extended mantra: "[The poor] may be as stupid and ungrateful as they like . . . but to be warm and comfortable instead of cold and hungry always makes a difference" (488). And to make a difference lies at the heart of Lucilla's endeavors. She anticipates with "the liveliest satisfaction" all "the disorder and disarray of the Marchbank village. Her fingers itched to be at it—to set all the crooked things straight, and clean away the rubbish, and set everything, as she said, on a sound foundation" (488). After imposing this middle-class regime locally, Lucilla anticipates a larger realm for her talents. She recalls that, although she has rejected the Member for Carlingford, "there are Members for counties too"; the thought "threw a gleam of light over the new world of ambition and progress which was opened to Lucilla's far-seeing vision" (493). After ten years in Marchbank, having honed her ability to forge groups and consensus, she will no doubt be prepared to take her place on the national scene. With her experience in constructing social meanings, manipulating the sociosexual traffic, and managing the middle and working classes, she will be prepared to make a substantial contribution to government.

Phoebe Junior's Performance of Middle-Class Ladyhood

Phoebe Beecham, the protagonist of Oliphant's *Phoebe Junior*, resembles her predecessor Lucilla Marjoribanks in her refined body and her aspirations after a career, defined as social influence. Like Lucilla, Phoebe has no sentimentality about dashing and handsome young suitors; as in *Miss Marjoribanks*, men serve to consolidate the protagonist's cultural currency. Phoebe readily relinquishes her "true lover"; although the young man is "very tender in his reverential homage, very romantic, a true lover," he is "not the kind of man who wants a wife or wants a clever companion to amuse him, and save him the expense of a coach, and be his to refer to in everything" (272). She chooses, instead, a man who is "not very wise, nor a man to be enthusiastic about" because he "would be a career" to her (234). The narrator bluntly states: "She did not think of it humbly like this, but with a big capital—a Career. Yes: she could put him into parliament, and keep him there. She could thrust him forward (she believed) to the front of affairs. He would be as good as a profession, a position, a great work for Phoebe" (234). This household goddess, like Lucilla Marjoribanks, has more of the Dives than the divine about her, more of the manager than *mon anges*. However, she dismisses wealth in its "superficial aspect as something meaningless and vulgar"; she accepts it only "in its higher aspect as an almost necessary condition of influence" (234). What attracts her irresistibly are "all the possibilities of future power," as they are inscribed on certain male bodies. The narrator asks, "Who can say that she was not as romantic as any girl of twenty could be? Only her romance took an unusual form" (234).[11]

The demystification of the angel and romance is accompanied by a general questioning of "nature" as a grounding for class and gender distinctions. Phoebe's romance of a Career culminates the work of three generations in their rise from the vulgarity of lower-middle-class shopkeeping to the gentility of upper-middle-class life. The title of the novel, *Phoebe Junior*, the moniker given the protagonist by her shopkeeping grandfather, expresses both the vulgarity of his diction in so designating her—a vulgarity she has transcended—and the novel's engagement of generations as well as of generational change. Phoebe Senior, the mother, provides the pivot between Grandfather and Grandmother Tozer and daughter, Phoebe Junior.

Women manage their family's class elevations in the same way that they manage everything else in the social world. The first Phoebe, daughter of shopkeepers, has early achieved a coup in marrying the minister of the dissenting congregation in Carlingford, Henry Beecham. The "certain something attached to the position of a clerical caste" allows the daughter of a butterman to snub her former friends, having "advanced over them to the honours and glories inalienable from the position of minister's wife." She quickly consolidates her new prestige by paying a visit to the Miss Hemmingses and shaking hands with the doctor's wife. Possessed of a "courage which developed from the moment of her marriage," this first Phoebe urges her husband to "find another sphere for your talents." She counsels him to seek a chapel in the north: "A different class of society, and better altogether. These Pigeons and Browns, and people are not the sort of society for you." He accedes to her suggestions, and soon Mrs. Phoebe finds herself "in much finer society, and [grows] rapidly in importance and in ideas." Mr. Beecham's own talent—"an unbounded wealth of phraseology"—coupled with

---

[11] Critics are less generous with *Phoebe Junior* than they are with *Miss Marjoribanks*. Leavis calls it a "tired novel" (144), and Merryn Williams briefly remarks that the novel "seems to me not completely successful. It is clever and amusing but has no central theme" (85–86). This generally dismissive tone can be only partially explained by the melodrama of the forgery plot. I suggest that class issues are emphasized in such a way that the protagonist seems not merely competent but callous.

her social skills facilitate their rise to ever more prestigious and wealthy congregations, until they achieve their "final apotheosis in a handsome chapel near Regent's Park," London, where they "were not above the amiable weakness of making it known that their house was in a line with that of Lady Cecilia Burleigh" (3, 5).

Whereas *Miss Marjoribanks* depicted the heroine's staged performance of various stereotypical roles, this novel emphasizes image management and the process by which individuals negotiate their class relationships with others. It also reveals the kind of performativity that underlies the overall narrative of Lucilla's rise: What Butler calls the "reiterative power of discourse to produce the phenomena that it regulates and contains" (*Bodies That Matter* 2).

The text remains quite clear about Mrs. Phoebe's role in the initial familial social elevation, pointing to it at first and emphasizing it at last. The effect of the sudden rise is so dizzying that the young bride needs command of all her faculties so as not to betray her shopkeeping origins and to master the signifying practices of each new rank: "Her sudden introduction to 'circles' which Mrs. Pigeon had never entered, and to houses at the area-door of which Mr. Brown, the dairyman, would have humbly waited, would have turned the young woman's head, had she not felt the overpowering necessity of keeping that organ as steady as possible, to help her to hold her position in the new world. Phoebe was a girl of spirit, and though her head went round and round, and everything felt confused about her, she did manage desperately to hold her own and to avoid committing herself" (6–7). The grandparents, who have "remained stationary," present a problem to the Beechams, inasmuch as the couple cannot snub their own relatives. But they have cleverly managed the class difficulty by escaping visits to Carlingford, where the vulgarity of the shop is unavoidable. They had "appointed meetings at the sea-side," where "Mr. Tozer, who was only a butterman at Carlingford, presented all the appearance of an old Dissenting minister out of it" (34). Through this process of image management, the children have been "trained in affectionate acquaintance with their grandparents" without being shocked by the shop.

The novel has set itself the explicit challenge of negotiating between familial claims and class aspirations, the "natural" versus the "constructed" social self. When the novel opens, Grandmother Tozer is ill and the Beechams, unwilling to lose inheritance of their share of the fortune amassed in the shop, need a delegate in Carlingford to represent their interests against the claims of Tom and "Mrs. Tom" Tozer, Phoebe's brother and his grasping wife, who are now running the business. Phoebe Junior volunteers and, although Mr. and Mrs. Beecham worry that their daughter will be distressed by the manners of her relations, they congratulate themselves that "Phoebe could manage them if any one could" (36). Phoebe emboldens herself by imagining she is "something like a Joan of Arc . . . going among barbarians" (38). The hyperbolic comparison both amuses and instructs the reader; familial blood is not thicker than the waters of social custom. Phoebe has more in common with utter strangers who share her manners, dress, and conventions of etiquette than she does with her own grandparents. Mr. and Mrs. Beecham, Phoebe's parents, have in fact elevated their daughter even above themselves. She has had an education unavailable to them and companions far superior to their own early acquaintances. The text thus makes us acutely aware of the mother's own inferiority to the daughter in manners and breeding. Her diction is less genteel: she refers to her husband as "Henery" and to herself as "more refined like" than her former Carlingford friends (32, 35). Mrs. Beecham also lacks her daughter's exquisite taste in dress, and Phoebe regrets her mother's penchant for bright colors that make her look "so much pinker and fatter than was needful" (337). Finally, Mrs. Beecham cannot escape the vulgarity of triumph in sending to Carlingford a daughter so clearly superior to her own former acquaintances. When Phoebe discerns her mother's intention that "she was to be made a show of to all the connection as a specimen of what the Tozer blood could come to," she feels mortified and regrets that "Mamma meant it too!" (91). And, finally, the parents' pride in their daughter's resourcefulness—"Phoebe might be safely trusted to take care of herself anywhere"—betrays their shopkeeping origins, as they read their daughter's body through petit-bourgeois rather than genteel-bourgeois values. The narrator ironically remarks that in the parents' "expression of their pride . . . the observant reader may see a proof of their own origin from the humbler classes. They would probably have prided themselves on her timidity and helplessness had they been a little better born" (80).

The text presents many similar challenges in "reading" behavior for its class markings. The "observant reader," in fact, undergoes instruction in the signs and signifiers of class, and the text works on us so that we increasingly appreciate the way an individual's identity is constituted or performed through these markers. For example, the confrontation between grandparents Tozer and granddaughter Phoebe illustrates the social construction of identity through a series of discursive practices. Dress is, of course, a central one. In Chapter 2, I mentioned a crucial episode in Oliphant's novel when Phoebe, in her garb as an elegant lady, accompanies her shopkeeping grandfather home. At another point, Mrs. Sam Hurst sees Phoebe, "a young lady, in appearance . . . nicely dressed, nothing vulgar or showy," with her grandmother, who looks "like an old washerwoman" (97–98). Phoebe attends punctiliously to her costume because she recognizes that the "question of dress was not a mere frivolity" (19). She complacently remarks, "I have never undervalued dress . . . as some girls do; I think it is a very important social influence" (75). The measure of that influence may be taken in Phoebe's visit to Carlingford.

As she anticipates seeing her grandparents, Phoebe consoles herself that "their ways of thinking, perhaps . . . are not those which I have been used to . . . but . . . I am myself whatever happens" (75). She adds, "Even if poor dear grandmamma's habits are not refined . . . that does not make me unrefined. A lady must always be a lady wherever she is" (75). Her thoughts and conversation are subsequently punctuated with similar reflections: her "consoling certainty that she could not suffer from association with her humble relations," her belief that "whoever saw her must do her justice," her conviction that "she would be herself, whatever happened" (85). The self she will be, however, is concretized in her dress and manner as a lady. When another young lady objects to Mrs. Hurst's categorizing and valuing Phoebe as a "twenty-guineas dress," she receives the sharp rebuke: "I can't know much about her moral qualities, can I?" (98). The answer is both no and yes. Her dress bespeaks class, which brings with it a whole constellation of values. When Phoebe dresses the part, she acts the part; she *is* the part. Her strict attention to dress wins her the attention of a wealthy young man, who falls "a hopeless victim to her fascinations" (20). And even though that young man early speaks of the "social suicide" in marrying someone like Phoebe with so small a fortune and so poor a lineage, in the course of the novel he learns his own lesson in the incalculable value of a woman so fully enabled by genteel society's discursive practices.

The signifiers of class prescribe a whole range of beliefs, behaviors, and relationships that eclipse consanguineous ties. Phoebe's appearance as a lady provokes poignantly humorous moments when she greets her grandfather in Carlingford and realizes that they must both fight against their mutual inscription within class behaviors and attitudes. She has to struggle to overcome her disgust for him while he is "half-frightened" by her. As the social superior, she, the child, has to initiate the conduct that will put them, ostensibly, on familial grounds. When Phoebe first sees her grandfather from the train window, she holds back for a moment "to overcome the shock": "He was not even like an old Dissenting minister, which had been her childish notion of him," the product of her parents' image management. What he appears to be now constitutes his "reality" for Phoebe and the reader: "He looked neither more nor less than what he was, an old shopkeeper, very decent and respectable, but a little shabby and greasy, like the men whose weekly bills she had been accustomed to pay for her mother" (83). In an instant, Phoebe understands that he "would call her 'Ma'am,' if she went up to him, and think her one of the quality" (83). To forestall this inappropriate response to a granddaughter, Phoebe alights from the train and calls out "Grandpapa!" before he can recognize her. Even so, he sustains a palpable shock: "He knew that his daughter had made great strides in social elevation, and that her children, when he had seen them last, had been quite like 'gentlefolk's children,' but to see this young princess step forth graciously out of a first-class carriage, and address him as 'grandpapa,' took away his breath" (84). She "kiss[es] him dutifully," although "she was half-disgusted, he half-frightened" (84). The scene is replayed when Tozer presents the granddaughter to his wife: "She, too, was somewhat frightened by the appearance of the young lady, who was her Phoebe's child, yet was so unlike any other scion of the Tozer race; and felt greatly disposed to curtsey and say 'Ma'am' to her" (86). Phoebe requires all of her courage and self-possession not to collapse under the extraordinary strain presented by the class gap: "She had expected 'a difference,' but she had not looked for her grandfather's greasy coat and wisp of neckcloth, or her grandmother's amazing cap, or the grammatical peculiarities in which both indulged" (87). All of her habitual responses must be substituted by conscious and careful manifestations of a familial regard that she does not feel. In short, the so-called natural relations are the ones that must be dutifully performed. The whole enterprise depends upon Phoebe; her grandmother remarks pessimistically: "She is a deal too fine for us, Tozer . . . she ain't one of our sort" (87). Only an ideology of "duty" enables Phoebe to cope with the class conflict and establish a relationship with her grandparents on some sort of intimate footing: "It was apparent that Duty was what she had to look to; Duty, and that alone" (85). Yet "duty" here, as it was in *Miss Marjoribanks*, is always the rubric under which the heroine

covertly pursues her own interests and those of her class while passing herself off as the very pattern of feminine propriety.

Phoebe *is* her class; its very constraints enable her successes.
When she consoles herself that "she would be herself, whatever
happened," she is reaffirming not a metaphysical essence but a class
identity built on dress, manner, and speech. Her appearance with
her grandparents provokes these same questions of identity in the
Carlingford onlookers. Ursula May, daughter of the Carlingford
high church rector, a gentleman, desires an acquaintance with
Phoebe, whom she has greatly admired in London when both girls
attended the Copperhead ball. Ursula has worshiped the elegant
young woman in black, whom she has perceived as her social superior, and is astonished and delighted to find her in Carlingford.
Phoebe, however, granddaughter of Tozer the butterman and dis-
senter, is doubly disqualified from becoming Ursula's social acquaintance. When Ursula is informed that Phoebe is "that Tozer girl," she
grows "first red and then pale with horror and dismay" (142). Mrs.
Hurst has earlier lectured Ursula never to "trust to appearances,"
because she would "have taken [Phoebe] for a lady if I had met her
in the street. It shows how one may be taken in" (98). This kind of
comment echoes the ideological confusion in the etiquette manuals,
which cautioned against dressing above one's class because one
would always be exposed. The manuals intend to forestall the social
parvenu and are oblivious to their contradictions in acknowledging
that dress signals class, and if one successfully dresses at a certain
rank, then one is of that rank. Phoebe herself explains, "I have no
right, I suppose, to stand upon being a lady, though I always
thought I was one" (204). No association with her grandparents can
change who Phoebe is; only a change in her dress, manner, or diction can effect that change. Ursula's father, impressed with Phoebe,
designates her a "very lady-like young woman" (141), and he asks
his daughter, "Is she an impostor, taking people in, or what is it all
about?" (143). Ursula responds by citing Phoebe's social credentials:
"An impostor! If you had seen her as I saw her, at a great, beautiful,
splendid ball. . . . I was Nobody there . . . but Miss Beecham!" (143).
And she continues to insist that "she is a lady in herself, as good a
lady as any one" (151), implicitly raising questions about the categories through which individuals understand identity. Ursula finally
wins her father's approval to pursue the acquaintance although he
makes it an exception to "principle": "It is quite necessary, in an
ordinary way, to think of a girl's grandfather. . . . No shopkeeping
friends for me; but in this individual case I am willing to make an

exception" (151). Apparently it is not necessary to think of a girl's grandfather if she does not herself recall him in her appearance.

Rather than condemn the class values that it represents so accurately, the novel affirms them. Phoebe herself has too much respect for social convention to try any attempt at disguising her relations with the Tozers. In fact, she must respect social conventions because they function to set her apart from the Tozers: she is *with* them but not *of* them. Thus, she frankly avows the relationship, an avowal that indirectly distinguishes her sharply from them. When Ursula first invites her to tea, Phoebe responds, "You must tell me first . . . whether you know who I am. If you ask me after that, I shall come. I am old Mr. Tozer's granddaughter, who had a shop in the High Street" (154). She then candidly adds, "I do not like it myself . . . and no one else can be expected to like it" (154). Phoebe is most "herself" when admitting that she cannot possibly like being with her grandparents. Nobody who is like her could!

The novel thus tackles directly the way all relationships are performed through social semiotics, and it makes short shrift of allegiances other than class. Celebrating as it does entrepreneurial ingenuity, the text must sacrifice the sanctity of familial affections. Phoebe herself raises the question implicit in her situation, whether one's obligations toward relatives continue: "To be educated in another sphere and brought down to this, is hard. One cannot feel the same for one's relations" (116). She questions: "Which is best: for everybody to continue in the position he was born in, or for an honest shopkeeper to educate his children and push them up higher until they come to feel themselves members of a different class, and to be ashamed of him? Either way, you know, it is hard" (116). Later, in conversation with Ursula and her brother Reginald May, Phoebe confesses to the "nasty disagreeable struggle with one's self and one's pride" (174) when she is forced to interact with her grandparents' acquaintances. These people are no longer her people; she shares more with the Mays and her gentleman acquaintance, Mr. Northcote, who are of her class, than with the Tozers, Pigeons, and Browns, who are shopkeepers.

The fact that the very signifying practices through which Phoebe constructs her identity are completely unintelligible to her grandparents dramatizes this conclusion. For example, winter encourages the young people to embark on skating parties, and the Mays always urge Phoebe to join them in the fun. However, she refuses all but the occasional invitation because she has no chaperone. She justifies her behavior to her grandparents by arguing that she wishes to stay at home to nurse her grandmother, but she confides to Ursula that "I have nobody of my own to go with. If I took grandpapa with me, I don't think it would mend matters. Once or twice it was possible, but not every day" (225). And Reginald fully justifies and does justice to "Phoebe's fine feeling": "He was much impressed by, and approved highly of this reticence, having a very high standard of minor morals for ladies, in his mind, like most young men" (225). Manners and morals, Phoebe fully grasps the connection, especially for eligible young men. It escapes her grandparents, though, for whom the "idea of a chaperon never entered their homely head. Such articles are unnecessary in the lower levels of society" (224). Phoebe's mastery of the discursive practices of upper-middle-class life puts her throughout in full control of her situation, however unfavorable circumstances might initially appear.

The novel's climax pits class constructions against consanguineous ties and is unhesitating in privileging the former. This melodramatic episode threatens the impecunious gentleman rector, Mr. May, with exposure for forging the more wealthy Tozer's name as security on a bill for £150. Phoebe quickly discerns the main facts of the case, and she "determined to be [Mr. May's] true protector" (298). When she tells his son Reginald to attend to her instructions and follow her advice, he agrees to do exactly as she directs and enthuses, "Only you or an angel would have done it" (301). Only this angel, with the control of the community in her hands, *can* do it. The resolution depends on class loyalty. Phoebe ultimately identifies herself with the Mays against the Tozers; she will excuse the economic debt Mr. May owes to her grandfather in order to dischange the social debt she owes the Mays for providing her with a congenial "home" in Carlingford, for she has been much more comfortable in the parsonage than at her grandparents' house, "where the 'tent' bed hung with old-fashioned red and brown chintz, and the moreen curtains drooping over the window, and the gigantic flowers on the carpet, made Phoebe's soul sick within her" (87). Her grandfather's rage, his "vindictive fierceness," and his physical violence shock her deeply because in her class she has "never met with such an outburst of coarse anger in her life" (293). These manifestations of his masculinity as constructed through his lower class repel her. Thus, like Lucilla Marjoribanks before her, Phoebe Beecham manipulates social signifiers to keep *her* community intact, to protect Mr. May's reputation and masculine gentility as well as the prestige and power of the middle classes.

Social capital works not only to protect the interests of the upper

middle class generally but also to enable skillful semioticians to realize additional material capital. Phoebe succeeds in securing a proposal of marriage from wealthy Clarence Copperhead, who has been
sent to Carlingford to be tutored by Mr. May because he has been
"ploughed" at Oxford. The Copperheads resemble, in certain ways,
the Beechams. Mr. Copperhead is, in fact, the "leading member" of
Mr. Beecham's congregation, the disposition toward dissent being a
function of class. He, too, derives from a lower class and has made
his fortune in business. His first wife and family have no more gentility than the Tozers, and he "somewhat despise[s] his elder sons,
who were like himself" because he sees, "oddly enough, the coarse-
ness of their manners, and even of their ways of thinking" (12). He
chooses his daughter's governess for his second wife, "one of those
naturally refined but less than half-educated, timid creatures" (10).
An "officer's daughter," the second Mrs. Copperhead brings social
distinction to the Copperhead name. It is, as we have seen, the
woman who determines the family's social position and expectations, and Mr. Copperhead's own crassness cannot abrogate their
standing in society. The son of this woman, Clarence, in due course
attends Oxford and possesses the air, manners, and diction of a gentleman, in contrast to his half-brothers, with whom he has no association and nothing in common. Although Mr. Copperhead ridicules
the gentility of his "well-bred wife" and "elegant University man,"
he also prizes it above all his merely material possessions. His ambition is to see his son in Parliament.

The novel's rigorous focus on class issues inflects the presentation
of the romance plot, which, for the level-headed parties concerned,
is a matter of consolidating and improving one's position. As in *Miss
Marjoribanks*, sexual desire is routed through the social formations;
women use men to consolidate their own and middle-class control.
Thus, although Mr. Northcote is alarmed that Phoebe might have
marked him out as eligible, "the idea that a small undistinguished
Dissenting minister should think her capable of marrying him, was a
humiliation which did not enter into Phoebe's head" (119). And
when sensible, intelligent Reginald May falls in love with her, she
rejects him for complacent, obtuse Clarence Copperhead and the
"Career" this inferior young man represents for her. Clarence Copperhead has inherited enough of his mother's pride so that he early
condescends to Phoebe, whom he has known since a child. Although Clarence is intellectually stupid and self-absorbed, he learns
in the course of the novel that a woman like Phoebe is exactly the
kind of wife he requires for his ambitions: "Who would look better

at the head of a table, or show better at a ball, or get on better in society?" (232–33). Who, in short, is more fully enabled by the social discourses of middle-class gentility? Moreover, Phoebe has the additional qualification of intellect: "A wife like Phoebe, what a relief that would be, in the way of education! No need of any more coaching. She was clever, and fond of reading, and so forth. She would get everything up for him, if he went into parliament, or that sort of thing; why, she'd keep him posted up. . . . She would save him worlds of trouble" (233). Although Mr. Copperhead threatens to disinherit him if Clarence marries Phoebe, ultimately he, too, comes around to his son's way of thinking. The happy conclusion to Phoebe's romance of a Career finds Clarence in Parliament. "The reader," announces the narrator, "perhaps . . . may have had the luck to read a speech in the morning paper of Phoebe's composition" (339). What remained only a gleam in the eye of Lucilla Marjoribanks becomes a reality for Phoebe.

It is worth noting that Oliphant, unlike George Eliot, does not indulge in regrets that a woman with Phoebe's talents will be wasted in middle-class management. Oliphant's text inhabits a different ideological universe than Eliot's *Middlemarch*. That kind of regret is built upon conventional ideologies of the Angel in the House. It presupposes that, except in their roles as wives and mothers, middle-class women are idle, dependent, and ineffectual. It affords no recognition of their managerial positions, either at home or in the larger society.

Oliphant is fully aware that women were limited in the society of her time, but she infuses the gendered plot with the bourgeois plot that details the social productivity of the signifiers controlled by women. Instead of focusing primarily on what women could not do, Oliphant kept her eye on what they could and did do, on their substantial contributions to the rise and consolidation of the middle classes. That focus enables her to tell a fascinating tale of class change and the sociosexual construction of identity. As we have seen, it is a story often mystified.

At the same time Oliphant's novels implicate readers in the practice of middle-class gentility. *Miss Marjoribanks* does this by endorsing Lucilla's assessment of Barbara Lake's vulgarity or the haplessness of the working class. Both *Miss Marjoribanks* and *Phoebe Junior* focus their stories through middle-class eyes: either sharing a middle-class horror at lower-class vulgarity or presenting the middle classes through a scrim of lower-class admiration and emulation. In this way, the novels themselves are complicit in the values of a Lucilla Marjoribanks or a Phoebe Beecham. Thus, the absence of the Tozers from their granddaughter's wedding is remarked only in its unremarkableness although, by bringing her into Carlingford, the grandparents had been the means of uniting Phoebe and Clarence: "Tozer and his wife cried together for joy on the wedding day, but they did not expect to be asked to that ceremony, being well aware that Phoebe, having now completely entered into the regions of the great, could not be expected to have very much to say to them" (336–37). Nonetheless, both grandparents do Phoebe the justice to comment that, were she there with them, "she'd just be the same . . . and wouldn't let nobody look down upon you and me" (337). Indeed, as Phoebe has recognized from the beginning, she is herself a lady, whatever happens (75). It is this kind of iteration of her identity, articulated simultaneously through gender and class, that has facilitated the production of a historical space for Phoebe distinctively different from that occupied by either her mother or grandmother.

Domestic women were engaged in a semiotics of status that yielded political power, which Oliphant's protagonists often manipulate self-consciously. These heroines are "unpleasant" partly because the chaste sexual desire attributed to tender virgins by Victorian myth is exposed here as a pragmatic sociosexual desire that has more to do with consolidating middle-class control than with loving a man. That unpleasantness also derives from Oliphant's representation of protagonists who are empowered by the social semiotics of bourgeois gentility and, further, capable of performing even their supposedly natural traits to achieve certain pragmatic ends. And Oliphant never arrests the play of the signifier. Thus, her novels "unpleasantly" disrupt conventional gender hierarchies based on difference and, equally unpleasantly, point to class as both produced and managed by a manipulation of signs.

7

Inventing Reality: The Ideological Commitments of George Eliot's *Middlemarch*

Margaret Oliphant claimed, "No one even will mention me in the same breath with George Eliot," adding: "And that is just" (*Autobiography* 7). Eliot's horror that she should be suspected of writing one of the *Chronicles of Carlingford* certainly helped to keep Oliphant humble, and Eliot's art has subsequently set the standard by which Oliphant's seems less significant. If we reverse the focal optic, however, Oliphant's politics of domesticity reveal Eliot's commitment to a politics of a different sort.

This chapter and the following one take two different trajectories in order to foreground the politics of bourgeois domestic management in canon production and subject formation. *Middlemarch*, often hailed as the greatest domestic novel of the nineteenth century, certainly elevated above the works of Gaskell and Oliphant, is analyzed here to demonstrate how George Eliot represents the domestic sphere to mute class relations as effected by women and so to efface the productive tensions generated by women's contradictory class and gender placements. This following analysis should significantly revise our understanding of cultural mystifications of female agency and canonical inscriptions of social ideology. In short, it illustrates the privileging of certain narratives over others in the historical construction of Victorian mythology. In the primacy accorded Eliot's massive *Study of Provincial Life*, we glimpse the process by which certain cultural configurations have achieved the status of the "real" and so blocked our recognition of a contestatory politics documented elsewhere. Focusing Eliot's representational emphases through the lens of Oliphant's narrational techniques and her inscription of domestic discursive practices, in this chapter I examine Eliot's narrative choices in *Middlemarch* and the gender and class politics they support.

Canon Fodder

Margaret Oliphant's compelling representations of bourgeois women as social and class managers provide a base from which to explore both Eliot's horror and the public's neglect of this prolific writer—to raise, in short, the issue of canons and their formation. Although many of Oliphant's eighty-plus novels do not achieve the trenchant insight into Victorian social semiotics of *Miss Marjoribanks* and *Phoebe Junior*, it is hard to explain why the cream, in her case, has not risen to the top as it has, for example, with Thomas Hardy. The "hardness of tone," early criticized by her publisher, John Black-wood, most likely alienated readers and played a role in Oliphant's literary disappearance. Blackwood identifies this hardness of tone in Oliphant's representations of her heroines and their disdain for marriage as a fate. But, as I suggested in Chapter 6, Oliphant revises much more than the romance plot, and the negative comments are also responding to her demystification of the angelic ideal, her ironic staging of the feminine roles of dutiful daughter and ingenue, and her unrelenting focus on women's work that stresses the close imbrication of the domestic with the political.

Oliphant's tendency to set sail against the winds of Victorian social convention in her domestic novels certainly shaped her reception by contemporaries. But the burden of my argument about Eliot, the representation of women, and the canon calls for an examination not only of what is expressed in one author but what is textually repressed or excised in another. And the juxtaposition of Oliphant with Eliot highlights aspects of the picture like the negative of a positive image. Class relations are inscribed in Eliot's *Middlemarch* in ways that reinforce the depiction of women's disability within patriarchy, that is, class and gender representations emerge as complementary or congruent discourses. The productive sociality that informs Oliphant's novels and contests images of women's disability, passivity, and inconsequence disappears in Eliot's; sociality emerges as a version of Ruskin's empty "playing at precedence."

An examination of the narrative choices in George Eliot's *Middlemarch* (1871–72) identifies a contrasting set of ideological assumptions in presenting society and women that have made the politics of one so much more acceptable than those of the other. Q. D. Leavis has cut through the received judgments of the two authors by calling attention to how Oliphant's *Miss Marjoribanks* "contributed quite considerably to *Middlemarch*" (147–48).[1] Leavis bases her claim on numerous points of similarity between the two female protagonists and their situations. In addition, she notes that "the Quarry for *Middlemarch* was not, it seems, begun before September 1868, whereas the last instalment of *Miss Marjoribanks* had appeared in 'Maga' in May 1866, having run for a year and a quarter there. It is inconceivable that George Eliot did not look through at least some of the installments in all that time . . . more especially as Blackwood, her own publisher, had initially the highest opinion of *Miss Marjoribanks* and great hopes for it, as she may well have heard" (145–46). To grasp the significance of Leavis's insights we must investigate what is omitted in George Eliot's representation of middle-class women's lives: the semiotics of social life, generating distinctions of rank and class, and its corollary, performative identities.

George Eliot early attracted the attention of twentieth-century feminist critics, who located in her novels a frank assessment of the meanness of opportunity available to substantive and rare creatures like Dorothea Brooke. Those critics became cathected to the noble heroines and lamented with them, "Since I can do no good because a woman, reach constantly at something that is near it."[2] From this perspective, they clearly embodied the fate of an aspiring feminine spirit in patriarchy. George Eliot's men made their destinies; the women simply fulfilled theirs. It seemed inevitable that so noble a creature as Dorothea should be known in certain circles only as a wife and mother, no matter how "incalculably diffusive" the effect of her being on those around her. Yet there was always a crucial discrepancy: the author somehow neglected to explain how the society that thwarted Dorothea produced George Eliot. And this representational gap fostered among critics passionate debates and im-

---

[1] Leavis states that "the possible influence of *Miss Marjoribanks* on the production of *Middlemarch* [is] . . . a possibility that I have never seen recognized elsewhere" (145). Recognition has been blocked partly by Eliot's vociferous objection to being considered the author of the anonymously published *Chronicles of Carlingford*. Leavis identifies one striking debt in the narrators' attitudes toward their heroines. She observes that "the attempt at ironical treatment and unsentimental appraisal of these two heroines is what distinguishes Dorothea and Gwendolen from all George Eliot's previous heroines." This "aloof, ironic view of a heroine," which stresses "the contrast between how she conceives herself and how she appears to others" was the legacy of Margaret Oliphant. Leavis continues, "George Eliot cannot maintain the uncongenial attitudes that . . . she absorbed unconsciously or tried to emulate," and so she "settles down, with the excuse of Dorothea's being unhappily married, into a more congenial compassion for her heroine and is weak enough to spoil her book by making Mrs Casaubon out to be a pathetic figure" (146–47).

[2] *Middlemarch*, epigraph, chap. 1.

passioned defenses and rejections of her heroines. It produced discussions such as "Why Feminists Are Angry with George Eliot" by Zelda Austin, and provoked the confession of Lee Edwards that *Middlemarch* could "no longer be one of the books of my life"[3]

The feminist debates provoked by Eliot's representations of women do not take us much further than the observation that Eliot does not allow her heroines the kind of scope she found in her own life, that she limits "the possibilities for directly willed feminist change."[4] Given Eliot's status as a realist, committed to narrative probability, not mere possibility, the limited fates of her heroines have been read as part of her compelling realism. It has not occurred to feminist critics to question the way Eliot constructs domestic women in her texts and what she *omits* to represent of their lives.

The perspective of a writer such as Oliphant on the Victorian angel as social manager clarifies aspects of Eliot's ideology. Because she was a subtle and sensitive observer of social life, Eliot persuades readers of the veracity of her picture by the sheer mass of detail and commentary in her novels, and she has assumed a place in the canon as a great, perhaps the great, realist of the nineteenth century. In the face of emerging alternative perspectives, however, critics have begun to recognize the seductions of that "real," and they are increasingly disposed to examine its ideological implications.[5]

No one would accuse George Eliot of building a world out of etiquette and the related domestic discourses that Oliphant details in her novels. Or, if someone did, there would be historical irony be-

---

[3] Zelda Austin's piece initiated a debate continued in Showalter, "The Greening of Sister George," and, more recently, renewed in Langbauer 216–23.

[4] Langbauer 231.

[5] Excellent analyses of the specific values encoded in Eliot's realism are Daniel Cottom, *Social Figures: George Eliot, Social History, and Literary Representation*, and Catherine Gallagher, *The Industrial Reformation of English Fiction*. Cottom analyzes the relationship between language and "reality," Gallagher, that between facts and values: Eliot "clung to the hope that a detailed recording of everyday life might automatically lead to moral progress" (Gallagher 221). Cottom defines his project: "In place of idealism of the sort with which Eliot identified, in which reality must always be other than the language that tells of it, I analyze uses of language in relation to those structurings of social life for which these uses constitute reality" (xix). Gallagher grounds her argument in a discussion of the politics of culture, concluding that "it is only after the separation of facts and values has become a programmatic element within the novel that realists can become fully conscious of the dynamics and potentialities of their own genre. The introduction of the politics of culture into the novel created just such a programmatic separation of the novel itself from the object of its representation. . . . Realism, then, is reshaped within the discourse about representation in the 1860s; it cannot remain the same after it has made war on its previous justifications by stressing the necessary discontinuity between facts and values" (266).

cause George Eliot fought shy of those discourses as a mark of "silly novels."[6] In contempt for what she regarded as certain "unessential" details—or as G. H. Lewes put it, *"detailism* which calls itself realism"—Eliot grounded her own philosophy of realism in emphases shared with Lewes and John Ruskin.[7] Of Ruskin, Eliot argued that "the truth of infinite value that he teaches is *realism*—the doctrine that all truth and beauty are to be attained by a humble and faithful study of nature, and not by substituting vague forms, bred by imagination on the mists of feeling, in place of definite substantial reality" ("Art and Belles Lettres" 626). This praise, linking fidelity to nature and definite substantial reality, privileges detail as a ground for higher knowledge in contradistinction to detail as semiotically variable. Lewes implies a similar value in distinguishing detailism— the inessential—from essential detail: "The painter who devotes years to a work representing modern life, yet calls for even more attention to a waistcoat than to the face of a philosopher, may exhibit truth of detail which will delight the tailor-mind, but he is defective in artistic truth, because he ought to be representing something higher than waistcoats."[8] The contrast Lewes establishes is telling: waistcoats versus philosopher's faces. Both are signs, but Lewes refuses status to the former; it cannot produce "artistic truth." In essence, he fundamentally refuses the instability of semiotics, arrogating truth to certain signs but not to others. What George Eliot and G. H. Lewes argue, in short, is that details differ in essence rather than in ideological construction.[9] Some conduce to truth and some do not. Both thinkers contemn the detailed semiotics of social life—of interest to tailors and upholsterers but not much else. The fluidity of meanings and the constructed nature of identities that delight artists such as Gaskell and Oliphant are uninteresting, perhaps even troubling to Eliot. Her narrator in *Adam Bede* famously

[6] Alison Booth, citing Eliot's "Silly Novel by Lady Novelists," points out: "As though she has completely seen through the cult of woman's mission with its exaltation of minutiae . . . she heaps scorn on *'mind and millinery'* novels, with their combination of exquisite accessories and ignorant philosophies" (71). Booth seems to share Eliot's interpretations of these details as "meaningless" minutiae.

[7] G. H. Lewes, *Principles of Success,* cited in Langbauer. I am indebted to Laurie Langbauer, whose excellent discussion of the role of details in Eliot's art, especially as it relates to the tension between realism and romance, has been stimulating to my own thoughts. See especially chap. 5, "Recycling Patriarchy's Garbage," 188–232.

[8] Lewes, quoted in Langbauer 204–5.

[9] Naomi Schor, who helpfully identifies contempt for the detail with its association with women, also notes the prominence of the detail in the theories of Barthes, Derrida, and Foucault: "Viewed in a historical perspective, the ongoing valorization of the detail appears to be an essential aspect of that dismantling of Idealist metaphysics which looms so large on the agenda of modernity" (3–4).

claims to give a "faithful account of men and things as they have mirrored themselves in my mind," acknowledging that the mirror is defective, perhaps, but not that the world itself is constantly changing its meanings (150). This narrator privileges "vulgar details," the kind found in Dutch genre painting: "I turn, without shrinking, from . . . sibyls, and heroic warriors, to an old woman bending over her flower-pot, or eating her solitary dinner, while the noonday light . . . falls on her mob-cap, and . . . her spinning-wheel, and . . . all those cheap common things which are the precious necessaries of life to her" (152). Eliot's homely details tend to typify if not essentialize her subject. And "woman" itself becomes an essential category in Eliot's novels. Laurie Langbauer persuasively documents the way "woman's association with detail quickly becomes her reduction to anatomical detail," a process implying that "anatomy equals destiny." Langbauer concludes that "this hidden trap of essentialism, so inimical to women, is built into Eliot's fiction; her realism seems to embrace it" (214–15). But that "almost obstetric accuracy of detail" was not the only possibility open to Eliot, nor are the meanings bound up in that kind of detail the only truths.[10] Therefore, what is *not*, or only minimally, represented must be exposed in order to gain a fuller grasp of Eliot's ideological position: the *other* kinds of details with *other* kinds of meanings that hover in the margins of Eliot's *Study of Provincial Life*

Middlemarch: The Devil Is in the Details

My axis of approach to the problematic issue of what is *not* in *Middlemarch* lies first in representations of two contrasting women: Rosamond Vincy and Dorothea Brooke. Rosamond sees society as a medium for her quest; Dorothea seeks to escape the life of a gentlewoman. George Eliot, by and large, excludes domestic discursive practices from her novels. Indeed, the hallmark of a character such as Dorothea Brooke is that she desperately wishes to accomplish something outside the domestic sphere that seems so utterly inconsequential to her. But what might be just one character's frustrated perspective on domesticity becomes the informing conception of the novel. Furthermore, when George Eliot does represent domestic details, she often detaches them from the social semiotics that ground their meanings in the novels of Gaskell and Oliphant, and she re-

[10] The quotation is from an early review of Eliot's novels in the *Examiner*, quoted in Langbauer 214.

lodges them within a dialectic of nature and artifice. Unlike Oliphant's Phoebe Junior, who comfortably reassures herself that she is "herself" whatever happens and who persuasively locates that self in her elegant apparel, her refined manner, and her exquisite discriminations of appropriate etiquette, George Eliot's Rosamond Vincy, a creature equally compounded of society's discursive practices, is depicted as armored in a hard social shell that protects the blind egoism of a vulnerable self. She is indicted by the narrator for her belief that behavior constitutes the person and for her complacent certainty that she never misbehaves no matter how unpleasant others may be. All her social graces signify her ensnaring artifice, symbolized by the chains she crafts and the plaits in which she braids her hair. The novel's events work to smash that protective shell, to leave "her little world . . . in ruins . . . and herself tottering in the midst of a lonely bewildered consciousness" (571–72). And the narrator applauds this pain as necessary and purifying, celebrating her emergence from a vision of the world as "an udder to feed our supreme selves" (156). Eliot's twin themes—egoism and its antithesis, fellow feeling—are both founded on a concept of an inherent self, independent of the discursive practices that seem otherwise to constitute the "self." And so Eliot's *Middlemarch* culminates in a contradictory picture of both nineteenth-century society and Victorian women. On the one hand, the "self" inevitably reflects society; on the other, it must resist society.

The novel presents performance as inauthentic and remains suspicious of all actors, who use theatrical stagings to carry out covert and destructive designs. By describing her as "by nature an actress of parts," the narrator subtly allies Rosamond with the murderous Laure, the object of Lydgate's first great passion.[11] The narrator ironically comments that Rosamond "even acted her own character, and so well, that she did not know it to be precisely her own" (87). But what can her character be apart from her actions? One might quarrel with the contradiction inherent in the narrator's notion that she is "by nature" an actress. But the narrator clings stubbornly to the idea that there exists a "natural" versus an artificial, or acted character. "The pride of Mrs Lemon's school," Rosamond was "always that combination of correct sentiments, music, dancing, drawing, elegant note-writing, private album for extracted verse, and perfect blond loveliness, which made the irresistible woman for the doomed man

---

[11] Laure, of course, has deliberately killed her husband while acting a part in a play. That the episode appears to be an accident is part of the performance, thus performance comes to seem a dangerous and deceptive thing.

of that date" (198). If we look at Rosamond from the perspective of the middle-class woman as social manager, it is hard not to laugh at the lugubrious melodrama of the phrase "doomed man of that date." Such a woman in an Oliphant novel would be presented as a positive asset. Having thus condemned Rosamond's character, the narrator pulls back with a characteristic invitation to pity her: "Think no unfair evil of her, pray: she had no wicked plots, nothing sordid or mercenary" (198). The assessment concludes by recognizing the cooperation of nature with art: "She was not in the habit of devising falsehoods, and if her statements were no direct clue to fact, why, they were not intended in that light—they were among her elegant accomplishments, intended to please. Nature had inspired many arts in finishing Mrs Lemon's favourite pupil, who by general consent (Fred's excepted) was a rare compound of beauty, cleverness, and amiability" (198). The entire passage is built on implied oppositions: nature, statement, and fact versus art, falsehood, and pleasing accomplishments.

Middlemarch participates in its own Victorian melodrama by writing women into and out of spiritual scripts. The "doomed man of that date," in this case Tertius Lydgate, falls prey to a moment of "naturalness" in Rosamond's behavior. Whereas Lydgate has been used to see her "lovely little face . . . under the most perfect management of self-contented grace," suddenly her act fails: "At this moment she was as natural as she had ever been when she was five years old: she felt that her tears had risen, and it was no use to try to do anything else than let them stay like water on a blue flower or let them fall over her cheeks, even as they would. That moment of naturalness was the crystallising feather-touch: it shook flirtation into love" (222). The distinction between an acted and a natural self figures throughout the narrative where social conventions of dress and etiquette are allied with artifice, superficiality, triviality, and femininity. And, Rosamond's face, rather than her household, is under "perfect management."

The dialectic of nature and artifice also grounds an opposition between nobility and commonness. The novel immediately signals that attention to clothing reveals one's commonness with its opening observation: "Miss Brooke had that kind of beauty which seems to be thrown into relief by poor dress." It first routes that sartorial choice through a social semiotic ("The Pride of being ladies had something to do with it. . . . Then there was well-bred economy") only to dismiss these reasons as implicitly frivolous and to locate a firmer ground: "In Miss Brooke's case, religion alone would have determined it" (5). It is a mark of Dorothea's innate nobility of spirit that she throws off various items of clothing like her bonnet and gloves "with an instinctive discarding of formality where a great question of destiny was concerned" (212). In the momentous interview between Rosamond and Dorothea, the former advances "wrapping her soft shawl around her," a sign that she "was inwardly wrapping her soul in cold reserve" (580). In contrast, Dorothea "had taken off her gloves, from an impulse which she could never resist when she wanted a sense of freedom" (580). Etiquette manuals cautioned ladies *not* remove outer garments during visits, and the ease with which Dorothea discards hers thus serves *here* as a powerful signifier to represent noble self-forgetfulness and "sincerity" in contrast to Rosamond's selfishness and artifice. If placed within a *social* grid, however, Mrs. Casaubon's freedoms might be read as presumption and condescension by the lower-ranked Mrs. Lydgate. Yet the novel does not make available that interpretive system to decode this particular detail. If one could read a character outside of an author's representational schemes—impossible though this is—one would have a potentially humorous encounter: a socially correct Mrs. Lydgate confounded by the arrogant presumption of Mrs. Casaubon because she is not privy to the narrator's new semiology governing the event, in which she is to "read" Dorothea's discarding of clothes as spontaneous, heartfelt compassion. Certainly, George Eliot was only minimally interested in "good society," but it does not necessarily follow that good society is therefore trivial and negligible in its effects. To leave it and its practices unexamined is to ensure its continued mystification and to excuse genteel women from their participation in the class project with its oppressions.

The artifice of social semiotics in Eliot's novel associates readily with the power of those systems to compromise inherent goodness. To emphasize society and its conventions as destructive rather than productive Eliot depicts a conversation between Lydgate and Farebrother on the importance of keeping oneself "independent": "Very few men can do that. Either you slip out of service altogether, and become good for nothing, or you wear the harness and draw a good deal where your yoke-fellows pull you" (129). Farebrother continues, "A good wife—a good unworldly woman—may really help a man, and keep him more independent" (130). This definition of a good wife as "unworldly" contradicts the notion of a good wife implicit and explicit in Oliphant's novels. There, worldliness enabled the social manager to further the affairs of men, to better their individual situations, to facilitate their success. After all, men must inhabit and negotiate the world.

Society in Middlemarch, however, emerges as a kind of noose from which one wants to keep one's neck clear. Despite discussions of provincial society that focus on "new consciousness of interdependence" and "fresh threads of connection" (70, 71), Eliot persistently represents social interaction as petty. In voting for the chaplain of the new hospital, Lydgate feels "for the first time . . . the hampering threadlike pressure of small social conditions, and their frustrating complexity" (133–34). The adjective "small" suggests both the physical and moral dimension of these conditions that thwart talent and intelligence. Lydgate learns that "this was one of the difficulties of moving in good Middlemarch society: it was dangerous to insist on knowledge as a qualification for any salaried office" (117). And, to the extent that Lydgate colludes in society's estimates, he is "spotted with commonness." The narrator warns us that "that distinction of mind which belonged to his intellectual ardour, did not penetrate his feeling and judgment about furniture, or women, or the desirability of its being known (without his telling) that he was better born than other country surgeons" (111–12). Although the narrator makes Lydgate the object of irony in his mental identification of women with furniture, the text itself repeatedly insists that women who do not rise above society's claims are little better than household furnishings.

Visiting, the central function through which good society established and maintained itself, is scarcely represented in *Middlemarch*. Mr. Brooke and his world—"that is to say, Mrs. Cadwallader the Rector's wife, and the small group of gentry with whom he visited in the north-east corner of Loamshire"(8)—meet only occasionally and largely for the exchange of gossip, the subject of which is usually Dorothea and her liaisons. When Dorothea is at Freshitt, Sir James stages just such a visit from Mrs. Cadwallader so that she can lecture the young widow on the unseemliness of contact with Will Ladislaw. Or Celia rushes to Lowick, in the only depicted visit after the requisite bridal one, to try to induce Dorothea to give up her engagement to Ladislaw. Dorothea herself sits day after day in a splendid isolation punctuated only by visits from Ladislaw or from Miss Noble as his emissary. In fact, Eliot represents Will Ladislaw as the only indefatigable visitor in the northeast corner of Loamshire, and his frequent calls on Rosamond Lydgate stimulate rumors. Dorothea thinks "with some wonder that Will was passing his time with

Mrs Lydgate in her husband's absence" (317). When women of the town visit, they either share idle gossip—such as the rumor that Lydgate was "a natural son of Bulstrode's"—or confide "their little troubles of health and household management to each other" (194, 217). The troubles are "little" just as society is "small."

The adjective "little" crops up fairly often in Eliot's descriptions of ladies' lives. For example, the narrator comments that "Dorothea seldom left home without her husband, but she did occasionally drive into Middlemarch alone, on little errands of shopping or charity such as occur to every lady of any wealth when she lives within three miles of a town" (315). This representation belittles the life of a lady and evacuates it of significance. There exists a still center, a blank, in Eliot's representation of women's lives. For example, in terms of the prescriptions of etiquette manuals and Rosamond's own social ambitions, it is certainly strange that Eliot portrays her as making no bridal visits. One would expect that the "flower of Mrs. Lemon's school" would attempt to consolidate the rise in status conferred by her marriage. Although Rosamond is depicted as the prototypical Victorian lady, the novel denies her any energy or resourcefulness, even what would be a negative energy for Eliot, that of social climbing. After all, Rosamond marries Lydgate for his good birth and "the prospect of rising in rank and getting a little nearer to that celestial condition on earth in which she would have nothing to do with vulgar people" (123). But, having married Lydgate, Rosamond simply sits in the drawing room all day, ignoring the Middlemarch social ladder, receiving suspect visits from Will Ladislaw, and angling for visits to or from Lydgate's relatives.

Further, given Rosamond's represented hypersensitivity to correct behavior and propriety—her sensitive nose "discern[s] very subtly the faintest aroma of rank" (123)—it is inconsistent that she would be insensitive to the impropriety—immediately grasped by Dorothea—of Will Ladislaw languishing over her piano and lolling on her carpets all day. Far more likely that Rosamond Lydgate, like Oliphant's "hard" Phoebe Beecham, would not participate in anything likely to jeopardize her reputation. After all, the narrator has been at pains to assure us that Rosamond is nothing but these social reflexes. Her very impenetrability to Lydgate's appeals depends on her conviction that she is "blameless." The text portrays her as massively deluded—a big vulnerable ego hiding within a shell of petty social refinement—but either Rosamond is socially competent or she is not. She is, when Eliot wants to criticize the emptiness of society, but Eliot shifts her representation when Rosamond's sociality might actually be productive of Lydgate's professional advancement because the novel is committed ideologically to unworldliness as a necessary condition of individual success.

George Eliot's representational choices lead to other narrative gaps. One of Rosamond's most pointed moments of defiance of Lydgate occurs when she writes to Sir Godwin to request his help in discharging their debt. Eliot has persistently represented this obstructive wife as sensitive to the merest whiff of vulgarity, "alive to the slightest hint that anything was not, according to Lydgate, in the very highest taste" (200). She would rather die than offend against propriety. Rosamond perceives that her mother's "tinge of unpretentious, inoffensive vulgarity" gives "more effect to [her own] refinement" for Lydgate, who recognizes that he is "descending a little in relation to Rosamond's family," but rejoices that he can give "that exquisite creature herself . . . a much-needed transplantation" (256).[12] The difference in refinement between Rosamond and Mrs. Vincy causes the daughter to blush deeply when the mother tells Lydgate, "I hope your uncle Sir Godwin will not look down on Rosy. . . . I should think he would do something handsome. A thousand or two can be nothing to a baronet" (261). The narrator relates that Lydgate, "pitied her so much that he remained silent and went to the other end of the room to examine a print curiously, as if he had been absent-minded" (261). Although here Rosamond can be painfully mortified by a mere suggestion from her mother, the novel later portrays her actually writing to Lydgate's uncle for money, an obvious violation of her own sense of honor and social propriety. The narrator comments pityingly, "Such was the force of poor Rosamond's tactics now she applied them to affairs" (481). Rosamond's sense of social correctness fails to protect her from egregious blunders like writing to Sir Godwin. And it takes only the most narrow and repulsive form of making her "shrink in cold dislike" from Lydgate, becoming "all the more calmly correct, in the conviction that she was not the person to misbehave, whatever others might do" (482). Rosamond is simultaneously convicted of shielding herself behind a mantle of propriety and letting it drop when she most needs it. Here as elsewhere, Eliot's representations engage with social details largely as a measure of individual character.

The novel stages its resistance to social semiotics in a climactic episode that echoes comparable scenes in both Gaskell's *Wives and*

---

[12] Vulgarity is, by definition, offensive. Eliot's oxymoron "inoffensive vulgarity" signals the narrator's approval of the "lower" life that only appears vulgar to those of false refinement.

Daughters and Oliphant's *Miss Marjoribanks*. When Lydgate is implicated in Raffles's death, Dorothea ardently believes in his innocence, and she hopes, by clearing him, to pave the way for his continued good work in Middlemarch. Similarly, Gaskell's Lady Harriet Cumnor uses her patronage of Molly Gibson, publicly walking and making calls with her, to stifle the vicious rumors about her indiscretions with Mr. Preston; once Lady Harriet has endorsed Molly, the Hollingford town families follow suit. In Oliphant's novel, Lucilla Marjoribanks likewise redeems Mr. Cavendish from exposure by a public demonstration of her support. After that endorsement, questions about his character and possible chicanery regarding his inheritance are forever silenced, reaffirming that social reality is constructed through discursive practices.

In contrast, *Middlemarch*'s narrator terms Dorothea's impulse to save Lydgate "impetuous generosity," suggesting its quixotic nature. Indeed, her "ardent faith" undergoes "a melancholy check" after she consults Mr. Farebrother. The narrator steers clear of socially evaluative terms in favor of the metaphysics of "justice and mercy" and "human fellowship" (537, 557). Ironically, Lydgate is suffering at the hands of society and his redemption must come at those hands, yet Eliot swerves away from such a resolution to focus on the merely individual encounter. Social reputations, however, lay firmly in the hands of women. Women drew and maintained the social lines. Neither a Lucilla nor a Lady Harriet would therefore dream of consulting men about their own conduct in a matter regarding a social reputation and the social fabric. Yet Dorothea, who once "liked [her] own opinions," submits to the dictum of Sir James: "Surely, a woman is bound to be cautious and listen to those who know the world better than she does. . . . You really should keep back at present, and not volunteer any meddling with this Bulstrode business." She contents herself with blurting out to Celia: "As if I wanted a husband! . . . I only want not to have my feelings checked at every turn," and remains inactive "in deference to her masculine advisers" (539, 557). By thus advocating the impotence of women even in the social world, exposing their apparent ignorance and inability to act effectively, the novel more seriously extends the power of the patriarchal realm it is seemingly criticizing.

What might have been an effective public demonstration turns into a private interview, in which Dorothea's support of Lydgate is represented as both high-minded and naive. Dorothea is "moved to show her human fellowship" to Lydgate; the "idea of some active good . . . 'haunted her like a passion.'" She speaks of clearing him with the "truth" and the wickedness of letting people "think evil of any one falsely." These are very fine sentiments, perfectly appropriate to the Victorian Angel in the House, but they accomplish nothing except to give Lydgate the "exquisite sense of leaning entirely on a generous sympathy." But that is Eliot's point: women have no meaningful sphere for social action. Instead of enjoying a restored public confidence, Lydgate is only allowed to bask in the "presence of a noble nature, generous in its wishes, ardent in its charity" and believe that "[he] too can be seen and judged in the wholeness of [his] character" (557–59). When Dorothea speaks of her crusade partially to restore Lydgate's reputation by persuading Mr. Farebrother, her uncle, and Sir James Chettam, the narrator tenderly mocks "this childlike picture of what she would do," spoken in a voice that "might have been almost taken as a proof that she could do it effectively." The narrator finds ironic the possibility that Dorothea could actually be socially efficacious in her advocacy and invites a smile at "the childlike grave-eyed earnestness with which Dorothea said all this" (559–60). "Childlike" echoes "little," the narrator's characterization of women's lives. Eliot consistently represents this interchange as infused by Dorothea's naive idealism, which is what she has to offer in a contaminated social world, "holding up an ideal for others in her believing conception of them" (565).

For Dorothea to control events through etiquette practices is unthinkable in this novel; she only reassures Lydgate that she "can say of [him] what will make it stupidity to suppose that [he] would be bribed to do a wickedness" (563). But, consistently, the scene focuses on the human tragedy: "to love what is great, and try to reach it, and yet to fail," and Lydgate's relief that in Dorothea's sympathetic response "he had found room for the full meaning of his grief" (560). His conclusion—"This young creature has a heart large enough for the Virgin Mary"—ensures that readers will stay focused on the pettiness of a society that has sacrificed the talents of both Lydgate and Dorothea to its narrow definitions of responsibility and propriety. Society emerges as a monolith of oppression rather than a medium for interactions.

The preceding episode helps to clarify certain tendencies in *Middlemarch*. Social life is represented only insofar as it confirms the triviality of women's lives. Social details are absent or are routed through another signifying system. Those women who find meaning and purpose in society are represented as comparatively shallow. To emphasize this point, we may consider the novel's opening pages, which contrast Dorothea and Celia. Unlike her idealistic sister who worries about "spiritual life," the "destinies of mankind," the "good of all," the "highest purposes of truth," the "great soul," "spiritual communion," and "the ends of life," Celia concentrates on her appearance and behavior (6, 12, 13, 15, 16, 20). Her dress, although still ladylike, "ha[s] a shade of coquetry in its arrangements," and she takes pleasure in being adorned by lovely jewels. Dorothea, in contrast, finds "the solicitudes of feminine fashion . . . an occupation for Bedlam. She could not reconcile the anxieties of a spiritual life involving eternal consequences, with a keen interest in guimp and artificial protrusions of drapery." While Celia assiduously practices piano for drawing room performances—"a small kind of tinkling which symbolised the aesthetic part of the young ladies' education"—Dorothea draws plans for cottages, and wins the narrator's ironic apologia: her "slight regard for domestic music and feminine fine art must be forgiven her, considering the small tinkling and smearing in which they chiefly consisted at that dark period" (48). "Small tinkling" and the derisive "smearing" echo the "little" affairs of ladies.

It is in part because George Eliot is so consistently caustic about the emptiness of ladies' lives that she has been hailed for her realism. Her vision coincides so perfectly with patriarchal orthodoxy about the inconsequence and inanity of society and woman's place within it that no one has questioned what might have been omitted. But, of course, Eliot's "realism" is the product of a highly selective representation in which the signifying practices through which women organized society are severed from their larger meanings and household management is erased as a topic. This severing produces some interpretive gaps in the novel. In contrast to novels by Dickens, Gaskell, and Oliphant, *Middlemarch* does not depict genteel middle-class women as managers.[13] Esther Summerson had scarcely removed her bonnet before she was presented with the housekeeping keys to Bleak House. But, although we are informed that Dorothea "presided in her uncle's household, and did not at all dislike her new authority," the novel never specifies in what that authority consists (8). Dorothea never speaks to a housekeeper about visitors or meals or schedules either at Tipton or Lowick. She never hires or fires, supervises or instructs. She never even superintends tea. The ubiquitous Tantripp serves as chaperone and ladies' maid at Tipton, Lowick, and in Rome.

[13] Eliot will, however, represent management among those of the lower middle class, like Mrs. Poyser in *Adam Bede*. Then, the wife also participates in the household work.

When Dorothea agrees to marry Will Ladislaw, she promises to "learn what everything costs," an ominous phrase in Eliot that dictates both financial and emotional exactions. But the novel represents Dorothea as coming to the question of "costs" rather late in her development, especially since she has already been a mistress in two establishments. And, whereas Tipton parish has the worst village in the novel, Lowick parish inexplicably boasts a model village where nothing whatever needs to be done by anyone. Dorothea peremptorily announces to Will, "There is no good to be done in Lowick" (267).[14] Later she wonders, "What was there to be done in the village? O dear! nothing. Everybody was well and had flannel" (589). Dorothea's role is circumscribed to urging reforms on her uncle and Sir James Chettam. Apart from moral exhortation, the text depicts Dorothea's world as requiring no meaningful exertion from her:

> There was the stifling oppression of that gentlewoman's world, where everything was done for her and none asked for her aid—where the sense of connection with a manifold pregnant existence had to be kept up painfully as an inward vision, instead of coming from without in claims that would have shaped her energies.—"What shall I do?" "Whatever you please, my dear:" that had been her brief history since she had left off learning morning lessons and practising silly rhythms on the hated piano. Marriage, which was to bring guidance into worthy and imperative occupation, had not yet freed her from the gentlewoman's oppressive liberty; it had not even filled her leisure with the ruminant joy of unchecked tenderness. (202)

"Silly" joins "little," "small," and "childlike." We end up with one of the nineteenth century's most dramatic examples of domestic labor erased. To the extent workers themselves are represented, they exist

[14] This is one of the points of similarity that Leavis has identified between *Middlemarch* and *Miss Marjoribanks*: "we can't read such passages as Dorothea's disappointment on visiting her future home at finding that Lowick, with its good cottages, well-found villagers and neither vice, dirt, nor poverty . . . without remembering Lucilla's satisfaction on visiting Marchbank before *her* marriage." Leavis is highly critical of George Eliot's indulgence toward her egotistical heroine: "There is a considerable egoistic impulse in her yearning to do good to others, a yearning which yet never achieved definition and which we are never given any reason to suppose her to have qualifications for actualizing. Far from this essential egoism being exposed for what it is, it is offered for our admiration" (148–49). Leavis then quotes Dorothea's lament: "'I am feeling something which is perhaps foolish and wrong,' answered Dorothea with her usual openness—'almost wishing that the people wanted more to be done for them here. I have known so few ways of making my life good for anything'" (149).

as an anonymous, efficient underclass laboring for an upper class entirely oblivious to their existence. To the extent the text does not represent them or their management, it contributes to the ideologies that cement the status quo. Dorothea's comment that "it seems to me we know nothing of our neighbours, unless they are cottagers" (238) risks arrogance because it presumes she can have intimate knowledge of the cottagers' lives when her own domestic servants are invisible.[15]

The invisibility of servants in *Middlemarch* is startling, most notably in the famous parable of the pier-glass and the candle. It begins somewhat colloquially, addressing the reader in the second person: "An eminent philosopher among my friends, who can dignify even your ugly furniture by lifting it into the serene light of science, has shown me this pregnant little fact" (194). The passage continues to invite the reader to identify with the narrator's perspectives: "Your pier-glass or extensive surface of polished steel made to be rubbed by a housemaid, will be minutely and multitudinously scratched in all directions." The syntax invites the reader to read through the phrase "by a housemaid." The housemaid disappears into a function—rubbing—even as she is produced; she is made both inevitable and invisible. That is, the presence of a housemaid is assumed in the novel's audience; it is naturalized. Further, the passive construction insidiously mystifies the real logic: these possessions, which signify a certain gentility, must be kept up to snuff by a range of domestic servants whom the mistress *makes* labor toward that end. The fact of management is effaced in the very moment it is produced, our intellectual vistas are not cluttered with pictures of menial labor, and objects seem to come with their own injunctions: to be cooked at eight, to be cleaned when dirty, to be polished when tarnished.[16]

In this context, we can better appreciate the judgment of one of George Eliot's contemporaries, who objected to her representation

[15] George Eliot remarks in "The Natural History of German Life" that peasants do not "stand out as individuals. . . . The cultured man acts more as an individual; the peasant, more as one of a group" (274).

[16] Bruce Robbins locates in the phrase "made to be rubbed by a housemaid" a potential destabilization of the whole system of values represented. For Robbins, the fact of the rubbing housemaid reveals "possible distortions" in the "mirror of realism." He adds, "Not only is the egoism of the characters pushing toward their fates deflected by servant interference, which revises and enlarges those fates, but more important, realism itself is 'placed' by their self-conscious exteriority" (160). This interpretation puts a lot of weight on the reader's actually noticing and pausing over the phrase, which, I would argue, invites us in its unobtrusiveness to naturalize the relations inscribed in the passage.

of Dorothea as a Victorian Saint Theresa. In 1875, Jane Ellice Hopkins explained her experience among the working classes: "It was this suburb, with its lawless population of roughs, that I chose as the sphere for my efforts; youthful heroism, when combined with Christianity, even though it cannot be a St. Theresa, having still some few outlets left in these degenerate days, despite the dictum of our great novelist George Eliot; not being quite reduced to the melancholy career she accords it as summed up in Miss Nightingale's words 'of first marrying an elderly literary impostor, and then quick after him an inferior sort of fawn'" (28).

Not only is Dorothea portrayed as idle in her extensive establishment, but so is Rosamond Lydgate, whose much more modest situation should demand some supervisory role. Before marriage, Lydgate anticipates that his wife will "create order in the home and accounts with still magic" (258). But rather than represent Rosamond trying and failing, like Dora Copperfield, the text suggests that Rosamond has nothing to do except cooperate with Tertius, whose ideal of management takes the negative prescription of hiring "servants who will not break things" (258). She remains as divorced from her own household affairs as if she were a guest. Her mother, Mrs. Vincy, also presides over a household remarkable only for the extravagance that has spoiled her eldest children, so that Rosamond thinks that "good housekeeping consist[s] simply in ordering the best of everything" (429). The possibility exists that, in Lydgate and Rosamond's failure of housekeeping, Eliot dramatizes how management has been socially mystified, so that neither character understands the dimensions of the task. In this interpretation, the newly married Lydgates suffer a fate common to their generation, described colloquially in *The Englishwoman's Domestic Magazine*: "They began with the chucky."[17] That is, falling prey to their culture's mystifications of household management, they overextended themselves financially. Such a reading would demand a consistent representation of the importance of domestic organization.

But this balancing portrayal is absent from *Middlemarch*. The only "housekeeper" with any pretensions whatever is Mrs. Garth, and

[17] "Many will remember the anecdote of the mother who, when asked why her married son and his wife failed in business, replied, 'Ah, sir? you see they began with the chucky.' By which she meant . . . that they had commenced housekeeping on a scale of expenditure superior to their income. . . . In this old lady's time her son's case may have been exceptional; now, at all events, similar instances of erroneous proceeding are by no means rare. Half the world now begins with the 'chucky'" (*Englishwoman's Domestic Magazine* 1 [1865]:89).

the text affirms her immersion in actual physical labor, which is evidently supposed to lend a homely authenticity to her character: "Mrs Garth at certain hours was always in the kitchen, and this morning she was carrying on several occupations at once there— making her pies at the well-scoured deal table on one side of that airy room, observing Sally's movements at the oven and dough-tub through an open door. . . . A tub and clothes-horse at the other end of the kitchen indicated an intermittent wash of small things also going on" (179). Immersing Mrs. Garth in the physical work of her household, the narrator erases any sense of her management role. We must conclude that Sally is the Garth's maid-of-all-work; she exists here as a signifier of the Garth's middle-class status, but she is sufficiently effaced so that she in no way detracts from the narrative tribute accorded to Mrs. Garth:

> It must be admitted that Mrs Garth was a trifle too emphatic in her resistance to what she held to be follies: the passage from governess into housewife had wrought itself a little too strongly into her consciousness, and she rarely forgot that while her grammar and accent were above the town standard, she wore a plain cap, cooked the family dinner, and darned all the stockings. She had sometimes taken pupils in a peripatetic fashion, making them follow her about in the kitchen with their book and slate. She thought it good for them to see that she could make an excellent lather while she corrected their blunders "without looking,"—that a woman with her sleeves tucked up above her elbows might know all about the Subjunctive Mood or the Torrid Zone—that, in short, she might possess "education" and other good things ending in "tion," and worthy to be pronounced emphatically, without being a useless doll. (179)

In acknowledging Mrs. Garth's too emphatic resistance to "what she held to be follies," the narrator affirms the convictions of this defiantly domestic character, who seems to have exceeded the bounds of decorum in marching her pupils about as she lathers clothes and kneads dough. At the same time, in representing her energetic activity in contrast to the inertia of the other ladies, the narrator endorses Mrs. Garth and encourages us to share her assessment of the others as "useless doll[s]." Sally, too, awkwardly posed by the oven and dough-tub, apparently exists to admire this English homemaker, who "reminded one of that delightful Frenchwoman whom we have all seen marketing, basket on arm" (180). The condescension implicit in the narrator's own assumed urbanity indicates that a "good" housewife belongs to labor, not to management. Mrs. Garth is narratively required to be hardworking, educated, and socially snubbed as a touchstone for the pettiness of Middlemarch society.

As housekeeper to Peter Featherstone, Mary Garth, like her mother, is ostensibly employed in management. Yet, the servants whom she supervises are invisible in the household. When she is not serving as nursemaid to her uncle, Mary seems to spend her time reading in a corner. Positioned as she is, she represents duty and integrity rather than efficient and thrifty management.

George Eliot shares with her contemporaries a firm grasp of the importance of domestic management. But she translates the women's sphere of effective supervision into another sphere for meaningful and valuable male activity. Mary and Mrs. Garth are only shadows of Caleb Garth, who figures in the text as the superior manager, serving the gentry and reconciling working men to the "inevitability" of their lot, quietly enacting the reforms that others make such a noisy business about. He is employed by Brooke, Chettam, Dorothea Casaubon, and, ultimately, Bulstrode as agent on their estates. He approves work that is "of a healthy kind while it is being done, and after it is done, men are the better for it" (402) However, his definition of "better" is grounded in the advancement of middle-class and upper-middle-class interests.

The critical scene depicting Garth at work centers around a Luddite-like conflict between labor and management. Surveying lands in Lowick parish to sell to the coming railways on Dorothea's behalf, Garth rallies to the side of the railway agents against the local laborers and then hectors the routed locals with the admonition that "you can't hinder the railroad: it will be made whether you like it or not. And if you go fighting against it, you'll get yourselves into trouble." Insisting that the "railway's a good thing," Garth meets eloquent opposition in the form of old Timothy Cooper, who parries, "Aw! good for the big folks to make money out on. . . [Railroads]'ll on'y leave the poor man furder behind. . . . This is the big folks's world, this is. But yo're for the big folks, Muster Garth, yo are." Garth has no effective reply except to concede that things are hard for poor men and they should not do "what will make things worse for themselves" (408–9). Garth's management facilitates the concentration of wealth in the middle classes and contributes to the disenfranchisement of the unhappy working classes. Poor management, like Brooke's, stimulates insurrectionary impulses, but Garth's efficiency works like an anodyne to silence dissent.

Mary and Mrs. Garth provide a support system that furthers

Caleb's success, but their own supervisory skills are not stressed in the way his are. For example, when Fred arrives to announce that he has entangled the Garths in his impecunity, Mrs. Garth, who has previously "remained ignorant of the affair," immediately assumes the reins of leadership: "Like the eccentric woman she was, she was at present absorbed in considering what was to be done, and did not fancy the end could be better achieved by bitter remarks or explosions" (171, 183). She points out to her abashed husband that "if I had only known I might have been ready with some better plan" (184). Her efficient management and thrift both ground and enable the reforms he enacts as land agent on the estates of Tipton, Freshitt, Lowick, and Stone Court. Similarly, it is Fred who is to manage Stone Court, and Mary who is to manage Fred. Mary does eventually take Fred Vincy in hand—"husbands are an inferior class of men, who require keeping in order"—but the way in which her efforts help to produce the *social* order is mystified.

In the marriage between Mary and Fred, who has "gone down a step in life" (414), individual integrity is kept separate from questions of social benefit through a rhetoric of false gentility. Mary has dissuaded Fred from pursuing a clerical career, arguing that "being a clergyman would be only for gentility's sake, and I think there is nothing more contemptible than such imbecile gentility" (379). Mary is lauded for not being "among those daughters of Zion who are haughty, and walk with stretched-out necks and wanton eyes, mincing as they go" (298). Although the two will consolidate their own wealth and that of upper middle classes generally, these are represented as activities different from aspiring to gentility.

Eliot's text persistently denigrates the kind of socially "good" marriage that Oliphant's heroines were desirous of making. Mr. Casaubon, middle-aged, unencumbered, and wealthy, is a highly eligible mate for a Miss Brooke, and the marriage will certainly consolidate wealth among the county families. A social scandal erupts, however, when Dorothea accepts Casaubon's proposal; the social propriety of the match is only grudgingly conceded by Mrs. Cadwallader: "However, Casaubon has money enough; I must do him that justice" (41). And Mr. Brooke's just reflections—"the match is good. I should have been traveling out of my brief to have hindered it, let Mrs. Cadwallader say what she will" (49)—appear in the text as the self-serving rationalizations of a weak-willed man. The depiction of society's horror at the match proleptically announces that marriage for Dorothea is nothing without passion, a curious stance for society folk to take.

Middlemarch is, in fact, committed to the cause of "love," which is manifest as an inverse ratio to all possible social motivation or benefit. Thus, Rosamond's marriage to Lydgate receives the greatest narrative disapprobation, and we, as readers, are invited to pretend ignorance of motivations like hers: "If you think it incredible that to imagine Lydgate as a man of family could cause thrills of satisfaction which had anything to do with the sense that she was in love with him, I will ask you to use your power of comparison a little more effectively, and consider whether red cloth and epaulets have never had an influence of that sort" (123). The narrator explicitly addresses a "reader" who is asked to endorse certain perspectives and values. Demands on our imagination are particularly acute in the instance of Rosamond, of whose passion we are informed that, "any one who imagines ten days too short a time . . . for the whole spiritual circuit of alarmed conjecture and disappointment, is ignorant of what can go on in the elegant leisure of a young lady's mind" (221). The unconnected stranger Bulstrode focuses narrative suspicion for having married into one of the best Middlemarch families, and shallow Celia, predictably, falls into the position her noble sister rejected, that of wife to Sir James.

The novel presents more admirable characters as disdaining social propriety and appropriateness in making matches. From this perspective, we can understand Dorothea Brooke's love for Will Ladislaw. No other character enjoys his amphibious status: sufficiently of society to be acquainted with her but otherwise unclassifiable. Lydgate describes him as "a sort of gypsy," claiming that "he thinks nothing of leather and prunella" (319).[18] Mr. Casaubon attempts to get rid of Will by arguing his violation of "certain social fitnesses and proprieties," his holding a "position unsuited to [Ladislaw's] rank as [Casaubon's] cousin" (272, 286). Will's grandmother initially forfeited her estate for marrying a poor man, conduct that in Casaubon's estimation "constitutes a forfeiture of family claims" (275). The county families share Casaubon's feelings; Mrs. Cadwallader denigrates Ladislaw as "an Italian carrying white mice" (361). And the disclosures about Bulstrode culminate in Will's being branded the "grandson of a thieving Jew pawnbroker," a "worse kind of placard on poor Will's back than the 'Italian with white mice'" (566).

---

[18] Lydgate alludes to Alexander Pope's "Essay on Man" (1733), 4:203–4: "Worth makes the man, and want of it, the fellow;/The rest is all but leather or prunella." I am indebted for this reference to Bert G. Hornback, ed. *Middlemarch* (New York: Norton, 1977), p. 301. Hornback explains, "Pope suggests that dress—the leather of the cobbler's apron, the prunella of the priest's cassock—means nothing; Lydgate says that Ladislaw knows this, and cares nothing for such irrelevant social distinctions."

Dorothea, of course, does not share these crude estimations of Will, which rouse "afresh [her] inward resistance to what was said about him in that part of her world which lay within park palings" (566). Indeed, the attraction Will exerts on Dorothea depends upon his socially suspect origins and upon his ability to take her "out of her proper rank," a kind of straitjacket from which she seeks release (597). The local gentry finally concur that "it is difficult to say what Mr Ladislaw is," and Mrs. Cadwallader sums up: "It must be admitted that his blood is a frightful mixture! . . . The Casaubon cuttle-fish fluid to begin with, and then a rebellious Polish fiddler or dancing-master, was it?—and then an old clo—" (599). She gets no further before her husband cuts her off. But the point has been made: he is not one of them. That is what the narrative requires for Dorothea. Her love is depicted as a redemptive force, beyond class claims. It functions, like the elements of nature with which Will and Dorothea's passionate embrace is associated, as a force to tear asunder the superficial garments in which society clothes us, and the novel works to locate their passion outside of social convention and custom.[19]

When Eliot focuses on social relationships, she often uses them to demonstrate the vulgarity of individuals who presume to stand on their superior gentility, as in the relationship between the Vincys and the Garths. Although Mr. Vincy himself has married down in choosing an innkeeper's daughter, he theoretically believes that "it's a good British feeling to try and raise your family a little" (95). Mrs. Vincy has felt her elevation sufficiently that she disdains the Garths, even though Mrs. Garth, a former governess who speaks standard English, would never be guilty of the vulgarisms of Mrs. Vincy. Fred has argued earlier that "all choice of words is slang. It marks a class," and he adds that "correct English is the slang of prigs" (73, 74).

Fred's observations and the fact that wives determined a family's social position—a truth promulgated by etiquette manuals and social histories—do not hold in Middlemarch, where Mrs. Vincy looks down on the Garths and Fred Vincy is admirable for steadfastly loving Mary Garth, despite his mother's distaste for the humble union. Mr. Farebrother also wins narrative points for being "fond of his

[19] Leavis compares the proposal scene in *Miss Marjoribanks* and its corollary in *Middlemarch*: "The dramatic scene of Lucilla's capture by and surrender to an overwhelmingly masculine lover in her dead father's library is very poorly emulated in the feeble, unintentionally ridiculous scene in the dead husband's library at Lowick, where it takes a thunder-and-lightning storm to bring Will and Dorothea together" (147).

parishioners the Garths" and using "to the full the clergyman's privilege of disregarding the Middlemarch discrimination of ranks" in
visiting them (295). The narrator wants to insist on the Garths' more
humble position apparently to bolster our sense not only of Fred's
nobility in his persevering attachment to Mary but also of Mr. Farebrother's disinterestedness in his. And the vicar's insistence to his
mother that "Mrs Garth was more of a lady than any matron in the
town" (295) functions as a sign of his superior discrimination, although, within the signifying systems of education and diction,
Mrs. Garth would certainly rank above the shopkeepers' wives of
Middlemarch.

Society, however, is not always represented consistently in Eliot's
novel. "Even when Caleb Garth was prosperous," we are told, "the
Vincys were on condescending terms with him and his wife, for
there were nice distinctions of rank in Middlemarch; and though old
manufacturers could not any more than dukes be connected with
none but equals, they were conscious of an inherent social superiority which was defined with great nicety in practice, though hardly
expressible theoretically" (170). The basis for Mrs. Vincy's condescension lies in Mrs. Garth's formerly being a governess—"a woman
who had had to work for her bread"—but George Eliot enjoys a
unique place among novelists and tractarians of the period for proposing that a prosperous innkeeper's daughter enjoyed more social
esteem than an impoverished educated woman. Eliot's novel tends
to emphasize middle-class society as a petty, unproductive medium
that consistently thwarts fellow-feeling and the achievement of human community. "Good society" simply impedes productive sociality and to the extent that Eliot has so represented it, women, who
are its chief arbiters, must either "transcend" it or become mired in
its pettiness. But the novel itself does not transcend the exploitation
of domestic labor and the naturalization of class differences in which
bourgeois women participated. As we have seen, when the supervisor is not dramatized, then the labor is even more mystified. We
can read right over the traces of labor in a way that confirms that, in
terms of domestic class arrangements if not gender ones, this is the
best of all possible worlds.

In contrast to her contemporaries Elizabeth Gaskell and Margaret
Oliphant, George Eliot depicts society's discursive practices not as
integral to the construction of meaning and identity but as a con-
stricting force to be transcended, something to be penetrated by distinction of mind. Lydgate must suffer for desiring it to be known
"that he was better born than other country surgeons" (111–12).

Ladislaw reaps rewards for positioning himself as "a sort of gypsy, rather enjoying the sense of belonging to no class," and for proudly declaring that he "never had any caste" (338).

This scouting of class claims has significant consequences for the representation of women, who controlled the signifiers of social status and managed the family's household and position. Once such claims are textually discounted as frivolous and unproductive, then prosperous middle-class women come to inhabit a narrative empty space, a still center of enforced inactivity—the "gentlewoman's oppressive liberty." At best, she can serve, like Dorothea, as a cheerleader for aspiring men, "holding up an ideal for others in her believing conception of them." At the worst, she is a basil plant like Rosamond, feeding on a murdered man's brains.

But this reality is as much a construction as any other, and its political implications become more striking when we consider that George Eliot persistently suggests how domestic values do significant public work but analyzes those connections largely through men and male activity, as we have seen in the portrayal of Caleb Garth. Her presentation of the national reform movement is grounded in the mismanagement of Mr. Brooke's private estate and the class tensions he is blind to. The narrative repeatedly insists on the truism that reform must begin at home, where Brooke should "reform his rent-roll." And it questions "what business has an old county man to come currying favour with a low set of dark-blue freemen" (262). The country wants, as Will asserts, "to have a house of Commons which is not weighted with nominees of the landed class, but with representatives of the other interests" (337). *Middlemarch* delineates the ways in which class prerogatives of the most homely sort commit us to large political agendas, how "our furniture, our dinner-giving, and preference for armorial bearings in our own case, link us indissolubly with the established order" (255). The last quotation refers, of course, to Lydgate and suggests that he, not Rosamond, functions as the housekeeper, the keeper of their status. Although Eliot is astute about the ways the homeliest details of domestic life play themselves out on the national scene, she continually erases the place of woman in domestic management and thus in the political life of Victorian England.

Mr. Vincy responds with irritation to Rosamond's insistence that her marriage take place, arguing that "Parliament [is] going to be dissolved . . . and an election [is] coming on." To her query, "What can that have to do with my marriage?" he answers, "A pretty deal to do with it!" (259). The possibility of a dissolving political order jeopardizes all Rosamond has striven for, although she is never depicted as comprehending how social chaos is intimately tied to domestic disorder and failures of management.

In *Middlemarch*, however, domestic order and "good society" are severed. Women participate only in the latter; men ensure the former, to the extent it exists. Mrs. Garth and Mary only partially abridge this narrative tendency, and they remain pointedly outside of good society. In contrast to Mary and her mother stands "this petty medium of Middlemarch," whose members aspire to that "middle-class heaven, rank" (139, 88). So represented, middle-class women seem unlikely to have become agitators for equality in politics, education, and opportunity. It is much easier to see daughters of a Phoebe Junior or a Lucilla Marjoribanks agitating for rights alongside the Pankhurst sisters than it is to see descendants of Dorothea Brooke in that role. For, it seems likely that middle-class feminism was forged, at least in part, in the smithy of women's social management, which gave women an inclination for professional work even as it taught them that they had the skills to pursue it. The bourgeois manager also helps explain the early and persistent class gaps among women, both in their feminism and in their aspirations and expectations. For middle-class feminism was built upon the assumption that another class existed to perform menial labor, and working-class women were constructed to bolster and facilitate the middle-class project.

The implications of this process in *Middlemarch* are integral to the novel's "moral" effects, which are acknowledged and validated in the canonical status accorded Eliot's *Study of Provincial Life*, the only novel, in Virginia Woolf's estimation, written for adults. The tension between bourgeois women's class and gender roles has been managed in such a way as to reinforce our sense of women's disability in patriarchy and to mute the discursive instability that was producing new images and new possibilities for female subjects. The result is a text that has been enormously attractive to feminist readers for its depictions of talented and thwarted women but equally frustrating in ways that have not been successfully articulated. As we see here, the difficulty of articulation lies in mystifications of the domestic realm and its dependency upon a female management that extended into the larger community. These mystifications are also inscribed in the canon, which relegates to an inferior status works that engage with domesticity and rely for meanings on the always already feminized and marginalized domestic detail.

8

Hannah Cullwick:
Deity of Dirt

The examination of *Middlemarch* provided one point of departure
from the main thesis, a departure intended to clarify the canonical
privileging of certain domestic ideologies inscribed in Eliot's novel.
An analysis of the diaries of domestic servant Hannah Cullwick extends the reach of this discussion by dramatizing in a particularly
vivid way the intrication of class and gender in the formation of
subjectivity. In this chapter I examine the social semiotics of middle-
class life from the perspective of a domestic servant elevated
through marriage to the middle class. Only by positing an identity
multiply constituted can we grasp the intractable difficulties of her
situation when Cullwick attempts to redefine herself as a "lady." In
Cullwick's diary narrative, we discover that what has been repressed in the formation of her identity cannot be recalled without a
traumatic destabilization of her sense of "self." It is not simply a
question of material elevation but an entire reconfiguration of her
gender identity and sexuality through different class terms.

In these two chapters—on Eliot's *Middlemarch* and Cullwick's diaries—I give center stage to two issues that were implicit in my earlier discussion of bourgeois domestic management: the tenacity of
dominant cultural mythologies and the way the "classing" of sexed
bodies and the sexing of "classed" bodies produce corollary repres-
sions so that a new class position threatens to destabilize the entire
entity. In critical studies the tendency persists to give priority to certain narratives of domestic life over others and to gender over other
terms in a psychosexual narrative that implicitly institutes sexual difference as *the* ground of difference. My analyses of *Middlemarch* and
Cullwick's diaries challenge those simple priorities, deepening our
grasp of the complex configurations of subjects in Victorian En-

gland, recasting questions of female agency, and facilitating our understanding of how social change might be effected.

The Housemaid's Tale

Hannah Cullwick's diaries record over thirty years of her life as a Victorian maidservant. Written at the express wish, indeed, virtual command, of her gentleman lover, Arthur Munby, the diaries chart the shifting construction of her identity through entwined discourses of gender, class, and race. In previous chapters I have illuminated conflicts in the discursive formation of middle-class womanhood, as represented in both literary and nonliterary works of the mid-Victorian period, and pointed to the ways some novels inevitably try to elide these representational gaps through a recourse to nature and an appeal to narrative telos. Because she helped to solidify an image of the middle classes, the bourgeois, managerial woman was transforming her own image, producing representations that would propel the emergence of the late-Victorian "new woman," a middle-class phenomenon that built its rationalizations along rigid class lines. In a corollary development, the working-class woman often found her subjectivity articulated through a discourse of degradation. The representations of middle-class women allowed us partially to gauge the tensions produced by a contradictory placement within patriarchal and bourgeois ideologies; Hannah Cullwick's diaries, however, throw that conflict into relief and thus make painfully explicit what is often only implicit in the other texts I have discussed.

By examining the relationship between Arthur Munby and Hannah Cullwick I reintroduce the initial inquiry of this book—that is, why the plot of the worthy working girl marrying her master disappeared from the novel, became non-narratable. This instance of interclass marriage provides further insights into the material realities that informed the myth of the Angel in the House and returns us to Richardson's plot. *Pamela* depicted just such a marriage between a servant girl and a gentleman immeasurably her social superior. If I initially seemed to suggest that the union was effortless, requiring only a lessening of his pride to accommodate her inferior status, in fact, the narrative structure exposes clear signs of strain. The marriage takes place two-thirds of the way into the novel, eliminating the aesthetic tension which focuses on the affective relationship between Mr. B and Pamela: will she be raped or married? At this point when the narrative interest is exhausted, fully one-third of the novel still remains because the narrative instabilities have not been resolved. Those instabilities focus on Pamela's qualifications for such social elevation, her ability to swim comfortably in the new waters of bourgeois life. Her success becomes the precondition for the novel's conclusion. She succeeds, of course, but that is the eighteenth century and a fiction, one that depicts a working-class heroine who is effectively middle class in all but her fortune. Hannah Cullwick's class-inflected subjectivity was not so readily transformed. The prospect of a class elevation destabilized her whole identity.

The process by which class lines hardened to facilitate the breaching of gender boundaries is poignantly traced in Hannah Cullwick's narrative. As a self-protective gesture, she attempts to suture together some kind of plausible subjectivity, but she is repeatedly forced to reexperience her fracturing by Arthur Munby's encouragement that she construct herself at once through discourses of degradation and elevation, expressed most succinctly in his simultaneous exaltation of her menial labor and social distinction. Thus, she imports a self-stylized racial performance to negotiate the conflicting class indentities of refined lady and child of the soil. Her narrative becomes an eloquent testimony to the instability of the female subject in Victorian woman.

The story of Arthur Munby and Hannah Cullwick became known only in the twentieth century. A few intimate friends and her family shared the secret of their marriage during their lives; his family remained unaware that he had married a working woman. The extreme clandestine nature of the relationship marks it as a site of some of the most intransigent problems of Victorian England. Unlike those members of the aristocracy whose rank allowed them to publish their irregular liaisons with members of the servant classes, Munby felt constrained. His less-elevated position no doubt bound him more firmly to the discourses of bourgeois respectability and propriety, just as his sense of duty made him aware of an increasing obligation to marry the domestic servant who had devoted her life to "Massa." He finally did so after eighteen years.

Munby, born in 1828, and Cullwick, born in 1832, inhabited an England dominated by the discursive practices I have been investigating throughout this book, practices that constructed an angelic image of middle-class woman and that bifurcated woman as signifier. The wedge of class became fully as intransigent as the wedge of gender because class rhetoric of Victorian England dematerialized middle-class women as bodies and, in a corollary movement, essentialized working and lower-class women as merely bodies, sexual and physical machines.

Although Munby's story is surely revelatory of his individual psychology, that story and his psychology seem characteristic of his age. Munby was early attracted to working women; indeed, we are indebted to him for the careful records he kept of their lives. Derek Hudson, Munby's biographer, has pointed to the "latent homosexual trend" evident in Munby's "interest in trousered, grimy, even disfigured women" (71), but the unfolding narrative of his life reveals the forms that ideology allowed for the expression of his homosexuality. Obviously, part of Cullwick's attraction for Munby lay in the fact that she was not a "woman" within his culture's signifying practices. Munby loved to contrast working women with ladies, depicting them both in the same drawing; inevitably, the signifiers of femininity are entirely absent in his representations of working women, who are characterized through bulky figures, blackened faces, shorn or covered hair, distorted features. His verbal pictures emphasize the same contrasts, evident in this description of a farm servant: "Altogether, a noble creature, refreshing to behold: simple & unconscious—thinking only, if she thought at all, that she was very dirty & not fit to be seen: and yet possessing all the charms of contour and colours that ladies strive for, and a large sinewy grace besides, that were neither proper nor possible for them" (17). Munby's conviction that "sinewy grace" is not "proper" for ladies speaks eloquently to the way bodies are inscribed within cultural expectations and practices. At one point, Munby cuts Cullwick's hair and remarks "though I should never have proposed the sacrifice—which she made of her own accord—it adds one more to the outward contrasts between her and fine-ladyhood, & so I like it" (148).

Just as Munby was searching for a "helpmate fit to labour," Cullwick was engaging in a reciprocal search for "someone above her own class" (15, 17). At one point in her diaries, Cullwick imagines a discussion in which a friend of Munby's expresses regret that she is not a lady and Munby replies: "But if she was a lady, you know . . . then she wouldn't be a *servant*, & that's *just* what I like her for, & she likes it too & I think it's certainly the same reason (only the exact opposite of course) why Hannah likes me. I love her for her ignorance, & she loves me for being *different*" (252). The imaginative value that Cullwick places in "difference" bespeaks her culture's investment in class and other markers. Cullwick later elaborates that difference through entwined race, class, and gender inscriptions. She defines herself as Munby's "slave," wearing literal chains and a padlock and addressing him as "Massa," to free herself, it seems, from the dependence dictated by compulsory heterosexuality within a class matrix. Cullwick asks herself: "Should I have felt *such* pleasure for a common working man? I *might* if I had found a working man as could love as purely & be as Massa is (I mean in everything but his learning) & honour him as much, but that's a difficulty I doubt, the finding such a one" (272–73). Cullwick recognizes that, of course, Munby bears the imprint of his class as surely as a working man bears the mark of his. She could love a working man if he were like Munby, but of course no working man could be like Munby.

Cullwick invokes a sense of fate to justify events retrospectively. As she meditates on the significance of their differences, she reauthorizes her relationship with Munby by attributing it to her having had a vision of him before their actual meeting: "And so when I was young & *did* meet with Massa (whose face I'd seen in the fire) I made my mind up that it was best & safest to be a slave to a *gentleman*, nor wife & equal to any vulgar man, still with the wish & determination to be independent by working in service and without the slightest hope o' been rais'd in rank either in place or by being married" (273). Her justification serves the purpose of freeing Cullwick from the class expectation that she would marry within her sphere, even as it reinscribes her identity *as* a working woman.

Cullwick elaborates the meaning of that "safest" course in loving a gentleman through an entangled discourse of selfhood, independence, and self-preservation. Earlier she has commented, "The greatest pleasure wears away & quickly too & I've so long learnt that to save disappointments one mustn't expect pleasures, & so I feel safest . . . when I'm at my regular work in service" (182). Later, she argues for the status quo in these same terms: "But tho' I'm never so happy as when I'm with him or working for *him*, yet I want to be still a servant & working so as to be independent & get my own living" (193). She frets that she never could "make my mind up to [married life]—it's too much like being a *woman*." When she finally capitulates to marriage, urged by Munby's sense of duty, Cullwick reaffirms the complexly negotiated freedoms purchased through her "slavery" to Munby: "I am as I am. A servant still, & a very low one, in the eyes o' the world. I can work at ease. I can go out & come in when I please, & I can look as degraded as ever I like without caring how much I'm despised in the Temple, or in Fetter Lane or in the streets. And with all that I have the inward comfort o' knowing that I am loved & honoured & admired & that I am united in heart & soul as well as married at church to the truest, best & handsomest man in my eyes that ever was born" (273).

By refusing to become a lady and by flaunting the signifiers of her degradation, Cullwick has forestalled the collapse of her selfhood in marriage that she feared. When Munby initially presented her with a marriage license, he demanded of her, "Doesn't this show how much I love you, & what do you say to it?" Cullwick responds, "I told him I had *nothing* to say about it, but I hoped he would never be sorry for it, nor *I*. Tho' I seem'd so cool & said so little I really *meant* what I said. I car'd very *very* little for the license or being married either. Indeed I've a certain dislike to either, they seem to have so little to do with our *love* & our union" (253). Cullwick employed a discourse of romantic love here and later—"after all this there can be do doubt of our being made for each other"—to suture the class and gender gaps opening between Munby's construction of her and her own self-construction (273).

A proud, intelligent, and handsome woman, Cullwick pursued distinction not by climbing the social ladder—as a kind of British Honoria Alger—but through enacting a fairy tale plot of love and marriage with a man her social superior. In doing so, of course, she was fulfilling a social script already laid out for her. Given the contradictory inscriptions of the working and middle classes, the narrative of her transformation from servant to lady did not exist as an alternative. Instead, the Cinderella tale became literalized in Cullwick's life as she repeatedly returned to the ashes, soot, and dirt of her work to be chosen over and over again by her elegant prince. All her forays into ladyhood were, like so many charades, to end when the clock struck twelve and her coach once more became a pumpkin, her gowns, common rags.

Dirt and Distinction

From its inception, the relationship between Munby and Cullwick was negotiated through signifiers of racial degradation that helped to displace the class and sexual tensions. Cullwick's appropriation of blackness and of chains and padlocks as the ultimate signs of her servitude reveals the extent to which both master and servant conceptualized her degradation in racial terms. Indeed, the intransigent class and gender tensions in their relationship could be negotiated through racial "games," in which Hannah's black, enchained body became the fetishized object of Munby's gaze and desire. Cullwick relishes her debasement and revels in her dirty appearance. She throws herself into cleaning frenzies of the most awful drudgery and filth entirely for Munby's viewing pleasure. A racially encoded dirty appearance had become the major signifier of class difference and sexual attractiveness. Within the year after she first met Munby, Cullwick began blacking her face, associating the practice with his presence in her lodgings: "There Massa came to see me again, & there was where I first black'd my face with *oil & lead*" (40). On one occasion Munby lodges at a rooming house at which Cullwick is employed, and she enters his room "in my dirt to do the grate up, & light the fire. I had a dirty face, & my arms was black too, on purpose for M. to see me as he had wish'd to" (69).

Ironically, Munby's presence was not necessary for the drama because Cullwick could re-present herself in the diary she kept at his behest. It is enough for Cullwick simply to imagine herself in her blackness as the object of Munby's gaze: "I wish'd much that M. could see me for I knew he would o' liked to see me so, & have loved me the more for it. But still I was satisfied that I was doing it for him & I could give him a nice account of it in writing" (66). Cullwick augmented her diary record with photographic representations and insists to one photographer, Mr. Stodart, that she wants "to be done thoroughly black like I am sometimes at work" and is disappointed when the picture "wasn't 1/2 so black as I was really" (75, 76). In a more dramatic instance of this racial self-fashioning, Cullwick prepares to clean a chimney by stripping herself "quite naked," tying an "old duster" over her hair, and ascending the chimney with a brush: "I swept lots o' soot down & it come all over me & I sat there for ten minutes or more, & when I'd swept all round & as far as I could reach I come down, & lay on the hearth in the soot a minute or two thinking, & I wish'd rather that Massa could see me. I black'd my face over & then got the looking glass & look'd at myself & I was certainly a fright & hideous all over, at least I should o' seem'd so to anybody but Massa" (139). Hannah's fetishized phallic body lends itself to psychoanalytic interpretation, but I want to focus on its role in the material construction of subjecthood. The racialization of Cullwick's sexuality stimulates a desire Munby is incapable of expressing for "women" in his culture, just as the racialization of Cullwick's class inscription facilitates her sense of control as she willingly and willfully blackens her body.

But Munby must have led Cullwick a tormented life because she could never be sure whether she was too black or not black enough. One evening Munby visited Cullwick "in [her] dirt, but he said [she] wasn't black enough" (116). Black enough for what? On another evening, Munby tells her to black her face "like it was that night I clean'd after the coalmen." Cullwick obeys and "got the dinner & clean'd the boots & wash'd up the things & Massa's feet with it black, & M. seem'd pleas'd wi' it" (138). Even after they are married, Munby periodically requires that his wife appear in blackface: "M. told me to kiss him afore I black'd my face. So I did, & then rubb'd my black hand across my face & arms, & when I'd to go down for a fresh [pail] o' water M. said he hoped to see me blacker still when I come back. So downstairs I black'd both my hands & wiped them all over my face & that pleas'd Massa & he said I was blacker even than any o' the pit wenches" (271–72). The dirtiness that was initially only the consequence of her labor quickly became a staged performance.

Yet blackness, that signifier of difference and desirability, could apparently collapse into one of simple filth, as when Cullwick, proud that she was "the *blackest* servant in the street of all the lodging house servants," decides to visit Munby "in my dirt . . . on purpose that he may see *how* dirty I got" (61). She is dismayed, however, to find that he is "disgusted" at her appearance: "My face was dirty (I'd been cleaning the dirty scullery out) & my arms black'd & my *hands* look'd swell'd & red, & begrimed with dirt— *grener'd* as we say in Shropshire. That is, the cracks in our hands ingrain'd with back lead" (61). Cullwick is hurt and bewildered by his insistence that she wash herself, and she thinks, "Massa was changed. . . . It seems he began to think I *was too low* & degraded & that he really pitied me" (61–62). His ambivalence is reflected in his own diary of 1860: "I found [Cullwick] dirty and unkempt, as she had been all day, she said; and the poor child evidently thought I liked to see her so" (51). Munby's condescending representation of Cullwick as the delusional "poor child" betrays his anxiety that the elaborate theater of color they've enacted will make it impossible for Cullwick to play the part of a lady, the role prescribed for her as his wife.

Indeed, having stabilized her class and gender identity through this racially inflected discourse of degradation and dirt, which served as prominent signifiers of her value, Cullwick increasingly resisted Munby's attempts to make her play the lady. Even early in the relationship, when she was more compliant, Cullwick never internalized the signifiers of ladyhood the way she had embraced the signifiers of degradation. The racial inflections of her identity seemed coterminous with the class inflections but served the important function of making unique her commonplace inscription as working-class woman, domestic servant. They further intensified the physical differences between a middle-class lady and herself.

A Fussy Fine Lady

In contrast, the signifiers of middle-class ladyhood, particularly those of bodily weakness and ineptitude, conflicted sharply with the others Cullwick had adopted. Cullwick prides herself on her weight, massive biceps and coarse, red hands, all signs of her physical capacity. She boasts that "my arm is 13-3/4 inches round the muscle & my hand 4-1/2 inches across the inside" (127). Then she continues to itemize her measurements in contrast to Munby's: "I put how thick my arm was round the muscle & it's 10 & a 1/2 inches round thick below [the] elbow—6 & 3/4 round my wrist. My neck is 13-1/2, so it's not so big as my arm—& Massa's muscle is but 13 & a half round" (128). Cullwick repeatedly contrasts her bulk with that of her mistresses', reading in their diminutive size the signs of their ineptitude: "Miss K thought me very strong, & so I am, 4 times stronger nor she is I should say, for she couldn't draw a cork, nor lift a saucepan. She could not *sew* well either, therefore a poor drudge like me is more use in a lodging house than her being a brought-up lady" (78). At times, the comparison stimulates pride in her own capacity; at others, contempt for what she sees as the lady's useless life: "*She* was fussy and *whining* like, & yet so small & feeble. It seem'd hard to be provoked so by her, & for me to be patient & meek to one as I could crush with one hand almost & I so much taller nor her" (89). Cullwick interprets the lady's life and clothes alike as stifling. On one occasion, her mistress feels compelled to lecture her on her church attendance, and, when Cullwick is released from her presence, she records: "I actually jump'd for joy & felt as if I was let out o' prison. The feeling is dreadful—that being stuck in a drawing room & having a fussy fine lady talking to you" (74).

The prison metaphor extends to the lady's clothes, which confine alike the body and its movement: "That's the best o' being drest rough, & looking '*nobody*'—-you can go any where & not be wonder'd at" (274). Cullwick's preoccupation with bare hands in contrast to gloved ones underlines her feelings about the freedoms of domestic servitude versus the confinements of ladyhood. She speaks of having "no need" for gloves in her life and chafes against Munby's requirement that she wear them as his wife: "I felt I'd much liefer feel my hands free as they used to be. But M. made me put the gloves on again, & I thought it was hard to be forced to wear gloves" (181, 266). Cullwick alleges her hands as the sign of her disqualification to be Munby's companion, positioning them as a metonym for her person: "Besides, I told M. my hands wasn't fit to go with him" (247). Describing a mistress, she notes that "her hand seem'd so tiny & thin in my big right hand, & I thought she herself look'd less than ever" (248–49). Cullwick uses her bare hands to clean out grates, drains, and sewers. She is seemingly proud of what her hands can do and where they can go, strengths and freedoms she arrogates to herself. They are the ultimate sign that she is herself a manual laborer.

What prevents Cullwick from simply crushing her mistress is her naturalization of class differences and her acceptance of class complementarity: "But she knew she was the lady & I knew I was her servant" (89). She tells Munby, "I was *born* to *serve*, & *not* to order," and she adds this note in her diary: "and I hope I shall always keep the same humble spirit—that of *liking* to serve others, & obeying instead of commanding" (85). Or she reflects: "And so we complemented one another, she for being a lady, & me for being a servant" (62). Cullwick experiences her greatest contentment when she is "serving a real lady." She comments that "I am a real happy maid of all work then, without restraint, working as hard as I like" (59). The "real" lady and "real" happy maid-of-all-work enter into a complementary economy in which one manages and the other labors. When her fellow servants refuse to perform some of the signifiers of class—for example, curtsying to a lady—Cullwick remonstrates with them, arguing, "I do think it's our duty to curtsy. . . . We do it when we're children, 'cause we're *teach'd* to do it, but how much nicer to do it from a real feeling of respect" (162–63). This "real" feeling helps to solidify Cullwick's identity as working class. One hears behind all of Cullwick's rationalizations the tension she feels as she struggles to negotiate the bourgeois demand not only that she do her assigned work but that she also perform her menial status.

In addition, of course, as the emphasis on size and strength indicates, Cullwick privileges labor over leisure in her self-construction. When her fellow servants express their desires to enjoy the privileges and comforts of ladyhood, she chastises them: "But for being among the grand folks or drest up like 'em & all that I'd fifty times rather be all black among the grate cleaning. And which is the most lasting o' the two, & which is the solidest & real pleasure?" (156).

The insistence on a "real" solid pleasure in physical labor plays on an implicit contrast to a lady's seemingly ephemeral existence.

When Cullwick finally marries Munby, she is forced to adopt the role she has so long alienated from her self-construction: that of a lady. At first, she attempts to perform the part as she had the racial inscriptions, as a kind of masquerade, a costume she dons on occasion. Munby, tickled by the new game, remarks, "For, is she not a servant during the day, and a lady in the evening? and fulfils either part so well, that for the time she seems incapable of the other" (Hudson 329). However, Cullwick's own representation of the transformation betrays the strain in the charade. She relates that "everywhere I was treated most respectfully, just as if I was a real lady." The "as if" betrays her real condition of being "almost ill-temper'd at being so muffled up." She is relieved to return home where she "doff'd all my best clothes & put my own on again—my dirty cotton frock & apron & my cap" (266). The "best clothes" are clearly not her "own," but those of a character she mimics.

Cullwick's most extended appearance as a "lady" occurred during a trip to France with Munby, a period she reflected on later in her diary. The musings occur after she has regrounded her identity in labor and dirt: "When I clean'd the water closet out last Saturday & I was so dirty I thought of the difference 'twixt me *then*, & when I was with Massa in France & being look'd on by everybody as a *lady*" (276). She adds that she found it strange to be "stopping at the best hotels & all as if I was ever so much a lady in reality," especially as "there was a many real ladies about" (277).

The tenacity with which Cullwick returns to the concept of a "real" lady who is not herself and her obsession with drudgery and dirt as signifiers of her value reflect her attempt to hold on to some stable identity. Munby's attempts to make her a lady and his corollary decision to free her from manual labor embittered and depressed Cullwick. She worked herself into a collapse, seeking to purchase his approval. She asks, "Massa . . . don't I do more work for you, nor all your other servants put together?" And Munby righteously writes in his diary, "This is her standing grievance, her one accusation against her husband: that he cannot & will not allow his wife to be his *only* servant" (424). Denied physical labor, Hannah simply refused to play any more at being a lady, and the debacle of their relationship led to increasing estrangement. Munby commented, "It seemed at first utterly sad . . . that all that sweet blossoming of ladyhood in her should be repressed once more, and she reduced to be a drudge again" (374).

But the "sweet blossoming of ladyhood" was only a romance

Munby had invented. More telling and more poignant are Cull-wick's later diary entries in which she reflects on why she can never be a lady, on what lies behind the "real" differences she has discerned. She thinks first of the difficulty for her—she who can perform Herculean feats of strength—of "pouring out tea for two gentlemen" (282). She finds an answer in varied modes of possession:

> Still, I felt that nothing could be done without self-possession, & which I've found out is the great difference 'twixt a lady & a servant, & which I must own too is scarcely possible for a thorough servant to *have* except in her own kitchen. And even there she must be what I call a presumptuous one except with the servants under her, 'cause it shows that she forgets the kitchen is *not* her own. Yet I pity the servants who always remember it, no one can tell her feelings who *does* remember that & forgets that she's working & earning all her wages. I went out to service too soon, before I really understood the meaning of it. (282)

This poignant revelation marks the constructed gulf between domestic servant and mistress, the one "born" to rule, the other to obey.

Cullwick's incisive grasp of what "seem'd to come natural" reveals the way class inflected gender and she was early written into a particular ideological script: "At the charity school I was taught to curtsy to the ladies & gentlemen & it seem'd to come natural to me to think them *entirely* over the lower class & as if it was our place to bow & be at their bidding, & I've never got out o' that feeling somehow" (282). Cullwick's intelligence gave her partial insight into the ideological formation of identity, just as it allowed her also to glimpse the system of representations governing her relationship to the society in which she lived.[1] But it did not allow her to change that system of representations or to alter substantially her relation to it. She, like her middle-class other, had been too successfully inscribed within the existing social texts.

Cullwick's obsession with manual labor, drudgery and dirt as signifiers of her value obviously reflected cultural ideology. She defined labor as menial, physical work, and she defined herself as a servant, maid-of-all-work. Those are the terms in which she was culturally constituted. She was completely alienated from the signifying

---

[1] As I noted in Chapter 1, Pierre Bourdieu theorizes this tendency to behave in specific ways in the social world in his concepts of *habitus* and *bodily hexis*. A habitus is a "set of *dispositions* which incline agents to act and react in certain ways"; they "literally mould the body and become second nature" (Introduction, *Language and Symbolic Power* 12). Bodily hexis is "political mythology *embodied*," an expression in body and thought of one's social position.

practices of the middle class; to be a lady was, for her, to be without identity. She could not cope with an ideology that would disembody her, render the material spiritual. Nor could she cope with labor defined as management. She rightly branded herself an "anomaly" in Munby's life. Cullwick finally confessed to her husband, "It *is* hard to be a slave to a littery person like you, as keeps on writin' books an' letters an' things, all day long!" (Hudson 424). Her dilemma pinpoints the mystification of middle-class work, the intervention of management between the worker and the product. Her sense of self depends on a class identity generally inimical to the middle-class definitions of gender and thus suggests other historical and potential definitions. Her ultimate refusal to become a lady bespeaks no insufficiency of nature; rather, it helps to constitute the class gulf in mid-Victorian England, where bourgeois women had become fully invested and centrally significant in the discursive practices that consolidated middle-class power.

Hannah Cullwick's diary narrative presents the tensions she experienced in trying to bridge class gulfs and, in its intelligence and sensitivity, helps to illuminate how that gulf is constructed—a process, as we have seen, often mystified in middle-class texts. The two perspectives together, bourgeois and working-class, paint a sobering picture of thousands of middle-class women marching toward gender equality over the bodies of their domestic servants.

9

New Women in
Old Guises

A brief formal survey of the novel from the late eighteenth to the late nineteenth century will bring into sharp relief the changed and changing representations of middle-class women—a genealogy of the female subject. In this overview I inevitably find myself constructing a narrative of a bourgeois female subject, but it is a narrative whose threads are constantly disrupted by discontinuities and complications. I chart cross-currents and instabilities rather than map the unfolding logic of a traditional historical narrative.

Evelina: From Birth to Breeding

From the beginning of Fanny Burney's *Evelina*, published in 1778, there is a mystery about the protagonist: Who is she? But the question could be reformulated in two different ways. Is she to be the acknowledged daughter of Sir John Belmont and the agent who will restore her betrayed mother's reputation? Or is she the "poor, weak, ignorant girl" she appears to be in her first London outing? The first question focuses on birth as a measure of social legitimacy, the second on breeding as a mark of eligibility. In posing both questions, the novel positions itself at the juncture of changing systems of value. Unlike Fielding's *Tom Jones*, however, in which a previously forbidden marriage is sanctioned through a sudden and surprising elevation of fortune occasioned by the discovery of genteel parents, Evelina does not require that revelation before Lord Orville sues for her hand. He needs to be assured, instead, that the awkward and ignorant behavior she displays at her first London assembly is not a true sign of her class.

In *Evelina*, birth takes a back seat to breeding in determining who is the eligible mate. The novel obliquely picks up the *Pamela* plot, in which a serving girl marries a man vastly her superior in social consequence. That is, the beauty of Evelina's grandmother, a barmaid, originally seduced the eye of her grandfather, a gentleman. This woman, Madame Duval, remarried after her first husband's death, has an incorrigible vulgarity of manner and deportment that might threaten to sink Evelina's prospects. In her "violence and vulgarity," in her "total ignorance of propriety," however, she instead serves both as a foil for her granddaughter's elegance of demeanor and as a cautionary exemplum of the importance of manner (205). Lord Orville will not fall prey, as Evelina's grandfather has done before him, to mere beauty without social cultivation. In this change, the novel marks the increasing importance of domestic discourses practiced by women.

Yet the novel also harkens back to an older system of aristocratic privilege and the prerogatives of birth, which authorize a grossness and violence, particularly against women, that disappear in representations of Victorian culture. This violence carries with it the explicit threat of physical harm. All of Madame Duval's vulgarity cannot make laughable the cruel and painful treatment she receives at the hands of Captain Mirvan, culminating in a physical assault by supposed robbers. The captain's violence always threatens to run out of control, and the man arouses deep fear not only in Madame Duval but also in Evelina. His wife, all elegance herself, is helpless to control or curb his license. And that violence is not limited to the captain. When Lord Merton and Mr. Coverley lay a wager that one can outrace the other in his phaeton, they are persuaded to confine their betting to situations that are less dangerous to themselves. Their substitute wager pits two old women in a foot race, "one of which was to be chosen by each side, and both were to be proved more than eighty years of age" (369). When Mr. Coverley's "agent" in this context loses, "he swore at her with unmanly rage, and seemed scarce able to refrain even from striking her" (391). Despite its pretensions to elegance, this world is still raw, very much in formation; it represents an early moment in the process through which behavior came under the control of social semiotics. Lord Orville and Evelina's guardian, the Reverend Villars, testify alone among the men to the value of gentility.

Otherwise, there lurks a generalized fear of potential violence against unprotected women. Unlike Emma Woodhouse, when Evelina speaks of danger, she means physical threat, and when she invokes the concept of safety, she expresses release from physical fear. Unaccompanied women are fair game in public settings such as Vauxhall and Marybone-gardens; in outings to both, Evelina becomes separated from her companions and is subjected to insult and physical abuse. The contrast between Evelina's situation, as represented, and that of the Victorian heroine is dramatic. So powerful had social semiotics become in establishing and disciplining class behavior by the mid-nineteenth century that an Esther Summerson is free to roam through the brickmaker's slums surrounding Bleak House, a Lady Dedlock to traverse the slums of London, a Margaret Hale to visit the slums of Manchester: and no one will touch a hair on their heads.

The need for an increase in gentility drives the plot; it is Evelina's social blunder at her first assembly rather than her "orphaned" state that produces the narrative instability from which the complications flow. She is invited to dance by a gentleman whom she finds ridiculous, so she refuses him, averring her intention not to dance at all. When the more attractive Lord Orville seeks her as partner, she accepts. Her inexperience makes her awkward, and she worries that he will find her a "simple rustic" (36). But she compounds her problems when Mr. Lovel, who had initially asked her to dance, returns, and she laughs in his face. Lord Orville "actually stared" at her, and Lovel, enraged, condemns her "ill manners" (40). Evelina, thunderstruck, confesses that she "had not once considered the impropriety of refusing one partner, and afterwards accepting another" (40).[1] This initial breach must be redeemed in her subsequent behavior, and the novel explicitly represents Evelina at another ball where, having refused one partner, she refuses all others. That scene serves as a touchstone of her social development. And when she ultimately learns to discipline her laughter at absurdity, she has achieved the very pattern of ladyhood.

[1] The etiquette manuals are explicit about proper decorum in this circumstance. According to *Etiquette for the Ladies* (1837): "When a gentleman offers to dance with you do not, unless for some very special reason, refuse. If you can establish what you consider a valid objection, such refusal by no means hinders you from accepting the next more auspicious invitation" (8–9). Of course, Evelina does not establish that "valid objection." *Etiquette for Ladies and Gentlemen* (1862) is even less flexible: "It is not considered polite for a lady to refuse the invitation of a gentleman to dance, unless she be previously engaged; to do so would be considered an insult" (85). *The Ladies Pocket-Book of Etiquette* (1840) fulminates against this maxim but is powerless to overturn it: "I must here observe, that I am surprised that our fair patronesses (whose will is law on these subjects) do not annul this most foolish and arbitrary imposition. A gentleman, though disengaged, is not obliged to dance with any lady to whom he has been introduced, merely because he is disengaged. Why then should a lady be compelled to dance with every fool . . . " (59).

It is not only that manner becomes one's ticket to polite society, but it also guards individuals from the vulgarity surrounding them. Once Evelina is surrendered to her grandmother and her more vulgar relatives, the only thing that can protect her from insult is her social demeanor. She worries that one importunate gentleman "seems disposed to think that the alteration in my companions authorises an alteration in his manners" (253). To check his presumption she becomes more consciously correct.

When Lord Orville proposes to Evelina, he seeks the hand of an elegant woman, not the daughter of Sir John Belmont; he is altogether unaware of her birth and circumstances. Her demeanor is sufficient to recommend her. Significantly, Lord Orville speaks also of Evelina's "natural love of virtue," of her "informed, sensible, and intelligent" mind, rhetoric more applicable to the earlier courtesy books than the later etiquette manuals (433, 434). But when asked to account for his sudden proposal, Evelina makes him "confess how ill he thought of me, upon my foolish giddiness at Mrs. Stanley's ball; but he flatters me with assurances, that every succeeding time he saw me, I appeared to something less and less disadvantage" (488). The discourses of courtesy and etiquette become entangled as proper behavior on all occasions becomes a sign of "virtue."

Emma: From *Noblesse Oblige* to *La Bourgeoise Corrige*

Jane Austen's *Emma* introduces a world in the process of reforming itself discursively. The traditional privileges of the aristocracy and landed gentry are being eroded under pressure from new monied classes, and, thus, the privilege formerly guaranteed by wealth is being re-articulated and reinforced by an increasingly elaborate set of social signs. Emma Woodhouse stands at the juncture of these competing systems of social meaning, and her relationship with George Knightley establishes the grounds of those contested meanings.

Mr. Knightley belongs to the landed gentry and enjoys a security about his and his neighbors' status that belongs to an earlier age. However, the tenacity with which he holds to traditional prerogatives may not be superficially apparent. Indeed, it is tempting to read Mr. Knightley as accepting of social mobility in his world: for example, when the Coleses propose their dinner party, Emma wants to teach them that "it was not for them to arrange the terms on which the superior families would visit them," a lesson "she very much feared, they would receive only from herself; she had little hope of Mr. Knightley" (218). But to conclude from such an episode that Mr. Knightley is the Robespierre of Highbury society ignores important dimensions of his representation. Knightley's discussion with Emma at the Coles' dinner party demonstrates his strong sense of noblesse oblige. When Emma chides him for frequently refusing to employ his carriage and praises his arriving at the Coleses' as befits his station—"This is coming as you should do . . . like a gentleman"—he seems to check her presumption in his response: "How lucky that we should arrive at the same moment; for, if we had met first in the drawing-room, I doubt whether you would have discerned me to be more of a gentleman than usual." Emma, however, holds her own and responds confidently, "There is always a look of consciousness or bustle when people come in a way which they know to be beneath them" (223). Emma's comments demonstrate the new importance that social behaviors have acquired in determining class status; Knightley's reveal his assumption of a "natural" superiority, which also informs the invitation he issues to Highbury society to pick strawberries at Donwell Abbey. Countering Mrs. Elton's suggestion that the company dine alfresco, "every thing as natural and simple as possible," Knightley responds that "the nature and the simplicity of gentlemen and ladies, with their servants and furniture, I think is best observed by meals within doors" (351). Checking Mrs. Elton's presumption by employing her own language of nature and simplicity against her, Mr. Knightley nonetheless colludes in a rhetoric that naturalizes the social order, both in applying the concept of "nature" to upper-class habits and in identifying servants with furniture as properly belonging to property.

Telling as is his conflation of servants with property, Knightley's traditional orientation toward his social world is most fully revealed in his responses to Harriet Smith and her marital prospects. "The natural daughter of nobody knows whom" (87), Harriet Smith operates in the text as a social sign in potentia. Emma reads her as deserving of a place among the class with which she herself visits, and thus she fixes first on Mr. Elton and then on Frank Churchill as proper husbands. Knightley reads Harriet as "naturally" inferior to the world in which Emma's patronage has suddenly placed her and refuses to acknowledge that she is good enough even for Robert Martin. Although Emma's high estimate of Harriet is certainly bound up in her own Pygmalianesque desire to create Harriet and her fate, Emma's stance also implicitly accepts the social volatility of Highbury and the increasing significance of social signs as indexes of social status; Knightley adheres to the old criteria of "birth and circumstances" (67), "birth [and] nature" (87). He vehemently argues that Robert Martin "is as much her superior in sense as in situation" (87). When Harriet is ultimately revealed to be the daughter of a prosperous tradesman, Emma seems to collude in Knightley's original judgment of natural inferiority: "The stain of illegitimacy, unbleached by nobility or wealth, would have been a stain indeed" (463). Yet Emma has already, through her efforts, "improved" Harriet, that is, readied her for assuming a respectable position as wife of a prosperous yeoman farmer; Knightley himself credits the change in Harriet to Emma and admits that Harriet will be an excellent wife for Martin.

Although the "stain of illegitimacy" cannot be overcome by social bearing, Emma is not wrong in asserting that elegant manners adequately equip one for high position, especially when the birth is unexceptionable. In her relative obscurity and impoverishment, Jane Fairfax resembles Harriet Smith, but she enjoys a respectable, though undistinguished, lineage that keeps open her options. As a result, her elegant demeanor can purchase for her a substantial elevation in social status. Although the marriage of Jane Fairfax and Frank Churchill "is not a connexion to gratify" (391), Knightley, more generous in Jane's case than in Harriet's, points to the "equality of situation . . . as far as regards society, and all the habits and manners that are important" (415). No one in the social community quarrels with the proposition that Frank gains from the marriage. And what he gains is a promising future ("he may yet turn out well.—With such a woman he has a chance"), in contrast to Mr. Elton, whose tendencies toward vulgarity have been confirmed in his marrying Augusta Hawkins, who styles her *cara sposo* "Mr. E."[2]

Despite Mr. Knightley's willingness to credit Emma for Harriet's improvement in sense and manner and his ability to see that manners do much in justifying a marriage, his "thick leather gaiters" signify the extent to which he remains tied to an old Tory landowning social sensibility and tradition.[3] Emma emerges as the semioti-

---

[2] Various etiquette manuals pinpoint this form of address as particularly egregious. *Etiquette for Ladies* (1837): "In speaking to her husband, a lady may address him by his Christian name. In speaking of him to others, it is more proper to style him Mr. ——. To degrade him to a mere initial, to call him Mr. A., or Mr. B., is worse than vulgar, it is heathenish!" (20). *The Ladies Guide to Etiquette* (1855): "Not on any account [should one address a husband] by his initials merely, which is disrespectful to him, and is also the very perfection of vulgarity" (18).

[3] Margaret Kirkham points out that Mr. Knightley's leather gaiters are those of a working farmer "and, although he is the owner of Donwell Abbey, he is plain *Mr*

cian for a shifting social order, an individual who recognizes the old prerogatives but is also fully alive to the way in which social meanings are being reconstructed through discourses of etiquette: calls, cuts, visiting, dinner parties, dances, and outings. Whereas Mr. Knightley promptly acknowledges the social importance of Miss Bates, whose "notice was an honor" in former times, Emma regards the association with horror, not only because of the old maid's tedious ramblings but more significantly because her home is a place where the social boundaries that separate the various ranks are breached.[4] Emma is sensible of her "deficiency" in regard to visiting Miss Bates, but nothing can "counteract the persuasion of its being very disagreeable,—a waste of time—tiresome women—and all the horror of being in danger of falling in with the second rate and third rate of Highbury, who were calling on them forever" (169).

The choice of word "danger" stands out here because it enters into a signifying chain that positions "danger" and its antipode "safety" entirely within social terms. The one physical threat in the novel—Harriet's encounter with the importunate gypsies—exists to initiate Emma's confusion over the object of Harriet's new infatuation. When the two women allude to the great "service he rendered," each understands a different "he" and a different "service." Emma imagines that Harriet has been enraptured by Frank Churchill, who so serviceably rescued her from the gypsies, while Harriet is convinced that she cannot be mistaken in her intention to signify Mr. Knightley's consideration at the ball when he saved her from the mortification of Mr. Elton's deliberate snub. *That* was the real danger—of social degradation, of being put in her "place." Because Emma herself conceptualizes danger entirely in these terms, it is ironic that she fails to understand Harriet, preferring to privilege the physical rescue of gothic romance over the social rescue so important to her own operations in Highbury. It is further significant that Emma authorizes Harriet's new attachment because its "tendency would be to raise and refine her mind—and it must be *saving* her from the *danger* of degradation" (339, my italics).

George Knightley, not *Sir* George Knightley" (128). But Mr. Knightley can chart a plain course because his inherited place as the owner of Donwell Abbey is so clearly established.

  [4]Julia Prewitt Brown, *Jane Austen's Novels: Social Change and Literary Form*, comments: "Miss Bates is perhaps the nearest symbol of Highbury; all classes join and cooperate in her, just as all gossip passes through her vacant mind. . . . [Emma] does not like visiting Miss Bates . . . because it sanctions class fluidity" (112). Brown interprets this resistance as a flaw in Emma, agreeing with Lionel Trilling that "she is a reactionary" (112).

The excessive and unwarranted concerns of Mr. Woodhouse over his daughter's "safety"—in being driven by James, in attending a party at the Coleses', in returning home after he is in bed—can be read, then, as a reinterpretation of amorphous social vulnerabilities as concrete and manageable physical ones. His insistence that "Serle and the butler should see that every thing were safe in the house, as usual," betrays the more general worry, encoded in his earlier assurance to his daughter, "You will be perfectly safe, you know, among your friends" (221).

It is this social safety that is obliquely invoked when Emma feels sure that the timing of a particular visit to Miss Bates should keep her "quite safe from any letter from Jane Fairfax" (169). Jane stands as Emma's social counter in elegance and her superior in achievement, so she constitutes a threat to Emma's "natural" superiority. Perhaps more accurately, she threatens the notion of Emma's superiority as natural. Or, when Frank Churchill comments about Jane that there is "safety in reserve, but no attraction," he both argues for a protective social demeanor and adds to the series of small deceptions that secures his secret engagement to Jane from the prying eyes of the neighborhood. Similarly, Mrs. Elton threatens Jane's position by hurrying her into service as a governess, an officious activity from which Jane must "save herself" (340). And, after the engagement between Frank and Jane is revealed, Mrs. Weston can reflect that she "must have been safe" from speaking ill of either party, whereas Emma enjoys no such confidence. Emma can assure everyone, however, that Frank's flirtations have not engaged her heart: "I was somehow or other safe from him" (415).

This discourse of safety finds its analogue in the narrative depiction of danger. Often, as I noted earlier, they are linked. After Elizabeth Martin has called upon Harriet, etiquette requires that Harriet return the visit. Yet Emma worries over what might be the "safest" way to fulfill the social obligation without incurring the "danger of a renewal of the acquaintance" (197). Her decision to have Harriet return the visit *in form only*, by limiting it strictly to fifteen minutes, disturbs Emma in its implicit ingratitude, but she argues that "it must be done, or what would become of Harriet?" (198). Obviously, on one level, Emma and her pretensions are laughable, but the plot enacts what Emma insists upon, that is, that she "could not have visited Mrs Robert Martin, of Abbey-Mill Farm" (80). At this point, early in the novel, Harriet is aghast at the prospect; she "had not surmised her own danger" (80). The conclusion of the novel finds Emma relieved that Harriet is "necessarily drawn away [from Hartfield] by her engagements with the Martins." Emma applauds the "gradual, natural manner" in which her intimacy with Harriet sinks "into a calmer sort of goodwill" (463). Again, the discourse of the "natural" is invoked to transform into a social propriety what Emma has represented to herself as a "danger."

The line between lower-middle-class prosperous yeoman farmers like the Martins and the upper-middle-class gentry is drawn all the more rigidly because society implicitly recognizes that divisions based on social manner and etiquette can be readily breached. Emma arrogantly pronounces to Harriet: "A young farmer, whether on horseback or on foot, is the very last sort of person to raise my curiosity. The yeomanry are precisely the order of people with whom I feel I can have nothing to do. A degree or two lower, and a creditable appearance might interest me; I might hope to be useful to the families in some way or other. But a farmer can need none of my help, and is therefore in one sense as much above my notice as in every other he is below it" (59). Emma's arrogance reveals, even as it attempts to conceal, the social threat posed by families like the Martins. Emma is uneasily impressed by Robert Martin's letter of proposal to Harriet, confessing to herself that "the style of the letter was much above her expectation. There were not merely no grammatical errors, but as a composition it would not have disgraced a gentleman" (77). If there is, indeed, nothing to divide the Woodhouses from the Martins but such differences of expression—or manners—then Emma has no choice but to reassert her earlier estimate, that Robert Martin is "illiterate and vulgar" or to insist that "with all his sense and all his merit" he is only a farmer (80, 88). Yet the contradictions continue to trouble her, and when Harriet accidentally encounters Elizabeth and Robert Martin in Ford's store, they behave with so much kindness and "genuine delicacy" that Emma has to rationalize again her actions: "But she had believed them to be well meaning, worthy people before; and what difference did this make in the evils of the connection?" Although Emma can argue that "it was folly to be disturbed by it," she cannot rationalize away her disturbance (192). At best she can justify her condescension to the Martins by falling back on a rhetoric of inherited privilege and sanctioned divisions, acknowledging, "It was a bad business. She would have given a great deal, or endured a great deal, to have had the Martins in a higher rank of life. They were so deserving, that a *little* higher should have been enough: but as it was, how could she have done otherwise?" (200).

Mr. Knightley's comments at the novel's conclusion reinforce this logic, which draws unobtrusively upon a naturalization of class differences. Seeking to reconcile Emma to Harriet's marriage to Robert Martin, Mr. Knightley concedes, "His rank in society I would alter if I could; which is saying a great deal I assure you, Emma" (454). Seemingly, despite his desires, Mr. Knightley must accept the order of things, represented as independent of his wishes and intentions.

But Emma has already betrayed, in innumerable ways, the tension between the old way of doing social business and the new way, informed by a complex discourse of etiquette, through which one signals one's social place through social demeanor. Whereas Mr. Knightley and Mr. Weston promptly accept the Coleses' invitation to dine, Emma intends to check their presumption in inviting "the superior families." Only when she is persuaded that the invitation is accompanied with all the proper social signals—"so much real attention in the manner of it—so much consideration for her father" (219)—does she reverse her decision. Only after her class superiority is clearly signified in the invitation and in her reception at the dinner can she be complacent about attending: "All that she might be supposed to have lost on the side of dignified seclusion, must be amply repaid in the splendour of popularity" (239).

Emma's major breach of social decorum—insulting Miss Bates at Box Hill—is one she recognizes and rectifies immediately. The Box Hill episode stands out because Emma punctiliously fulfills social decorum on other occasions, motivated by "pride" and "propriety," for example, in making a prompt call on Mr. Elton's new bride and in deciding that she must host a dinner for the Eltons because she "must not do less than others" (273, 291). Despite Mrs. Elton's failing herself to fulfill decorum and patronizing Emma—"the idea of her being indebted to Mrs Elton for what was called an *introduction*"—and the vulgarity of her conversation with her "Knightley," and "Mr. E." and "*caro sposo*," Emma does not fail in politeness and elegance, distinguishing herself as immeasurably the superior (278, 281).

The social volatility of this world is most fully signified in the discourse of "evil," one of the most prominent words in Jane Austen's novel. Entirely stripped of religious and spiritual meanings, "evil" functions, with "safety" and "danger," as a signifier of social instability and potential upheaval. The novel opens famously characterizing the "real evils" of Emma's situation as "the power of having rather too much her own way, and a disposition to think a little too well of herself" (37). These are "evils" because the machinations they encourage threaten to destabilize the Highbury community.

Disruption of Mr. Woodhouse's comfort is a "present evil," just as Harriet's "evil stars" lead her into possible mortification and threaten her with the "evils" of a connection to the Martins. Or Emma can be stunned by Frank Churchill's "indifference to a confusion of rank" as an "evil" of which he is an inadequate judge. Or she is dismayed by the prospect of Mr. Knightley's marrying Jane Fairfax: "evil to himself; a very shameful and degrading connection" (233–34). She sees "nothing but evil in it" (236). Emma's hyperbolic response, of course, betrays her own unacknowledged interest in Mr. Knightley, but the discourse of evil is always hyperbolic in *Emma*. The Eltons' feelings are "evil"; Jane Fairfax's "days of insignificance and evil" are finally over; Harriet's confession of her love for Mr. Knightley falls on Emma as a "burst of threatening evil." Emma has "brought evil on Harriet, on herself"; Jane Fairfax has involved herself in "evil"; Emma, a "source of evil," has done "evil and good" to Jane; Emma's prospective marriage to Mr. Knightley is an "impending evil" for Mr. Woodhouse. Anything that threatens the status quo, anything that threatens one's social self-interest, is an evil.

Emma's lessons in the novel have all focused on refining her social instincts, on training her how to preserve her prerogatives from the dangers that threaten them among shifting social signifiers. The "small band of true friends" that witnesses the marriage of George Knightley and Emma Woodhouse at the novel's conclusion is secure from social upheaval with Emma at its helm. She will steer the group safely through the dangers of the social Scylla and Charybdis, neither assuming an automatic privilege nor succumbing to vulgarity among those scrambling to assert their position. The modesty of her wedding—no "finery or parade"—testifies to the discretion she has achieved. She has conquered the "real evils . . . of [her] situation" by yoking the power of having her own way and a disposition to think well of herself with a command of the social medium in which she must enact her self-construction.

Emma will make an excellent wife for Mr. Knightley. Less inclined than he to rest on inherited privilege, she has shown herself to be an apt semiotician of the emerging discourses of gentility. She not only knows how to fill her position but knows as well how to keep her position against parvenus like Mrs. Elton. From this perspective Emma is not simply rewarded by union with Knightley or, alternatively, squelched by marriage with this lecturing father-figure; rather her talents complement his, making her fully his equal, ready from a reinforced position of inherited wealth and rank to wield a more absolute social authority in Highbury.[5]

The Course of True Ideology Never Did Run Smooth

Austen's novels, poised between traditional and emerging signifiers of privilege, set the stage for the mid-Victorian works that construct the middle-class woman as proto-professional manager. By the 1860s, writers such as Margaret Oliphant were foregrounding images that had been mystified in earlier novels and tracts although that mystification returned under another guise in George Eliot's *Middlemarch*, in which the managerial functions of bourgeois women were often effaced.

The gap that had been opened in the construction of women—between patriarchal and bourgeois discursive formations—produced other historical and potential representations. Sensation novels that emerged in the 1860s portrayed a different kind of middle-class woman. Indeed, what made them sensational depended, in part, on depictions of devilish corruption beneath an angelic demeanor. In the words of Eliza Lynn Linton, writing for the *Saturday Review*, "their worst sinners are in all respects fashioned as much after the outward semblance of the ideal saint as [the sensation novelists] have skill to design." The heroine is, according to the *Westminster Review*, "no longer the Angel, but the Devil in the House." Certainly, the emergence of sensational novels has been tied to a changing role of women and a "discontent with old ways."[6] That dissatisfaction has been linked, especially, with the repression of female sexuality and passion, and the sensation novels often luridly illustrate both its repression and its expression.[7] But of more interest

[5] Joseph Litvak identifies as a function of "patriarchal criticism of *Emma*" the tendency to take Knightley's side. He is one of the few critics to argue for balance in the relationship.

[6] Reviews quoted in Helsinger et al., 3: 125; ibid. 126. There are, of course, multiple accounts possible for the origin of any literary genre or subgenre. Helsinger et al. summarize the generic aspects of sensationalism as they pertained to Victorian women. They stress that these novels "written by women were primarily about women and are largely for women" (123). They point to the tension between the subversive and orthodox elements—"shocking novels that boasted morally impeccable endings" (125). And they read in that tension a feared threat to social life itself from women's emergence as independent agents.

[7] D. A. Miller reads Wilkie Collins's sensation novel *The Woman in White* as representing the coercive normalization and policing of male sexuality, the enforcement of mandatory heterosexuality (146–91).

here than the represented passion is the introduction of split depictions of the middle-class domestic woman: the emergence of a mannish "new woman" to stabilize representations of the feminine bourgeois woman.

Wilkie Collins and Elizabeth Braddon, who pioneered the sensation novel, introduced this split in similar ways: the heroes of Collins's *Woman in White* and Braddon's *Lady Audley's Secret* find attractive two very different women, one a passive, dependent, "feminine" angel already reined in by patriarchal mandates, the other an independent, active rebel, who will be curbed in the novel's end, in part through her desire to please the hero. We can see in these opposing representations the two aspects that had uneasily cohabited in the mid-Victorian angel/manager; the tension has been worked through here by splitting off the managerial function, muting its class function, and designating it in gender terms as "mannish."

Yet this "masculine" heroine is, surprisingly, also depicted as sensually attractive, part of a narrative strategy to make her independence and competence appear more threatening because her autonomy implies a certain sexual freedom and responsiveness. The "figure" of Collins's Marian Halcombe immediately seduces the eye of middle-class hero, Walter Hartright, who glimpses her back from across a room. Entranced by the grace and sensuality of a figure "undeformed by stays," Walter is in "a flutter of expectation to see her face clearly" (25), a flutter that is rudely arrested with his realization that "the lady is ugly!"[8] Subsequent descriptions of Marian, who directs monetary and household affairs for both herself and her half sister, highlight the way representations of the competent, self-sufficient woman combine masculinity with sensuality to suggest the dangers of female independence. Presented as possessing a complexion "almost swarthy," "dark down on her upper lip" that "was almost a moustache," and "a large, firm, masculine mouth and jaw," Marian ultimately repels the hero by her anomalies, "by the masculine form and masculine look of the features in which the perfectly-shaped figure ended" (25).

Rejecting the frank sexuality he reads in Marian's face, Walter initiates a triangulation of sexual desire, expressed in the love that both Marian and Walter acknowledge for the childlike, asexual Laura

[8] Miller argues that this response confirms that Walter, who has previously been infected with a woman's nervousness and who has revealed that "he is not, so to speak, the man he is pretending to be," is, in fact, a real man. In Miller's view, Walter discovers that Marian is a "dog," and real men don't like dogs (151–52). I am interested in a different pattern, that is, the interrelationship posited among managerial competence, masculinity, and sensuality.

Fairlie and repress in their relations with each other. In contrast to Marian, Laura is described without the same immediacy, remembered only as she is imaged in a water-colour drawing. She is, therefore, from her initial depiction, at a remove, rendered onto paper. Almost ephemeral, she represents to Walter, and the male reader to whom he appeals, that "woman who first gives life, light, and form to our shadowy conceptions of beauty, fills a void in our spiritual nature that has remained unknown to us till she appeared. Sympathies that lie too deep for words, too deep almost for thoughts, are touched" (41–42). The echoes of Wordsworth place this essence of the feminine within a tradition of woman-as-muse, woman-as-inspiration. Further, she is represented as having a "childish earnestness" that resonates ominously with the hero's disturbing response that "mingling with the vivid impression produced by the charm of her fair face and head . . . was another impression, which, in a shadowy way, suggested to me the idea of something wanting" (42). His inability to decide if it is "something wanting in *her*" or in himself prepares us for the process by which he casts out the something wanting in himself—the feminine—en route to middle-class manhood, and her childishness becomes a mental enfeeblement that proleptically justifies her incarceration in an asylum.[9] The vacuous, infantile creature whom Walter Hartright marries in the novel's conclusion is one revision of the Angel in the House.[10]

Collins's novel betrays an anxiety about female competence in the managerial domestic woman, who must be humbled in a violent way, and then reinscribed within the domestic order through a chastening process of menial labor. This angel's alter ego—the masculine, competent woman Marian—first suffers a ritualistic debilitating illness so that she, too, can be reined into the harmonious domestic circle. Tellingly, the fever follows an escapade in detection that requires her to strip off her women's gown and underclothing, which "took up the room of three men at least," and don a garb that

[9] Miller has powerfully traced the motif of women's incarceration in male bodies as part of his larger exploration of homosexual representations in *The Woman in White*. He alludes to the Victorian definition of homosexuality as *anima muliebris in corpore virili inclusa*, which he translates as "a woman's breath caught in a man's body" (154).

[10] In a compelling discussion that addresses class issues from a different perspective, Ann Cvetkovich traces the "relation between capitalism and affective life" in Collins's novel, and she argues that *The Woman in White* uses sensationalized events and appearances to mask the more materialist narrative of Walter Hartright's rise in the social hierarchy through marriage to Laura Fairlie. Cvetkovich analyzes the ways in which "class differences are secured by the management of sexual desire" (95, 77). Walter's love for Laura, therefore, is not independent of his class identity but a product of his desire to change it" (78).

gives her the mobility of a man (292). Just at the moment that the wily villain Count Fosco praises her for possessing "the foresight and the resolution of a man," she collapses into "a useless, helpless, panic-stricken creature," who must suffer Fosco's penetration of her private diary as a final humbling indignity (296, 306). Partially "restored" to her femininity by this rape, Marian willingly undergoes an even more troubling degradation by housework to ensure that the lesson takes.

The terms of Marian's further humiliation are familiar from my earlier discussion of the bourgeois manager. But, now, she must herself submit to her own class degradation as a sign of her femininity. We witness in Collins's resolution a collapse of the distinction between the bourgeois and patriarchal discourses as a means of containing the threat of the emerging new woman. Collins's novel has, from its opening line, relied on an oppositional gender structure: "This is the story of what a Woman's patience can endure, and of what a Man's resolution can achieve." Man/resolution/achieve versus Woman/patience/endure. The story itself represents the threatened collapse of these seemingly stable cultural encodings of identity, a process Roland Barthes has identified in his description of the symbolic code, the "place for multivalence and for reversibility." Nowhere is the transgressive possibility of the symbolic code more pointedly in evidence than in the confusion of identity between self and other, between Laurie Fairlie, the heiress, and Anne Catherick, the woman in white who has escaped from a mental asylum. This confusion drives the plot: Laura Fairlie must be proved to be Laura and her son declared heir of Limmeridge to arrest the narrative's instability and achieve closure. So this transgressive violation of self is partially stabilized through what Barthes has called the novel's hermeneutic and proairetic codes.[11] But the equally prominent gender oppositions that trouble the narrative are not contained by the hermeneutic code and stabilizing them demands manly action and resolution from Walter and a whacking great chunk of household drudgery and enforced patience from Marian. When Walter returns a new man from the wilds of South America, having encountered and conquered plague, attack by Indians, and shipwreck, he is ready to replace Marian as Laura's defender. Marian is returned to the household as her proper sphere, and her fate is played out through the dialectics of menial labor and management that charac-

[11] Barthes defines the hermeneutic code as "the various (formal) terms by which an enigma can be distinguished, suggested, formulated, held in suspense, and finally disclosed," the proairetic code as actions that "can fall into various sequences" (19).

terized the bourgeois domestic home. The extreme secrecy with which Walter and Marian must proceed in trying to reestablish Laura's identity forces them to forego the assistance of a servant. Servants have been implicated in the novel as tools of the patriarchy: crass, grasping, or readily manipulated. In short, they cannot be trusted. The novel has worked to ensure our acceptance of Walter's explanation, "The house-work, which, if we had dared trust a stranger near us, would have been done by a servant, was taken on the first day, taken as her own right, by Marian Halcombe" (398). The lower-class encodings of this newly domestic woman testify to the way the class distinctions that middle-class women worked to enforce are broken down to break the women down. Marian says, "What a woman's hands *are* fit for . . . early and late, these hands of mine shall do." Her words are followed by a depiction of a chastened Marian: "[Her hands] trembled as she held them out. The wasted arms told their sad story of the past, as she turned up the sleeves of the poor plain dress that she wore for safety's sake; but the unquenchable spirit of the woman burnt bright in her even yet." She cries, signifier of her new femininity, and pleads, "Don't doubt my courage, Walter . . . it's my weakness that cries, not *me*. The house-work shall conquer it, if *I* can't" (398, 399). Thus, while "in the heart of civilised London" Walter enacts the "stratagem[s] against suspected treachery" he had first learnt "in the wilds of Central America," Marian is counseled to pursue women's work: to endure patiently, to "have the courage to wait" (418, 543).

In a corollary scenario, Marian's evident sexuality, which first attracted Walter, must be recontained. The foreign villain, Count Fosco, provides the mechanism for this process. Not only does the count lust after Marian, confessing that "at sixty, [he] worshipped her with the volcanic ardour of eighteen" (558); at the same time, his enormous fat softness images and evokes a woman's sensuality and sensibility. "He is," Marian claims, "as nervously sensitive as the weakest of us." He becomes, thus, a locus both of Marian's bodily desires and of her desirability, and she admits that when he looks at her, he "causes me sensations . . . which I would rather not feel" (197). The count's fatness, his softness, his nervousness, his love of sweets, and his passion for small, helpless animals underscore not only his femininity but also represent the foreignness, the exoticism, and the decadence in women's sexuality that threatens good middle-class Englishmen. Marian is made to collude in the destruction of her sexual potential just as she acquiesced in her humbling by housework. She herself urges Walter to "begin [his revenge] with the Count! . . . For my sake, begin with the Count" (415).[12] She receives her reward in the last phrases of the story when Walter designates her as "the good angel of our lives." He adds, "let Marian end our Story" (584). Appropriately and ironically, that *is* the end of the story: Marian's silence. The managerial woman who developed in the mid-Victorian household met a grim demise within the formal requirements of sensation fiction, which demanded that the bourgeois housewife be recontained within the ideology of domesticity.

Lady Audley's Secret requires a less extended analysis because Mary Elizabeth Braddon borrows from Collins's plot in *The Woman in White*, and she leaves intact the structural and representational features that are of interest here. The lawyer-hero, Robert Audley, pursues his scheming aunt remorselessly while negotiating between two possible love interests: one his cousin Alicia, the other, Clara, the sister of his apparently murdered friend, George Talboys. Robert feels a certain obligation to his cousin, who he knows likes him, and he counsels her that, "if you'll only be patient and take life easily, and try and reform yourself of banging doors, bouncing in and out rooms, talking of the stables, and riding across country, I've no doubt the person you prefer will make you a very excellent husband" (84). In short, Alicia needs to be more ladylike, less masculine; Robert bemoans on another occasion "her rather limited stock of patience" (148). Alicia's chances with her cousin are obliterated, however, when he meets Clara Talboys, who has suffered patiently under her father's mandates against her brother. All of her energy is channeled into submission to her father and love for her brother, and in her Robert Audley finds his ideal of womanhood: "Her beauty was elevated into sublimity by the intensity of her suppressed passion. She was different to all other women that he had ever seen. His cousin was pretty, his uncle's wife was lovely, but Clara Talboys was beautiful. Niobe's face, sublimated by sorrow, could scarcely have been more purely classical than hers" (132). Robert's acquaintance with Clara transforms his previously idle character into one of resolution; she, like Collins's heroines, functions as man's muse and inspiration.

The reinscription of middle-class woman's passive role accompanies a dismantling of her character as manager. Women's manag-

---

[12] Bram Stoker's *Dracula* also depicts a woman's sensuality as foreign and dangerous. The Transylvanian count Dracula, in the process of his nightly feasting, turns good, modest English girls into lascivious tarts. There, too, the brave English boys must destroy what is foreign and decadent to restore "their" women to purity.

erial talents undergo a variety of sea changes in a long diatribe
launched against women by Robert, who resents being coerced into
action. First, the domestic woman is represented as a goad and virago: "Who ever heard of a woman taking life as it ought to be
taken? . . . She dresses for it, and simpers and grins, and gesticu-
lates for it. She pushes her neighbors, and struggles for a good place
in the dismal march. . . . She drags her husband on to the woolsack,
or pushes him into Parliament." The bourgeois wife is blamed for
"incompetent men . . . in high places": "The square men in the
round holes are pushed into them by their wives." Her virtues are
reinterpreted as vices: "It is because women are *never lazy*. They
don't know what it is to be quiet. . . . If they can't agitate the universe . . . they'll make mountains of warfare and vexation out of
domestic molehills, and social storms in household teacups." Their
household role is rewritten as captious backbiting: "Forbid them to
hold forth upon the freedom of nations and the wrongs of mankind,
and they'll quarrel with Mrs. Jones about the shape of a mantle or
the character of a small maid-servant." Their desires for a larger
scope are reinscribed as hyperactivity: "They want freedom of opinion, variety of occupation, do they? Let them . . . be lawyers, doctors, preachers, teachers, soldiers, legislators—anything they like—
but let them be quiet if they can" (136–37). Of course, we are meant
to be amused by this diatribe—a lazy Robert Audley making a last-
ditch effort to rest on his inherited privileges—but it achieves many
interesting ends, not the least of which is to link middle-class housewives with feminist agitators. By collapsing stereotypes of housewives and feminists, the text exposes the threat of bourgeois management, which it then works to recontain as Robert asserts himself,
solves the mystery, incarcerates his aunt in a mental asylum, subdues his bouncing cousin, and marries the monument of patience,
Clara. He also secures his deepest wish of restoring to "life" his
friend, George, who joins Clara and him in their "fairy cottage"
(285), a telling example of male bonding through trafficking in
women.[13] The patriarchy is reasserted, and Clara takes her pitiable

---

[13] I allude here to the work of Luce Irigaray, who writes in "Women on the Market"
that "reigning everywhere, although prohibited in practice, hom(m)o-sexuality is
played out through the bodies of women, matter, or sign, and heterosexuality has
been up to now just an alibi for the smooth workings of man's relations with himself,
of relations among men" (*This Sex* 172). Sedgwick, *Between Men*, tellingly develops
"the historicity of the female" in this process of homosocial bonding as depicted in
certain mid-Victorian texts, which *Lady Audley's Secret* recalls: "Each [novel] treats the
compulsory routing of homosocial desire through heterosexual love more or less as a
matter of course. Nevertheless, in each text that routing is both stressful and heavily
freighted with political meaning. Perhaps the most generalizable and important for

place in the "fairy cottage" that has become a temple to patriarchy, any notions of class management implied by Sarah Ellis's broader phrase "fairy order" have been all but erased.

Gissing's Odd Women: Old Wine in New Bottles

George Gissing's *Odd Women* has been credited by critics with formulating a new and revolutionary statement about women's possibilities. Feminist critics have joined in praise of this "astonishingly contemporary and relevant" novel that scouts romantic love, refuses to condone "the sexual double standard," and "takes the feminist cause seriously."[14] Theoretically, then, this novel challenges "the most deeply held beliefs and attitudes of the culture" and breaks sharply with Victorian domestic ideology. The extent of that break, however, is questionable. In fact, the new woman is the logical heir to the middle-class domestic manager in a genealogy of the female subject that remains suspicious of the culture's own generalizations about itself.

What in the new woman is "new"? Her insistence on autonomy? Her professional orientation? Her sexual freedom and frankness? The last, certainly. But one reason I have routed this final chapter through the sensation novels of the 1860s is to demonstrate how those narratives stabilize patriarchal ideology through the representation of a threatening female sensuality that is recontained. And by linking manly, managerial independence with woman's capacity for sexual desire, the text reins in the threat of female autonomy at the same time that it curtails the possible expressions of her sexuality.

Gissing's *Odd Women* is willing to point more frankly than earlier novels to women's sexuality, but it does so in ways that rigidify class representations and keep in place the bourgeois ideology that fueled the domestic novel. Gissing's personal commitments and experiences suggest that he might have broken down the Victorian class stereotypes of women and reintroduced the non-narratable plot of interclass marriage. After all, he himself married two women of the lower classes, first a young prostitute with whom he became

our ongoing narrative is this. . . . The sexually pitiable or contemptible female figure is a solvent that not only facilitates the relative democratization that grows up with capitalism and cash exchange, but goes a long way—for the men whom she leaves bonded together—toward palliating its gaps and failures" (160).

[14] Elaine Showalter, introduction to the Meridian edition of *The Odd Women*, pp. vii–viii.

entangled when she was only seventeen and the other a working woman from Camden Town.[15] Gissing, however, was irked by and ashamed of his wives; he attributed his disastrously incompatible marriages to his own peculiar nature, "a strange compound of the bohemian and the bourgeois."[16] But one might read in them as well Gissing's construction by the class ideologies of his culture. Lower-class women represented a certain sexual availability and predisposition that may have attracted a man who saw his own fate as governed by "sexual delinquency."[17] Certainly, Gissing reproduces in *The Odd Women* the sexual dichotomies between lower- and middle-class women that are a consistent feature of mid-Victorian domestic novels. In fact, those sexual encodings by class remain a consistent feature of nineteenth-century fiction and figure equally prominently in the work of Gissing's contemporary Thomas Hardy, whose desexualized middle-class new woman, Sue Bridehead, contrasts sharply with the sexually practiced peasant, Arabella Donn.[18]

Gissing's *Odd Women* elucidates and consolidates the class distinctions that have been partially masked in the works of Dickens, Gaskell, and Oliphant, and it does so explicitly in the context of the emerging bourgeois, professional, "new" woman. The text persistently distinguishes middle- from lower-class women at the levels of both character representation and narrative commentary. Mary Barfoot and Rhoda Nunn have begun a typewriting business to benefit the half million "odd" women in England: those for whom the surplus of women to men makes marriage unlikely and those to whom the institution of marriage is simply undesirable. From the outset the two women have limited their philanthropy to the educated

---

[15] See Gillian Tindall, who examines the interrelationship between sex and class in Gissing's life and work: "His attitudes to the opposite sex were imbued through and through with an awareness of class, whether he showed his heroes reaching up in vain towards ladies or stretching downwards to lift the humble or the fallen. In the same way, his attitudes to class were permeated with sexual awareness, so that the class struggle . . . becomes a sexual conflict, and class prejudice is inextricably mixed with sexual aversion" (158).

[16] Gissing, *Letters to Gabrielle Fleury* 32.

[17] John Sutherland speaks of the ruin of Gissing's autobiographical hero, Denzil Quarrier, in these terms (*Longman Companion* 248).

[18] Read in this light, *Jude the Obscure* is another novel about a lower-class man wishing to enact a rise in class through marriage with an appropriate woman. Tellingly, Hardy's "sympathetic" sexual woman, Tess Durbeyfield, belongs to the lower classes, a representation that reinscribes cultural values that have prevailed since the beginning of the century. When Angel is apprised of Tess's sexual liaison with Alec, he accuses her of both aristocratic decadence ("belated seedling of an effete aristocracy") and peasant bestiality, uninitiated into "the proportions of social things" (206). Further, Tess is made to convict herself by arguing that she is "only a peasant by position, not by nature!" leaving intact the category of the natural peasant woman (206).

middle classes, a strategy meant to ensure their success but one that also marks a complacent class contempt. Rhoda explains that "Miss Barfoot hasn't much interest in the lower classes; she wishes to be of use to the daughters of educated people" (24). The rhetoric of usefulness, tied only to a specific group, transforms a generally philanthropic project into another scheme for class hegemony. Miss Barfoot meets any appeal that she not "limit [her] humanity . . . by the artificial divisions of society" with the response, "I think those divisions are anything but artificial. . . . In the uneducated classes I have no interest whatever. You have heard me say so" (58). That the narrator describes her as speaking "good-humouredly" marks her comfortable reliance on the principles she has enunciated. As represented in this scene, she was early cued to her response by the quiet comment of a companion that the particular supplicant in question "never was a lady" (58). When accused of being "narrow," Mary complacently remarks: "Perhaps so. I choose my sphere, that's all. Let those work for the lower classes (I must call them lower, for they are, in every sense), let those work for them who have a call to do so. I have none. I must keep to my own class" (59). The idea of a special "call," what Rhoda Nunn terms an admirable "missionary enterprise," instantiates the gulf that exists between working women and ladies. Keeping the former in their "place" as a kind of unredeemed native species facilitates the professional emergence of the latter. When their disappointed interlocutor insists that she "aim[s] at the solidarity of woman" and appeals to one of the school's pupils, who has already benefited by the typewriting scheme, that pupil dutifully affirms her middle-class allegiance: "I really don't think . . . that there can be any solidarity of ladies with servant girls" (59). Closed case; Christian charity be damned. These women are talking about social, not religious, progress. And they are effectively continuing a process of class hegemony enacted in the households of their domestic mothers. Their attitudes help to perpetuate the idea of necessary separation from lower-class women, a policing that had been carried into the home through the policies governing domestic service.

The real solidarity—that of middle-class women—is affirmed when the narrator describes Mary Barfoot in terms that lodge her within the domestic discourses governing the representations of household managers. This unmarried revolutionary for middle-class women wears a "style of dress, gracefully ornate," that "would have led a stranger to presume her a wedded lady of some distinction" (55); these telling signifiers of dress have always facilitated a class project. Although the narrator insists that Mary's "abilities were of a kind uncommon in women, or at all events very rarely developed in one of her sex," he nonetheless represents this "new" woman in familiar terms of domestic managerial competence: "She could have managed a large and complicated business, could have filled a place on a board of directors, have taken an active part in municipal government—nay, perchance in national." Ironically, this narrator even serves up the same mystifications of female professionalism: "And this turn of intellect consisted with many traits of character so strongly feminine that people who knew her best thought of her with as much tenderness as admiration. . . . Her quiet work was probably more effectual than the public career of women who propagandize for female emancipation" (59–60). Feminine, tender, quiet: the narrator rounds up all the old culprits and then concedes that this new woman is not so new, after all, not one of those propagandists for emancipation. But that's what we should have suspected all along. The gender project provides a subterfuge for the class project.

The novel's own naturalizing of class differences proceeds quietly through a discourse of nature, nativity, and instinct, which underwrites and justifies systematic discrimination. Monica possesses "native elegance" (12). Her sister Virginia "could not have been judged anything but a lady. She wore her garments as only a lady can . . . and had the step never to be acquired by a person of vulgar instincts" (19). Mary Barfoot tells Rhoda that "the girls of our class are not like the uneducated, who, for one reason or another, will marry almost any man rather than remain single" (67). After all, such uneducated women are "mere lumps of human flesh" and capable of attracting young men "so frantic as to marry girls of the working class" (115).

The novel also erects the by-now familiar barriers between the shabby genteel and the truly genteel. "Young gentlewomen," cast into penury by the sudden death of their father, are forced to serve as governesses in the homes of "more or less well-to-do families in the lower middle class—people who could not have inherited refinement, and had not acquired any, neither proletarians nor gentlefolk, consumed with a disease of vulgar pretentiousness, inflated with the miasma of democracy" (17). The rhetoric of disease and miasma makes short shrift of democratic ideals. In the mid-Victorian domestic novels, the bourgeois manager was always positioned above that imaginary divide between gentlefolk and the vulgar. She was superior both to the working class, whom she regulated, and to the lower middle class, whom she patronized. And those same class prerogatives persist in her legitimate daughters, the new women.

These features of the "new woman" novel declare it as the logical heir to mid-Victorian domestic fiction. That is, we recognize the affinities between representations of the domestic woman and the new woman. The novel itself, however, is at some pains to disguise these, and it retools former representations of domesticity in new images. Disturbingly, the text's manipulations of other gender and class issues reinscribe highly traditional familial values and continuing mystifications of the homemaker. In its opening chapters, Gissing's novel depends on that distinction between shabby and true gentility to position both Mary Barfoot and Rhoda Nunn clearly on the genteel side of the class question, a location that helps to justify Rhoda as a love interest for Mary's cousin, Everard Barfoot. But once Rhoda enters into this dialectic of masculine/feminine love, her class currency suffers a devaluation. Everard is at first simply curious about this "masculine" woman—a gender encoding familiar from the sensation novels, in which the managerial woman is transformed into the mannish woman. Associated with her manly freedom is the suggestion of sensuality; Everard is stimulated by this sexual "type," which is "remote indeed from the voluptuous, but hinting a possibility of subtle feminine forces" (22). Force is the operative word here, as each is aroused by a desire to gain power over the other, to make the other submit. The "strength of her muscles" ultimately fires Everard's interest in Rhoda, who had initially "no sensual attraction for him" (114, 144). The rhetoric of romance rapidly mutates to a familiar discourse of subjugation, submission, brutality, and violence, ironic in a relationship that was to epitomize true equality between the sexes. Everard early admits that "love revives the barbarian; it wouldn't mean much if it didn't. In this one respect I suppose no man, however civilized, would wish the woman he loves to be his equal. Marriage by capture can't quite be done away with" (208). He intends to overcome "the womanly resistance, which is one of [her] charms" (209). Finally, the reductio ad absurdem: "Delighting in her independence of mind, he still desired to see her in complete subjugation" (299). A mark of her new womanhood, however, is Rhoda's refusal to capitulate; "she stood on her dignity, would bring him to supplication" (317). Nonetheless, what is lost in these clashing wills is Rhoda's dignity and gentility. She loses not only the man but her class. She seems just a little bit crass, exposed as she finally is to Everard's pity. "He began to think: If this woman had enjoyed the social advantages to which Agnes Brissenden and those others were doubtless indebted for so much of their charm, would she not have been their equal, or more? For the first time he compassionated Rhoda" (373).[19]

"Agnes Brissenden" is a trope for a new, more desirable gentility. She exists in the novel as a shadowy presence, evocative of elegance and refinement. She is presented only through Everard's appreciation of her. She is the site at which Gissing can instantiate a new, improved domestic ideal. The old ideal, described as girls "pottering about the house, because they have nothing better to do," has become somewhat tarnished (111). The best that the novel represents in the way of marriages is the long-delayed union of a math tutor with his wrinkled love of twenty years. A beaming groom Micklethwaite greets his former pupil, Everard, with the words, "there are angels walking the earth in this our day" (199). His bride, a resuscitated Angel in the House, has some lingering, familiar features of the class disciplinarian. We are informed, for example, that "the little servant who opened to [Everard] exhibited a gentle, noiseless demeanour which was no doubt the result of careful discipline" (198). But there are striking differences as well. Mrs. Micklethwaite participates with her servant in a domestic drudgery that would have been unthinkable to her antecedents. When the narrator reveals that "the dinner, which she herself had cooked, and which she assisted in serving, aimed at being no more than a simple, decorous meal but . . . even the vegetables and the bread seemed to him to have a daintier flavour than at many a rich table" (199), there is recognizably tendentious work being performed by this idealized portrait. One can almost hear echoing in the background Mrs. Bennet's asperse reply to Mr. Collins that "they were very well able to keep a good cook, and that her daughters had nothing to do in the kitchen" (45), or Mrs. Gibson's injunction against Molly's presence in the kitchen, or the etiquette manuals' stipulation that a good manager should know how meals are properly prepared but never condescend to cook herself.[20] The novel here collapses as "pretentious emptiness" the role of middle-class homemakers. There is a certain logic in Gissing's reduction of the housewife at the moment that the new woman manager is taking her place in the business world. It ensures the masking of the linkages we have identified between the constructions of mid-Victorian homemakers and late-Victorian new women.

[19] Showalter argues that "Everard Barfoot pities Rhoda; but he never understood or appreciated her. No serious reader need share his view" (xxvi). Unfortunately, as Showalter's special pleading makes clear, the text invites the reader to share his view.

[20] In Austen's *Pride and Prejudice* and Gaskell's *Wives and Daughters*, respectively.

The novel's conclusion soars into the ether with a heavy dose of mystification as Everard Barfoot marries the idealized Agnes Brissenden, confirming the double threat to the new woman: loss of her femininity and loss of her caste. He looks forward to his changed circumstances as he is "making friends in the world with which he had a natural affinity; that of wealthy and cultured people who seek no prominence, who shrink from contact with the circles known as 'smart,' who possess their souls in quiet freedom. It is a small class, especially distinguished by the charm of its women" (366). This diction of "quiet freedom" and "charm" is not difficult to decode. These are individuals whose wealth and class insulate them completely from quotidian problems. Everard gradually recognizes "the full extent of his sympathy with the social principles these men and women represented." Basically, these principles ensure this class the right to "liberal criticism" and protect it from an obligation to act: "These persons were not in declared revolt against the order of things, religious, ethical, or social; that is to say, they did not think it worthwhile to identify themselves with any 'movement'; they were content with the unopposed right of liberal criticism. They lived placidly; refraining from much that the larger world enjoined, but never aggressive" (366–67). Of course, neither revolt nor aggression is necessary when the world is already arranged for one's convenience. This kind of rhetoric makes Rhoda's struggles appear so heated, so profitless, and so tacky. The novel tends to represent Rhoda's pluck as rather vulgar. Depictions of Rhoda's sexuality and the brutality it elicits from Everard link her more with the working women "lumps of human flesh," who seduce and ruin vulnerable young men, than it does with genteel Agnes Brissenden, who has "subdued his masculine self-assertiveness" and led him to "appreciate the perfection of his own suavity, the vast advance he had been making in polished humanism" (367). Rhoda concludes the novel a gloomy monitrice, somberly regarding Monica's orphaned daughter. Her brave words, "we flourish like the green bay-tree. . . . The world is moving," are betrayed by her final speculation: "Poor little child!" (386). She might as well say "girl."

By Way of Conclusion

When I initially charted the course of this book, I speculated that it might end with Gissing, where I anticipated discovering a return of the plot of interclass marriage, especially because Gissing twice tried the experiment himself. But if his experiences had any effect evident in *The Odd Women*, it was to teach him an almost religious reverence for the prerogatives of class. Ineluctable in this novel is the way class figures as prominently as gender in representations of the new woman, just as it had figured in representations of the mid-Victorian domestic woman. The managerial skills of Gissing's new women are class prerogatives.

To articulate this genealogy of the female subject in Victorian England is, it turns out, to generate a more complex picture of development and change than the one that emerges from a single focus on gender and individual agency. Ironically, I had expected to celebrate the emergence of the domestic woman into the new woman as a rather simple affirmation of change through ideological conflict. But, of course, to discover such an uncomplicated genealogy would be to reintroduce here the idealist historical narrative whose validity I have questioned. Everything seems much messier from a perspective that stresses multiply constituted subjects: class and gender have generated complex configurations of the female subject, some revisionary, some reactionary. A focus on the ephemera, the material dimensions and social semiotics of women's lives, challenges the traditional bourgeois historical narrative, and both disrupts the historical narrative I am tempted to substitute and "make[s] visible all of those discontinuities that cross us" (*Foucault Reader* 95). It is crystal clear, however, that such complex models of subject formation are necessary as we examine more closely issues of agency and change. Indeed, the insights generated by this method testify to its limitations and exclusions, to what we might learn if we inflected gender and class with race or nationality or ethnicity. Hannah Cullwick's appropriation of blackness as a signifier of both her degradation and her distinction provides a glimpse of one way that race worked through these discourses. Her diaries illuminate how race functions in Victorian discourse as a repressed term, what Toni Morrison in *Playing in the Dark* has called "Africanisms."

The two terms I have implicated here, gender and class, help us to explain, in part, what Carol Dyhouse has described as the "'spectrum of feminisms' coexisting in England around the beginning of the present century." To define that spectrum is one goal Dyhouse articulates in *Feminism and the Family in England, 1880–1939*. She distinguishes the "individualism of many middle-class feminists" from the family-oriented feminist analysis developed by working-class women within the Labour movement, "which first and foremost asserted the value of a woman's role as domestic worker and child-rearer within the family" and which pursued "policies to 'protect' wives and mother in the working-class family and the labour market, most crucially through the defense of the ideal of the 'family wage'"(4–5).[21] Whereas working women were articulating their rights through a rhetoric of domesticity that had framed the lives of middle-class women in the nineteenth century, bourgeois women, struggling to escape that rhetoric, focused on individual rights. Dyhouse ties middle-class feminism to the dissatisfaction of bourgeois women with "their experiences of the Victorian patriarchal family—their experiences as dependent wives and daughters" (6). And, surely, she is not wrong, but this familiar picture of female dependency seems too limited in light of my analysis here. The emplacement of bourgeois women as class managers was far more likely than dependency to produce individualism and independence. And the corollary emplacement of working-class women as domestic servants would have helped to inscribe lower-class women within cultural discourses of domesticity and the family that prevailed at the end of the century. These divergent late-nineteenth-century feminisms thus testify to the success of the mid-Victorian bourgeois ideological project.

Middle-class women, particularly those of the upper ranks, did realize substantial changes in their prospects and opportunities. But this was not an enfranchisement that extended far down the social ladder, and it was also a process that generated an inevitable backlash that was carried out on the cultural level in renewed images of the idealized, idle domestic woman, especially now for working women. In *Woman's Work*, Ann Oakley notes: "The idea that work outside the home for married women was a 'misfortune and a disgrace' became acceptable to the working classes only in the last decades of the nineteenth century. In the early years of the twentieth century working-class married women were increasingly likely to follow the middle-class pattern, choosing the role of non-employed housewife even in cases where their employment would have improved the family's standard of living" (50). Such is the power of cultural ideology that working-class women were persuaded to jeopardize their economic well-being. Furthermore, Oakley recognizes the phenomenon I have explored here, that "middle-class wives chose housewifery as an occupation long before their working-class sisters partly because they did not actually have to *do* housework" (51). Oakley does not pursue the implications of the split between

---

[21] Dyhouse borrows the phrase "spectrum of feminisms" and the conclusions about working-class women within the Labour movement from Caroline Rowan.

manager and menial labor. She shifts instead to a point at which the situations of working-class and middle-class women theoretically converged because of the servant shortage in the early twentieth century (52). She concludes that "the mid-nineteenth-century role of housewife-supervisor became the twentieth-century role of house-wife-worker." She leaves unanalyzed the profound implications arising from the different ideological positions of bourgeois and working-class subjects, emphasizing instead a supposed role merger when "middle- and working-class married women [were both cast] in the modern role of housewife" (53). One burden of my argument has been to explore some consequences of that definitive difference between manager and menial labor in the emergence of differing female subjects at the turn of the century. There we see the effects of criss-crossing ideologies in destabilizing certain subject formations and producing others, a process of change initiated and carried out in the private, domestic sphere. It was as widespread and enduring as any movement launched in the public realm.

The tracing of these patterns of agency in the private sphere is particularly relevant for women in their domestic positions, who as individuals and classes are misrepresented by stereotypes of Victorian women's passivity and total subordination. Dethroning the angel who reigns in the house of Victorian domestic ideology opens up contestatory alternative narratives of female subjects.

Works Consulted

Allen, Dennis. *Sexuality in Victorian Fiction*. Norman: University of Oklahoma Press, 1993.

Armstrong, Nancy. *Desire and Domestic Fiction: A Political History of the Novel*. New York: Oxford University Press, 1987.

Armstrong, Nancy, and Leonard Tennenhouse, eds. *The Ideology of Conduct: Essays on Literature and the History of Sexuality*. New York: Methuen, 1987.

———. *The Imaginary Puritan: Literature, Intellectual Labor, and the Origins of Personal Life*. Berkeley: University of California Press, 1992.

Ashley, Rev. F. B. *The Domestic Circle; or, The Relative Duties*. London: Hatchard, Hamilton & Adams, [1852].

Auerbach, Nina. *Communities of Women: An Idea in Fiction*. Cambridge: Harvard University Press, 1978.

———. *Woman and the Demon: The Life of a Victorian Myth*. Cambridge: Harvard University Press, 1982.

Austen, Jane. *Emma*. Ed. Ronald Blythe. Harmondsworth: Penguin, 1966.

———. *Pride and Prejudice*. Ed. Tony Tanner. Harmondsworth: Penguin, 1972.

Austin, Zelda. "Why Feminist Critics Are Angry with George Eliot." *College English* 37 (February 1976): 549–61.

Bailey, Rufus William. *The Family Preacher; or, Domestic Duties*. New York: John S. Taylor, 1837.

Barrett, Michele, and Mary McIntosh. *The Anti-social Family*. Thetford, U.K.: Thetford Press, 1982.

Barthes, Roland. *S/Z*. Trans. Richard Miller. New York: Hill and Wang, 1974.

Baylis, T. Henry. *The Rights, Duties, and Relations of Domestic Servants and Their Masters and Mistresses*. 3d ed. London: Butterworths, 1873.

Beer, Patricia. *Reader, I Married Him: A Study of the Women Characters of Jane Austen, Charlotte Brontë, Elizabeth Gaskell, and George Eliot*. New York: Barnes and Noble, 1974.

Beeton, Isabella. *The Book of Household Management*. 1861. London: Chancellor, 1982.

Belsey, Catherine. *Critical Practice*. New York: Methuen, 1980.

Besant, Walter. *Fifty Years Ago*. London: Chatto & Windus, 1888.

Boone, Joseph Allen. *Tradition Counter Tradition: Love and the Form of Fiction*. Chicago: University of Chicago Press, 1987.

Booth, Alison. *Greatness Engendered: George Eliot and Virginia Woolf*. Ithaca: Cornell University Press, 1992.

Bossche, Chris Vanden. "Cookery Not Rookery: Family and Class in *David Copperfield*." *Dickens Studies Annual* 15 (1986): 87–109.

Bourdieu, Pierre. *The Field of Cultural Production: Essays on Art and Literature*. Ed. Randal Johnson. Cambridge: Cambridge University Press, 1993.

——. *Language and Symbolic Power*. Trans. Gino Raymond and Matthew Adamson. Ed. John B. Thompson. Cambridge: Harvard University Press, 1991.

——. *The Logic of Practice*. Trans. R. Nice. Cambridge: Polity Press, 1990.

Bowers, Bege K., and Barbara Brothers, eds. *Reading and Writing Women's Lives: A Study of the Novel of Manners*. Ann Arbor, Mich.: UMI Research Press, 1990.

Braddon, Mary Elizabeth. *Lady Audley's Secret*. New York: Dover, 1974.

Briggs, Asa. *Victorian Cities*. New York: Harper, 1965.

——. *Victorian Things*. Chicago: University of Chicago Press, 1988.

Brontë, Charlotte. *Jane Eyre*. Ed. Richard J. Dunn. New York: Norton, 1971.

Brown, Julia Prewitt. *Jane Austen's Novels: Social Change and Literary Form*. Cambridge: Harvard University Press, 1979.

Browne, Phillis. *Common-Sense Housekeeping*. London: Cassell Petter & Galpin, [1877].

——. *What Girls Can Do: A Book for Mothers and Daughters*. London: Cassell, Petter, Galpin, [1880].

Browne, Phyllis. *The Young Idea: Talks with Mothers on the Home Training of Children*. London: Elliot Stock, 1911.

Browne, W. A. F. *Sisterhoods in Asylums*. London: J. E. Adelard, 1866.

Browning, Elizabeth Barrett. *The Complete Works of Elizabeth Barrett Browning*. Eds. Charlotte Porter and Helen A. Clarke. 6 vols. 1900. Rpt. New York: AMS Press, 1973.

Brumberg, Joan. *Fasting Girls: The Emergence of Anorexia Nervosa*. Cambridge: Harvard University Press, 1989.

Buck-Morss, Susan. *The Dialectics of Seeing: Walter Benjamin and the Arcades Project*. Cambridge: MIT Press, 1989.

Burdett-Coutts, Angela, ed. *Woman's Mission: A Series of Congress Papers on the Philanthropic Work of Women by Eminent Writers*. London: Sampson Low, Marston, 1893.

Burman, Sandra, ed. *Fit Work for Women*. New York: St. Martin's, 1979.

Burney, Frances. *Evelina; or, The History of a Young Lady's Entrance into the World*. Ed. Frank D. MacKinnon. New York: Oxford University Press, 1930.

Butcher, John. *Instructions in Etiquette for the Use of All*. 3d ed. London: Simkin, Marshall, 1847.

Butler, C. Violet. *Domestic Service: An Enquiry by the Women's International Council*. London, 1916. Rpt. New York: Garland, 1980.

Butler, Judith. *Bodies That Matter: On the Discursive Limits of "Sex."* New York: Routledge, 1993.

——. *Gender Trouble: Feminism and the Subversion of Identity*. New York: Routledge, 1990.

Careful, Martha. *Domestic Hints to Young Mothers, with Practical Receipts for House and Nursery*. London: Dean & Son, 1862.

——. *Household Hints to Young Housewives*. London: Dean & Son, 1853.

——. *A Young Wife's Guide to Housekeeping, or How to Obtain Comfort on 60, 80, or 100 Pounds Year*. London: W. Strange, 1844.

Cassell's Book of the Household. London: Cassell, [1890?].

Cassell's Household Guide: Being a Complete Encyclopedia. London: Cassell, Petter, and Galpin, [1869–71].

Chalmers, Frederick. *The Christian Home; or, Seven Sermons on Domestic Duties*. London: J. Hatchard & Son, 1849.

Clarke, H. G. *The English Maiden; Her Moral & Domestic Duties*. London: H. G. Clarke, 1849.

Cobbett, Anne. *The English Housekeeper; or, Manual of Domestic Management, the Whole Being Intended for the Use of Young Ladies Who Undertake the Superintendence of Their Own Housekeeping*. London: W. J. Sears, [1835].

Collins, Wilkie. *The Woman in White*. Ed. Harvey Peter Sucksmith. New York: Oxford University Press, 1973.

Copley, Esther. *Cottage Comforts, with Hints for Promoting Them*. London: Simpkin & Marshall, 1841.

Corbett, Mary Jean. *Representing Femininity: Middle-Class Subjectivity in Victorian and Edwardian Women's Autobiographies*. New York: Oxford University Press, 1992.

Cottom, Daniel. *Social Figures: George Eliot, Social History, and Literary Representation*. Minneapolis: University of Minnesota Press, 1987.

Crow, Duncan. *The Victorian Woman*. New York: Stein, 1971.

Culler, Jonathan. "Literary Theory." Gibaldi 201–35.

Cullwick, Hannah. *The Diaries of Hannah Cullwick, Victorian Maidservant*. Ed. Liz Stanley. New Brunswick: Rutgers University Press, 1984.

Curtin, Michael. *Propriety and Position: A Study of Victorian Manners*. New York: Garland, 1987.

Cvetkovich, Ann. *Mixed Feelings: Feminism, Mass Culture, and Victorian Sensationalism*. New Brunswick: Rutgers University Press, 1993.

Danahay, Martin. "Housekeeping and Hegemony in *Bleak House*." *Studies in the Novel* 23 (Winter 1991): 416–31.

David, Deirdre. *Intellectual Women and Victorian Patriarchy: Harriet Martineau, Elizabeth Barrett Browning, George Eliot*. Ithaca: Cornell University Press, 1987.

Davidoff, Leonore. *The Best Circles: Women and Society in Victorian England*. Totowa, N.J.: Rowman, 1973.

Davidoff, Leonore, and Catherine Hall. *Family Fortunes: Men and Women of the English Middle Class, 1780–1850*. Chicago: University of Chicago Press, 1987.

Davidoff, Leonore, and Ruth Hawthorn. *A Day in the Life of a Victorian Domestic Servant*. London: George Allen & Unwin, 1976.

Davies, Jennifer. *The Victorian Kitchen*. London: BBC Books, 1989.

Day, Charles. *Hints on Etiquette and the Usages of Society; With a Glance at Bad Habits*. 2d ed. London, 1836.

Deane, William J. *A Manual of Household Prayer, for Morning and Evening*. London: Rivingtons, 1857.

De Lauretis, Teresa. *Technologies of Gender: Essays on Theory, Film, and Fiction*. Bloomington: Indiana University Press, 1987.

Derrida, Jacques. *Limited, Inc*. Ed. Gerald Graff. Trans. Samuel Weber and Jeffrey Mehlman. Evanston: Northwestern University Press, 1988.

Dickens, Charles. *Bleak House*. Ed. Morton Dauwen Zabel. Boston: Riverside, 1956.

——. *David Copperfield*. New York: Oxford University Press, 1948.

——. *Little Dorrit*. Ed. John Holloway. Harmondsworth: Penguin, 1967.

——. *Our Mutual Friend*. New York: Oxford University Press, 1952.

Donzelot, Jacques. *The Policing of Families*. Trans. Robert Hurley. New York: Pantheon Books, 1979.

Dreyfus, Hubert, and Paul Rabinow, eds. *Michel Foucault: Beyond Structuralism and Hermeneutics*. 2d rev. ed. Chicago: University of Chicago Press, 1983.

Duties of Happiness of Domestic Service. London: Charles Dolman, 1851.

Dyhouse, Carol. *Feminism and the Family in England, 1880–1939*. London: Basil Blackwell, 1989.

——. *Girls Growing Up in Late Victorian and Edwardian England*. London: Routledge, 1981.

——. "Mothers and Daughters in the Middle-Class Home, c. 1870–1914." Lewis 27–47.

Eagleton, Terry. "Fredric Jameson: The Politics of Style." *Diacritics* 12 (1982): 14–22.

Edwards, Lee R. "Women, Energy, and *Middlemarch*." *Massachusetts Review* 13 (1972): 222–38.

Eliot, George. *Adam Bede*. Ed. John Paterson. Boston: Riverside, 1968.

——. "Art and Belles Lettres." *Westminster Review* 9 (January/April 1856): 625–50.

——. *The George Eliot Letters*. Ed. Gordon S. Haight. 9 vols. New Haven: Yale University Press, 1954–78.

——. *Middlemarch*. Ed. Gordon S. Haight. Boston: Riverside, 1956.

——. "The Natural History of German Life." Pinney 266–99.

——. *Scenes of Clerical Life*. Ed. David Lodge. Harmondsworth: Penguin, 1973.

——. "Silly Novels by Lady Novelists." Pinney 300–324.

Ellis, Sarah. *Daughters of England*. London, 1842.

——. *The Women of England: Their Social Duties, and Domestic Habits*. London: Fisher, 1839.

Engels, Friedrich. *Karl Marx—Frederick Engels: Selected Correspondence*. New York: International Publishers, 1942.

Englishwoman's Domestic Magazine. London: S. O. Beeton, 1860–68.

Etiquette for Ladies. London: Knight and Son, 1851.

Etiquette for Ladies and Gentlemen. London: Frederick Warne, 1876.

Etiquette for Ladies and Gentlemen; or, The Principles of True Politeness. Halifax: Milner and Sowerby, 1862.

Etiquette for Ladies; or The Principles of True Politeness. Halifax: Milner and Sowerby, 1852.

Etiquette for the Ladies: Eighty Maxims on Dress, Manners, and Accomplishments. London: Charles Tilt, 1837.

Etiquette, Social Ethics, and Dinner-Table Observances. London: Houlston and Wright, 1860.

Family Manual and Servants' Guide. London: H. G. Collins, [1856].

Fielding, Henry. *The History of Tom Jones, a Foundling.* New York: Modern Library, 1950.

Flint, Kate. *The Woman Reader, 1837–1914.* New York: Oxford University Press, 1993.

Fonblanque, Albany. *Rights & Wrongs. A Manual of Household Law.* London: Routledge, Warne & Routledge, 1860.

Foucault, Michel. *The Archaeology of Knowledge.* Trans. Alan M. Sheridan. New York: Pantheon, 1972.

——. *Discipline and Punish: The Birth of the Prison.* Trans. Alan M. Sheridan. New York: Random House, 1979.

——. *The Foucault Reader.* Ed. Paul Rabinow. New York: Pantheon, 1984.

——. *The History of Sexuality.* Vol. 1. New York: Random House, 1978.

——. "The Subject and Power." Dreyfus and Rabinow 208–26.

Fraiman, Susan. *Unbecoming Women: British Women Writers and the Novel of Development.* New York: Columbia University Press, 1993.

Francis, E. Warren. *A Scheme for the Education of the Daughters of Working Men.* London: Houlston & Wright, [1862].

Freeman, Sarah. *Mutton and Oysters: The Victorians and Their Food.* London: Victor Gollancz, 1989.

Gagnier, Reginia. *Subjectivities: A History of Self-Representation in Britain, 1832–1920.* New York: Oxford University Press, 1991.

Gallagher, Catherine. *The Industrial Reformation of English Fiction: Social Discourse and Narrative Form.* Chicago: University of Chicago Press, 1985.

——. "Marxism and the New Historicism." Veeser 37–48.

Gallagher, Catherine, and Thomas Laqueur, eds. *The Making of the Modern Body: Sexuality and Society in the Nineteenth Century.* Berkeley: University of California Press, 1987.

Garnier, Rev. Thomas. *Domestic Duties: A Series of Sermons Preached in Trinity Church, St. Marylebone.* London: J. Laver, 1851.

Gaskell, Elizabeth. *Cranford; Cousin Phillis.* Ed. Peter Keating. Harmondsworth: Penguin, 1976.

——. *The Letters of Mrs. Gaskell.* Ed. J. A. V. Chapple and Arthur Pollard. Manchester: Manchester University Press, 1966.

——. *The Life of Charlotte Bronte*. Ed. Alan Shelston. Harmondsworth: Penguin, 1975.

——. *Mary Barton: A Tale of Manchester Life*. Ed. Stephen Gill. Harmondsworth: Penguin, 1970.

——. *North and South*. Ed. Dorothy Collin. Harmondsworth: Penguin, 1970.

——. *Ruth*. Ed. Alan Shelston. New York: Oxford University Press, 1985.

——. *Wives and Daughters*. Ed. Frank Glover Smith. Harmondsworth: Penguin, 1969.

Gibaldi, Joseph, ed. *Introduction to Scholarship in Modern Languages and Literatures*. 2d ed. New York: Modern Language Association, 1992.

Gilbert, Sandra, and Susan Gubar. *The Madwoman in the Attic: The Woman Writer and the Nineteenth-Century Literary Imagination*. New Haven: Yale University Press, 1979.

——. *No Man's Land: The Place of the Woman Writer in the Twentieth Century*. New Haven: Yale University Press, 1987.

Girouard, Mark. *Life in the English Country House*. New Haven: Yale University Press, 1978.

——. *The Victorian Country House*. New Haven: Yale University Press, 1979.

Gissing, George. *Letters to Gabrielle Fleury*. Ed. Pierre Coustillas. New York: New York Public Library, 1964.

——. *The Odd Women*. New York: Meridian, 1983.

Green, Gayle, and Coppelia Kahn, eds. *Making a Difference: Feminist Literary Criticism*. New York: Methuen, 1985.

Grogan, Mercy. *How Women May Earn a Living*. London: Cassell, Petter, Galpin, [1880].

Guide to English Etiquette with the Rules of Polite Society. London: C. Mitchell, [1844].

Habits of Good Society: An Handbook of Etiquette for Ladies and Gentlemen. London, [1875–78].

Hall, Catherine. "The Early Formation of Victorian Domestic Ideology." Burman 15–32.

Hardy, Thomas. *Jude the Obscure*. Ed. Norman Page. New York: Norton, 1978.

——. *Tess of the D'Urbervilles*. Ed. William E. Buckler. Boston: Riverside, 1960.

Harrison, Antony H. *Victorian Poets and Romantic Poems: Intertextuality and Ideology*. Charlottesville: University Press of Virginia, 1990.

Hartshorne, Henry. *A Household Manual of Medicine, Surgery, Nursing & Hygiene*. London: Sampson Low, 1887.

Haskins, C. W. *How to Keep Household Accounts: A Manual of Family Finance*. New York: Harper & Brothers, 1903.

Hay, Rev. David. *Domestic Servants & Their Interests and Duties*. London: John Mason, 1852.

Helsinger, Elizabeth, Robin Sheets, and William Veeder, eds. *The Woman Question: Society and Literature in Britain and America, 1837–1883*. 3 vols. London: Garland, 1983.

Henderson, Mrs. *The Young Wife's Own Book: Her Domestic Duties & Social Habits*. Glasgow: W. R. M'Phun, 1857.

Hewitt, Margaret. *Wives and Mothers in Victorian Industry*. London: Rockliff, 1958.

Higgs, Edward. "Domestic Service and Household Production." John 125–50.

Hiley, Michael. *Victorian Working Women: Portraits from Life*. Boston: David R. Godine, 1979.

Hobsbawm, E. J. *Industry and Empire*. Harmondsworth: Penguin, 1968.

Homans, Margaret. *Bearing the Word: Language and Female Experience in Nineteenth-Century Women's Writing*. Chicago: University of Chicago Press, 1986.

——. "The Powers of Powerlessness: The Courtships of Elizabeth Barrett and Queen Victoria." In *Feminist Measures: Soundings in Poetry and Theory*, ed. Lynn Keller and Cristanne Miller. Ann Arbor: University of Michigan Press, 1994.

——. "'To the Queen's Private Apartments': Royal Family Portraiture and the Construction of Victoria's Sovereign Obedience." *Victorian Studies* 37, no. 1 (Autumn 1993): 1–41.

Hopkins, Ellice. *On the Early Training of Girls and Boys*. London: Hatchards, 1882.

Hopkins, Jane Ellice. *An Englishwoman's Work among Working Men*. New Britain, Conn.: John A. Williams, 1875.

Horn, Pamela. *The Rise and Fall of the Victorian Servant*. New York: St. Martin's Press, 1975.

How to Behave; a Pocket Manual of Etiquette and Guide to Correct Personal Habits. London: Houlston & Wright, [1865].

How to Behave; or, Etiquette of Society. London: Ward, Lock & Tyler, [1879].

How to Woo; How to Win; and How to Get Married. Glasgow: W. R. M'Phun, 1856.

Hudson, Derek. *Munby, Man of Two Worlds: The Life and Diaries of Arthur J. Munby*. London: Murray, 1972.

Irigaray, Luce. *This Sex Which Is Not One*. Trans. Catherine Porter, with Carolyn Burke. Ithaca: Cornell University Press, 1985.

James, Henry. *Notes and Reviews*. 1921. Freeport, N.Y.: Books for Libraries, 1968.

Jameson, Fredric. *The Political Unconscious: Narrative as a Socially Symbolic Act*. Ithaca: Cornell University Press, 1981.

John, Angela V., ed. *Unequal Opportunities: Women's Employment in England, 1800–1918*. New York: Basil Blackwell, 1986.

Johnson, Edgar. *Charles Dickens: His Tragedy and Triumph*. New York: Viking, 1977.

Joyce, Patrick. *Visions of the People: Industrial England and the Question of Class, 1840–1914*. Cambridge: Cambridge University Press, 1991.

Kaplan, Cora. "Pandora's Box: Subjectivity, Class and Sexuality in Socialist Feminist Criticism." Green and Kahn 146–76.

————. *Sea Changes: Essays in Culture and Feminism*. London: Verso, 1986.

Kaplan, Fred. *Dickens: A Biography*. New York: William Morrow, 1988.

Kasson, John F. *Rudeness and Civility: Manners in Nineteenth-Century Urban America*. New York: Hill and Wang, 1990.

Keating, Peter. Introduction. Gaskell, *Cranford* 7–30.

Kincaid, James. *Child-Loving: The Erotic Child and Victorian Culture*. New York: Routledge, 1992.

Kirkham, Margaret. *Jane Austen, Feminism and Fiction*. New York: Methuen, 1986.

Kotz, Liz. "The Body You Want: Liz Kotz Interviews Judith Butler." *Artforum*, November 1992, 82–89.

Ladies' Guide to Etiquette, and Rules of True Politeness, as Observed by the Middle & Upper Classes of Society. London: H. Elliot, [1855].

Ladies' Pocket-Book of Etiquette. London, 1840.

Ladies' Science of Etiquette. Edinburgh: Paton & Ritchie, 1851.

Langbauer, Laurie. *Women and Romance: The Consolations of Gender in the English Novel*. Ithaca: Cornell University Press, 1990.

Leavis, Q. D. *Collected Essays: The Novel of Religious Controversy*. Vol. 3 of 3 vols. Cambridge: Cambridge University Press, 1989.

Lerner, Laurence. Introduction. Gaskell, *Wives and Daughters* 7–27.

Levy, Anita. *Other Women: The Writing of Class, Race, and Gender, 1832–1898*. Princeton: Princeton University Press, 1991.

Lewis, Jane, ed. *Labour and Love: Women's Experience of Home and Family, 1850–1940*. Oxford: Basil Blackwell, 1986.

Litvak, Joseph. "Reading Characters: Self, Society, and Text in Emma." *PMLA* 100 (October 1985): 763–71.

Lummis, Trevor, and Jan Marsh. *The Woman's Domain: Women and the English Country House*. New York: Viking, 1990.

Macherey, Pierre. *A Theory of Literary Production*. Trans. Geoffrey Wall. Boston: Routledge & Kegan Paul, 1978.

Manners and Tone of Good Society. London: Frederick Warne, [1879].

Manners of Modern Society: Being a Book of Etiquette. London: Cassell, Petter, and Galpin, 1872.

Manual of Etiquette for Ladies; or, True Principles of Politeness. London: T. Allman & Son, 1856.

Marcus, Steven. *The Other Victorians: A Study of Sexuality and Pornography in Mid-Nineteenth-Century England*. New York: Basic Books, 1966.

Mason, Michael. *The Making of Victorian Sexuality*. New York: Oxford University Press, 1994.

Mayhew, Henry. *London Labour and the London Poor*. 1861. 4 vols. New York: Dover, 1968.

McBride, Theresa M. *The Domestic Revolution: The Modernisation of Household Service in England and France, 1820–1920*. New York: Holmes & Meier, 1976.

McKeon, Michael. *The Origins of the English Novel, 1600–1740*. Baltimore: Johns Hopkins University Press, 1987.

Mercer, Kobena. "Welcome to the Jungle: Identity and Diversity in Post-modern Politics." Rutherford 43–71.

Miller, David A. *The Novel and the Police*. Berkeley: University of California Press, 1988.

Miller, Nancy K., ed. *The Poetics of Gender*. New York: Columbia University Press, 1986.

Morrison, Toni. *Playing in the Dark: Whiteness and the Literary Imagination*. Cambridge: Harvard University Press, 1992.

Mr. Punch's Victorian Era. London: Bradbury, Agnew, 1887.

Munich, Adrienne Auslander. "Queen Victoria, Empire, and Excess." *Tulsa Studies in Women's Literature* 6 (Fall 1987): 265–81.

Murray, Alexander. *The Domestic Oracle; or, A Complete System of Modern Cookery and Family Economy*. London: H. Fisher, [1826?].

Musselwhite, David. *Partings Welded Together: Politics and Desire in the Nine-teenth-Centure Novel*. New York: Methuen, 1987.

New System of Domestic Cookery. London: John Murray, 1833.

Newton, Judith Lowder. "History as Usual? Feminism and the 'New Historicism.'" Veeser 152–167.

Nietzsche, Friedrich. *The Portable Nietzsche*. New York: Viking, 1954.

Nightingale, Florence. *Cassandra*. 1852. Old Westbury, N.Y.: Feminist Press, 1979.

Oakley, Ann. *Woman's Work: The Housewife, Past and Present*. New York: Pantheon Books, 1974.

Oliphant, Margaret. "The Anti-Marriage League." *Blackwood's Magazine* 159 (January 1896): 135–49.

——. *The Autobiography of Mrs. Oliphant*. Ed. Mrs. Harry Coghill. Chicago: University of Chicago Press, 1988.

——. *Hester: A Story of Contemporary Life*. Harmondsworth: Penguin, 1984.

——. *Miss Marjoribanks*. Harmondsworth: Penguin, 1989.

——. *Phoebe Junior*. Harmondsworth: Penguin, 1989.

Perkin, Joan. *Women and Marriage in Nineteenth-Century England*. Chicago: Lyceum Books, 1989.

Pinney, Thomas, ed. *The Essays of George Eliot*. London: Routledge and Kegan Paul, 1963.

Poovey, Mary. *Uneven Developments: The Ideological Work of Gender in Mid-Victorian England*. Chicago: University of Chicago Press, 1988.

Porter, Carolyn. "Are We Being Historical Yet?" *South Atlantic Quarterly* 87 (Fall 1988): 743–86.

Prochaska, F. K. *Women and Philanthropy in Nineteenth-Century England*. Oxford: Clarendon–Oxford University Press, 1980.

Reddy, Maureen K. "Men, Women, and Manners in *Wives and Daughters*." Bowers and Brothers 67–85.

Reeve, Mrs. Henry. "Mistresses and Maids." *Longman's Magazine* 21 (March 1893): 497–504.

Robbins, Bruce. *The Servant's Hand: English Fiction from Below*. New York: Columbia University Press, 1986.

Rose, Michael. "The Disappearing Pauper: Victorian Attitudes to the Relief of the Poor." Sigsworth 56–72.

Rose, Sonya O. *Limited Livelihoods: Gender and Class in Nineteenth-Century England*. Berkeley: University of California Press, 1992.

Routledge's Manual of Etiquette. London, [1875?].

Rowan, Caroline. "Women in the Labour Party, 1906–1920." *Feminist Review* 12 (October 1982): 74–91.

Ruskin, John. *Sesame and Lilies*. 1865. London: Macmillan, 1933.

Russett, Cynthia. *Sexual Science: The Victorian Construction of Womanhood*. Cambridge: Harvard University Press, 1989.

Rutherford, Jonathan, ed. *Identity, Community, Culture, Difference*. London: Lawrence & Wishart, 1990.

Said, Edward. *Culture and Imperialism*. New York: Knopf, 1993.

St. George, Andrew. *The Descent of Manners: Etiquette, Rules, and the Victorians*. London: Chatto and Windus, 1993.

Schor, Naomi. *Reading in Detail: Aesthetics and the Feminine*. New York: Methuen, 1987.

Sedgwick, Eve Kosofsky. *Between Men: English Literature and Male Homosocial Desire*. New York: Columbia University Press, 1985.

Sharpe, Jenny. *Allegories of Empire: The Figure of Woman in the Colonial Text*. Minneapolis: University of Minnesota Press, 1993.

Showalter, Elaine. "The Greening of Sister George." *Nineteenth-Century Fiction* 35 (December 1980): 292–311.

——. Introduction. Gissing, *The Odd Women*, vii–xxvi.

——. *A Literature of Their Own: British Women Novelists from Brontë to Lessing*. Princeton: Princeton University Press, 1977.

——. *Sexual Anarchy: Gender and Culture at the Fin de Siècle*. New York: Viking, 1990.

Sigsworth, Eric, ed. *In Search of Victorian Values: Aspects of Nineteenth-Century Thought and Society*. Manchester: Manchester University Press, 1988.

Sloan, John. *George Gissing: The Cultural Challenge*. New York: St. Martin's Press, 1989.

Smiles, Samuel. *Physical Education; or, The Nurture and Management of Children*. London: Marshall, 1838.

——. *Self-Help; with Illustrations of Character & Conduct*. London: John Murray, 1859.

Spirit of Etiquette or Politeness Exemplified. London, 1837.

Stang, Richard. *The Theory of the Novel in England, 1850–1870*. New York: Columbia University Press, 1959.

Stedman Jones, Gareth. *Language of Class: Studies in English Working-Class History, 1832–1982*. Cambridge: Cambridge University Press, 1983.

Stone, Lawrence. *The Family, Sex, and Marriage in England, 1500–1800*. New York: Harper & Row, 1979.

Stone, Lawrence, and Jeanne Stone. *An Open Elite? England, 1540–1880*. New York: Oxford University Press, 1984.

Stoneman, Patsy. *Elizabeth Gaskell*. Bloomington: Indiana University Press, 1987.

Stubbs, Patricia. *Women and Fiction: Feminism and the Novel, 1880–1920*. Sussex: Harvester Press, 1979.

Sulloway, Alison G. *Jane Austen and the Province of Womanhood*. Philadelphia: University of Pennsylvania Press, 1989.

Summers, Anne. "A Home from Home—Women's Philanthropic Work in the Nineteenth Century." Burman 33–63.

——. "In Separate Spheres." *Times Literary Supplement* 7–13 April 1989, 357–58.

Sutherland, John. *The Longman Companion to Victorian Fiction*. Harlow: Longman, 1988.

Thackeray, William Makepeace. *Vanity Fair: A Novel without a Hero*. Boston: Riverside, 1963.

Thomas, Brook. "The New Historicism and Other Old-fashioned Topics." Veeser 182–203.

Thompson, Dorothy. *Queen Victoria: Gender and Power*. London: Virago, 1990.

Thompson, E. P. *The Making of the English Working Class*. New York: Vintage, 1963.

Thompson, F. M. L. *The Rise of Respectable Society: A Social History of Victorian Britain, 1830–1900*. Cambridge: Harvard University Press, 1988.

Thompson, John B. Introduction. Bourdieu, *Language and Symbolic Power* 1–31.

Tindall, Gillian. *The Born Exile: George Gissing*. New York: Harcourt Brace Jovanovich, 1974.

Trollope, Anthony. *Barchester Towers; The Warden*. New York: Modern Library, 1950.

Uppark. Original guidebook by Lady Meade-Featherstonhaugh, revised by C. H. B. Hertfortshire: Stellar Press, 1985.

Veeser, H. Aram, ed. *The New Historicism*. New York: Routledge, 1989.

Vicinus, Martha. *Independent Women: Work and Community for Single Women, 1850–1920*. Chicago: University of Chicago Press, 1985.

——. *The Industrial Muse: A Study of Nineteenth-Century British Working-Class Literature*. New York: Barnes & Noble, 1974.

——, ed. *Suffer and Be Still: Women in the Victorian Age*. Bloomington: Indiana University Press, 1972.

——, ed. *A Widening Sphere: Changing Roles of Victorian Women*. Bloomington: Indiana University Press, 1977.

Watkins, Henry George. *Friendly Hints to Female Servants*. London: John Hatchard, n.d.

Watt, Ian. *The Rise of the Novel: Studies in Defoe, Richardson, and Fielding*. Berkeley: University of California Press, 1957.

Weintraub, Stanley. *Victoria: An Intimate Biography*. New York: E. P. Dutton, 1987.

White, Hayden. *Tropics of Discourse*. Baltimore: Johns Hopkins University Press, 1978.

Why Do the Servants of the Nineteenth Century Dress As They Do? Brighton: William Simpson, [1859].

Williams, Merryn. *Margaret Oliphant: A Critical Biography*. New York: St. Martin's Press, 1986.

Woolf, Virginia. *The Death of the Moth and Other Essays*. New York: Harcourt, Brace, 1942.

——. *A Room of One's Own*. New York: Harcourt, Brace & World, 1929.

Young Husband's Book; A Manual of Domestic Advice. London: Hamilton, Adams, 1837.

Index

Reading Women Writing

A SERIES EDITED BY

Shari Benstock and Celeste Schenck